Gene Tierney

Contemporary Approaches to Film and Media Series

A complete listing of the books in this series can
be found online at wsupress.wayne.edu.

GENERAL EDITOR

Barry Keith Grant
Brock University

Gene Tierney

STAR OF
Hollywood's Home Front

Will Scheibel

WAYNE STATE UNIVERSITY PRESS
DETROIT

Library of Congress Control Number: 2022939253

ISBN (paperback): 978-0-8143-4821-5
ISBN (hardcover): 978-0-8143-4820-8
ISBN (e-book): 978-0-8143-4822-2

On cover: Early 1940s publicity photograph of actress Gene Tierney. Courtesy of
Wikimedia Commons.
Cover design by Vi-An Nguyen

An early version of chapter 1 was published in *Camera Obscura* 22, no. 2 (98) (2018)
and is reprinted here by permission of Duke University Press. An early version of
chapter 4 was published in *Resetting the Scene: Classical Hollywood Revisited*, edited
by Philippa Gates and Katherine Spring (2021), and is reprinted here by permission
of Wayne State University Press.

Wayne State University Press rests on Waawiyaataanong, also referred to as
Detroit, the ancestral and contemporary homeland of the Three Fires Confederacy.
These sovereign lands were granted by the Ojibwe, Odawa, Potawatomi, and
Wyandot nations, in 1807, through the Treaty of Detroit. Wayne State University
Press affirms Indigenous sovereignty and honors all tribes with a connection to
Detroit. With our Native neighbors, the press works to advance educational equity
and promote a better future for the earth and all people.

Wayne State University Press
Leonard N. Simons Building
4809 Woodward Avenue
Detroit, Michigan 48201-1309

Visit us online at wsupress.wayne.edu.

They are not long, the days of wine and roses:
Out of a misty dream
Our path emerges for a while, then closes
Within a dream.

—Ernest Dowson, "Vitae summa brevis
spem nos vetat incohare longam"

Contents

Introduction

"The Girl in the Portrait"

Johnny Mercer's lyrics to the theme melody for the film *Laura* (Otto Preminger, 1944) referred to the eponymous character as "the face in the misty light," echoing the Ernest Dowson poem that Waldo Lydecker (Clifton Webb) quotes on his radio broadcast at the end of the film.[1] "That was Laura," the song goes, "but she's only a dream."[2] *Was* Laura "only a dream"? Kristin Thompson has proposed that the film's ending leaves open two possibilities for the viewer. First, Laura Hunt (Gene Tierney), the presumed murder victim, was actually alive and Det. Lt. Mark McPherson (Dana Andrews) has successfully rescued her from another attempted murder. Second, when Mark investigates Laura's apartment halfway through the film and falls asleep under her painted portrait, believing her to be murdered (fig. 1), he remains asleep and the subsequent events of the story comprise his wish-fulfillment dream, which suggests that the film achieves a unique sense of closure for Classical Hollywood narrative (i.e., within a dream).[3] In this respect, theater and film historian Foster Hirsch is absolutely correct when he notes that the leads "look and sound like sleepwalkers."[4]

Several months after Twentieth Century–Fox released the film, the studio commissioned Mercer to write lyrics for David Raksin's haunting theme, and Woody Herman's 1945 jazz vocal recording sold over one million copies, perhaps encouraging the second reading.[5] Although Mercer's lyrics are not heard in the film, the song was indelibly linked to the screen visage of Laura, and she with the star who played her, Gene Tierney.[6] As she stated in her 1978 autobiography *Self-Portrait*, "The role most often identified with my career was that of the title character in *Laura*. The part was unusual in that Laura dominated the story as a presence, felt but unseen, for half the movie." Tierney continued, "I am not being modest when I say that people remember me less for my acting job than as the girl in the portrait, which is the movie's key prop."[7] The film, of course,

Fig. 1. Dana Andrews as Mark McPherson under the portrait of Laura
Hunt (Gene Tierney), in *Laura* (Otto Preminger, 1944).

was a hit and went on to become a Hollywood classic, replayed on television ad infinitum, and not to mention one of the first U.S. films to be
labeled "film noir" by French cinephiles writing after the Nazi occupation
(when the embargo on U.S. film imports had been lifted).[8] In 1999, it was
selected for preservation in the National Film Registry of the Library
of Congress among films deemed "culturally, historically, or aestheti-
cally significant."[9] And as the American Film Institute cycled through its
"100 Years . . ." series from 1998 to 2008, it was included on three lists
celebrating the centenary of narrative-feature filmmaking in U.S. cinema: "100 Years . . . 100 Thrills: The 100 Most Thrilling American Films"
(2001), "100 Years of Film Scores" (2005), and (in the category of "Mystery") "10 Top 10: The 10 Greatest Movies in 10 Categories" (2008).[10]

Like the character Laura, and arguably *because* of the slips between
actress and character, Tierney herself has been "framed" as an idealized
image of feminine beauty, fixed in gendered assumptions and mystified
into a dream apparition of 1940s Hollywood. Even the name Laura has
been made synonymous with femininity in classic film noir, as in the noir

pastiche *Brick* (Rian Johnson, 2005), to cite one example, which puts high school characters in archetypal noir roles. (Nora Zehetner plays femme fatale Laura, a popular, upper-class brunette.) Tierney was recognized by her narrow green eyes, dark hair, and heart-shaped face, with a slight overbite that pursed her lips into a romantic pout.[11] Movie buffs today know her as "the most beautiful woman in movie history," according to the often repeated pronouncement of Fox's head of production Darryl F. Zanuck, a legacy preserved on *Laura*'s DVD and Blu-ray packaging.[12] Popular writing on cinema tends to rehearse the received wisdom of her great beauty without querying the historical and ideological conditions of her reputation as a star "better known for her beauty than her talent."[13] For example, David Thomson remarks that in the film *Whirlpool* (Otto Preminger, 1950), she "seldom got past her own gorgeousness," while Otto Friedrich calls her "a girl of considerable beauty but without either great talent or that animal ambition that vivified a Joan Crawford or a Barbara Stanwyck."[14]

Dismissive comments of this sort are consistent with how reviewers appraised her acting during her career, as if it were impossible to take seriously a star as beautiful as Tierney. Bosley Crowther of the *New York Times*, the preeminent film reviewer in the United States after World War II, described her acting style in *The Ghost and Mrs. Muir* (Joseph L. Mankiewicz, 1947) as "customarily inexpressive." "She is a pretty girl," he wrote, "but has no depth of feeling as an actress."[15] Writing about *Dragonwyck* (Joseph L. Mankiewicz, 1946), he called her "fairly ornamental in the role," adding that "she plainly creates no more character than the meager script provides."[16] In his scathing review of *Leave Her to Heaven* (John M. Stahl, 1945), he compared her performance to "a piece of pin-up poster art," reifying Tierney as "the girl in the portrait" put on display in *Laura*.[17] Such is the case for Hollywood sex symbols, as Amanda Konkle observes in her book on Marilyn Monroe, *Some Kind of Mirror*. For Konkle, Monroe's performances were especially complex because "at the same time as they acknowledged and resisted the conventions of the sexpot, they also mirrored, or reflected, the concerns and anxieties of many postwar Americans. Monroe played the sexpot role, but she also challenged that role with humor, sensitivity, and cultural relevance."[18] However much Monroe was objectified, what critics ignored or failed to see was how she was also "an empowered woman whom other women admired."[19] Tierney poses a similar problem for critics and historians in that she was identified with a literal image of beauty (a portrait), in some ways the purest essence of Hollywood stardom, but only understood in equivalent terms as a passive aesthetic object (a beautiful but untalented actress). On the contrary, this book argues that Tierney should be taken seriously for how her films textually foreground such static social imaginings of women and how her American star image during World War II and the immediate postwar years gains contextual meaning from an active, dynamic female presence.

Tierney did in fact pose for pinup photos in the war period, published in official military magazines such as *Brief* and *Yank*, and her 1940 studio biography even promoted her as "the living embodiment of the sort of beauty that has made the Petty girl adored by millions of grads and undergrads from Yale to Cal Tech."[20] The "Petty girl" here is a reference to the *Esquire* pinup paintings by George Petty, which achieved a cultural prominence during World War II when they were reproduced as "nose art" on the fuselage of warplanes. Fox photographer Frank Powolny, who immortalized Betty Grable in her swimsuit and poodle hairdo to promote *Sweet Rosie O'Grady* (Irving Cummings, 1943), actually shot many photos of Tierney—including the *Laura* portrait, which the studio enlarged and lightly brushed to create the illusion of a painted likeness.[21] It is worth adding that Fox remade *Sweet Rosie O'Grady* as *That Wonderful Urge* (Robert B. Sinclair, 1948), with Tierney in Grable's role, and that Tierney was Zanuck's first choice star in *That Lady in Ermine* (Ernst Lubitsch, 1948) as another girl in a painting come to life, a role that ultimately went to Grable. *Laura*'s director Otto Preminger completed the latter film after Ernst Lubitsch died during the shooting.[22]

For moviegoers, however, Tierney was more than a pinup model. During World War II, as one of Fox's female "war workers," she engaged in different forms of war effort and U.S. propaganda, including selling war bonds and appearing at the Hollywood Canteen, a nightclub created by industry guilds and unions and staffed by volunteer stars, where uniformed servicemen could enjoy an evening's entertainment free of charge. Married to Hollywood costume designer Count Oleg Cassini, she was both a fashion icon and a "war bride," holding down the fort while Cassini was stationed in Fort Riley, Kansas, serving in the U.S. Army Cavalry. The couple wed in 1941 and eventually had two daughters,

Daria (in 1943) and Christina (in 1948). Immediately after the war, Tierney was at the peak of her career when she starred in *Leave Her to Heaven*, Fox's highest-grossing film by 1946,[23] and she received an Academy Award nomination for her performance, although Joan Crawford won the Oscar for *Mildred Pierce* (Michael Curtiz, 1945). When Grauman's Chinese Theatre resumed casting stars' hands and feet in concrete slabs, Tierney was reportedly the first star selected to leave impressions in the theater's forecourt (her one condition was that Sid Grauman perform the same ritual, and he agreed).[24] Based on *Variety*'s combined annual rankings from 1946 to 1949, she was one of the ten top stars of the late 1940s and the only star who emerged in that period to achieve "top stardom."[25] She graced the cover of almost every influential fan magazine at some point in the decade, including *Photoplay*, *Modern Screen*, *Screenland*, *Silver Screen*, *Screen Guide*, *Motion Picture*, *Movie Show*, and *Movie Stars Parade*. By the late 1950s, during psychiatric treatments for what today would likely be considered a bipolar disorder, or "manic depression," she also became one of the first major Hollywood stars institutionalized in the public eye.[26]

This book does not presume to recover and speak for the "real" Tierney, nor does it speculate about her thoughts and feelings, which one cannot ever "really" know. But it does seek to restore some of her historical subjectivity that her monolithic reputation obscures. Despite the homogeneity of her contemporary image as the "the girl in the portrait," the structuring absence in *Laura*, her star-making, unmaking, and eventual remaking suggests considerable variability as a pinup girl, worker in a public labor force, army wife, mother, female psychiatric subject, and comeback star. Hollywood participated in the creation of a public sphere that allowed for the negotiation of women's everyday lives contemporaneous with the war and its aftermath—what we might call a "home-front modernity"—and gave rise to stars such as Tierney, whose home-front activities will be the subjects of the chapters that follow. The Hollywood star system in 1940s was different from what audiences had seen previously because, as Sean Griffin states in the introduction to his collection *What Dreams Were Made Of*, "stars increased their actual physical presence among the rest of the population, strengthening their connections to the general public."[27] Studios helped maintain these connections by staging conversations about wartime and postwar experiences for the

U.S. home front, a space emotionally and psychologically affected by World War II even if geographically distant from where it was fought. Here, stars such as Tierney appeared to share similar experiences as their audiences. Contextualizing the processes that made Tierney one of Fox's top stars of the 1940s, this book aims to understand her stardom through a "domestic" history of her period, an alternative to masculinist narratives of war effort and postwar trauma, at the same time as it hopes to redress the generalizations about her career.

Interpreting Star Images and Subjectivities

The methodology of this sort of project is not biographical per se (McFarland published a biography by Michelle Vogel in 2009 with a foreword by Tierney's daughter Christina Cassini). Rather, it comes from the academic field of "star studies," which in large part accounts for why stars get tied to certain social groups and historical periods and how they come to represent certain human experiences.[28] For nearly the past twenty years, film scholars have been steadily writing critical monographs on individual Hollywood stars as case studies in labor, ethnicity, gender, sexuality, age, embodiment, genre, and fandom (or some combination thereof) during the period of the studio system.[29] Like Adrienne L. McLean's *Being Rita Hayworth*, this book is about the "discursive agency" of a star, and historical evidence therefore lies in the "discursive signs that at once indicate and produce struggles between being and doing, between working at making films and working at having a private life, between defining oneself and being defined by others."[30] I make use of biographical information insofar as it evidences the discursive construction of Tierney's subjectivity and the interpretive strategies available to the U.S. moviegoing public in the 1940s and 1950s.

Following Richard Dyer's thesis in his foundational *Stars*, uncovering the historical significance of film stars requires an awareness of the different media texts that circulated in culture and formed a star's image intertextually. To that end, my book draws from Tierney's promotion, or the material that indicated the studio's conception of her image and apparently deliberate efforts to make that image accessible to the public: pinups and fashion photographs, staged interviews, studio-written biographies and film production notes released to the press, film trailers, and studio-created marketing guides called "pressbooks," which provided exhibitors with production background, advertising copy and illustrations, and ideas for exploitation campaigns to sell particular films.[31] For example, the pressbook for *The Ghost and Mrs. Muir* recommended print and radio advertising tie-ins with Royal-Crown Cola that featured Tierney and mentioned the film, as well as illustrations of Tierney modeling five different ensembles that could be used for fashion pages and tie-ins with department and dress stores.[32] Other primary sources include publicity in newspapers, trade papers, general-circulation magazines, and fan magazines, constituting what the press allegedly discovered or what Tierney herself may have revealed. Publicity could be "disguised" promotion; the studios still controlled much of this information and used it to build up a star.[33] Harry Brand was the head of Fox's publicity department, and Tierney credited publicist Peggy McNaught for her star treatment at the studio.[34] Moreover, this book relies on criticism and commentary written about Tierney that molded public opinion during her career.[35] All these media texts help collapse the boundary between the star's private life and the films in which she appears as an on-screen performer.

A star study must also deal to some extent with the films of the star in question. For certain kinds of film stars, claims Dyer, "their celebrity is defined by the fact of their appearing in films."[36] Films are generally the most important of the media texts related to a star, he maintains, especially given how studios often built films around a star's image (i.e., star "vehicles").[37] Tierney exemplifies this phenomenon, and her films will therefore occupy a privileged place in the subsequent chapters. Elsewhere, Dyer has advised scholars of film stardom to pay close attention "to how stars function within the films themselves, that is, how the films articulate, carry, inflect or subvert the general ideological/cultural functions" of a star. Focusing on how the star's image "is variously used in relation to other elements, such as the construction of character, narrative, mise-en-scène, and so on[,]" grounds the wider historical significance of a star in aesthetic specificity.[38] The reversing polarities of Tierney's star image—presence and absence, mobility and stasis, resistance and containment—could apply to female stardom in general, if not women's experiences in any patriarchal-capitalist system, but they also serve narrative and thematic functions in Tierney's films that warrant scrutiny. We cannot think of *Laura* merely as a product of the star system (i.e., a vehicle for Tierney) but also as a film that exposes the conditions of female stardom in a way that makes them hypervisible.

A transmedia methodology such as the model Dyer advances does not intend to gather a totalizing meaning of a star based on determining the "correct" sources, the way a biographer verifies what happened to a star and when. Star studies instead acknowledges the many different, even contradictory possible meanings a star's image may hold in tension (either at a particular moment or over time). Dyer insists that stars matter to society precisely for this reason: "Stars frequently speak to the dominant contractions in social life—experienced as conflicting demands, contrary expectations, irreconcilable but equally held values—in such a way as to appear to reconcile them. In part, by simply being one indivisible entity within an existence in the 'real world,' yet displaying contradictory personality traits, stars can affirm that it is possible to triumph over, transcend, successfully live out contradictions."[39] Bound by an image that the industry's economic demands and ideological expectations shaped at the time, Tierney publicly worked to resolve the contradictions in women's social roles even if those contradictions remained never fully settled in her own life. In this way, her story supports McLean's position that "studies of Hollywood stars in the postwar era—even, if not especially, stars whose personal lives were as important as their films—can quite easily be folded into other revisionings of the 1950s as the crucible for, rather than the barrier to, the emergence of second wave feminism in the 1960s."[40]

I am not arguing that Tierney is necessarily the prime example of female stardom in Hollywood of the 1940s or even that she was unique among her peers, but that she was actually quite *typical*. Potentially overshadowed by other stars from her period, she tends to be viewed more through nostalgia than history, the details of her labor largely eclipsed by the portrait that looms so large in public memory, and she remains understudied and underappreciated. And yet McLean's interest in Hayworth runs parallel to mine in Tierney: her "image perhaps helped some women (and, one hopes, men) to begin to articulate overtly feminist feelings of dissatisfaction, frustration, and anger with the impossible double binds of their lives."[41] Tierney's ordinariness demonstrates the range of different meanings a single star produced and the different uses to which it could be deployed in the 1940s, helping us to recognize not only her significance but also the significance of Hollywood's female stars of the era more generally. The important work that stars perform does not lie in the domain of the select few who shine the brightest in the star system (the most popular, cultish, canonical, "talented," or subversive) but exists in a constellation that includes even the most ordinary. Identification with stars, as McLean and others have illustrated, "is often based on similarity rather than difference." That is to say, "we attach ourselves most easily to those with whom we share particular attributes—age, gender, class, nationality, or whose attributes we would most like to share."[42] Ordinary stars in a particular cultural-historical context can therefore teach us about the most commonly held similarities among a group of stars and their value to an audience as aspirational figures or objects of identification.

Part of this ordinariness was a result of rhetorical strategies used in the promotion and publicity of female stars in Hollywood between about 1930 and 1950. In their book *Reframing Screen Performance*, Cynthia Baron and Sharon Marie Carnicke find that "writing about screen performance often considers things more accessible than acting technique and more in tune with leisure interests, with the popular press consistently emphasizing film actors' beautiful bodies and winning personalities."[43] Baron and Carnicke's research shows how "publicity surrounding screen actors has often actively suppressed information about training, preferring instead the myth of the born performer whose natural talents and genuine feelings are first captured by the camera and then presented on screen." The studios wanted to demystify star acting for audiences; a star was to be valued as a social ideal, not a worker in a particular craft. Behind-the-scenes coverage attributed an actor's work merely to "instincts" and "a few tricks of the trade," crediting hair and makeup men or male publicists with the tough labor of stardom.[44] Virginia Wright Wexman puts forth a similar contention in *Creating the Couple*, her book on Hollywood stars and the performance of love and marriage. Both on and off the screen, the jobs performed by young women of a marrying age "do not appear to involve any activity that the audience could construe as work," what Wexman calls "productive labor."[45] Denying female stars their skilled expertise and labor was a means of turning them into models of heterosexual companionship rather than competitors with men. Constructed out of cosmetic and cinematic artifice but presented as "naturally" beautiful, female stars represented the ultimate in romantic desirability. Thus, despite their financial independence, Wexman concludes that they retained a certain passivity in their images as long as their labor was understood as less meaningful than that of men.[46]

Gene Tierney: Star of Hollywood's Home Front contributes to the growing body of recent scholarship that has shown how female stars engaged in their own artistic labor—however publicly concealed or distorted it might have been—and opened a discursive space for feminist identification as women working under and against the constraints of the Hollywood star system. There are many reasons one might *not* think of Tierney in the context of female star labor at this time. Her films are commonly identified by genre (e.g., film noir, "woman's film" melodrama) or credited to their directors, several of whom are now considered auteurs (e.g., Ernst Lubitsch, Otto Preminger, Joseph L. Mankiewicz). She neither formed her own production company like Rita Hayworth's Beckworth Corporation or Marilyn Monroe Productions nor worked as a producer, director, or writer like Ida Lupino, who established the independent company The Filmakers with her husband Collier Young.[47] She was neither a freelance star nor what Dyer calls an "independent" type, such as Bette Davis, Joan Crawford, and Katharine Hepburn.[48] Not unpopular by any means, Tierney also was not *as* popular as some of her contemporaries such as Betty Grable or Greer Garson.[49] Tierney was not a singer or a dancer, and she never studied a particular school of acting the way Marilyn Monroe learned the Method.[50] Exercising some control over her image, Monroe even bargained for financial compensation and required director approval in her contract (films were created with her in mind and productions would shut down if she did not arrive for work).[51] If the subtitle of a recent television documentary on Tierney's life is any indication of her current status in the general public, she is in many ways "a forgotten star."[52] For these very reasons, apart from obviously liking her, I have selected her as the subject of a star study, as this book aims to expand on understandings of what Hollywood's female labor and "ability" looked like during and immediately after World War II.

Hollywood and the U.S. Home Front in the 1940s

Tierney's ordinariness placed her at the intersection of multiple different star types between 1942 and 1950, the period of her career that this book primarily covers, during which time Fox featured her most prominently and she played her best-remembered roles. Whereas older stars such as Claudette Colbert, Ginger Rogers, and Barbara Stanwyck represented the American Everywoman (wives and mothers in wartime), her contemporaries such as Betty Grable at Fox and Rita Hayworth at Columbia were "pinup girls," wartime sex symbols who posed in bathing suits or nightgowns for photos "pinned up" on barracks walls.[53] Tierney could fit in both types, but Fox never entirely typecast her in either (Grable and Hayworth were also both dancers, and Grable sang to boot, star qualities that put them in a different category altogether). Brunettes such as MGM's Hedy Lamarr from Austria, Universal's Maria Montez from the Dominican Republic, and Paramount's U.S.-born "Sarong Queen" Dorothy Lamour embodied a cool, dark glamour and a sexualized Otherness, and we will see how Fox attempted to reconcile Tierney's image as an "average American girl" with her sexual "exoticism." Fox's biography in 1946 proudly read, "[The studio] had been trying to type her, but now they found that she did not fit into any one category. Gene Tierney could be anything they wanted her to be, in any language and with sex in all of them." Regarding her as a "very contradictory type," the studio labeled her "one of those rare anomalies of filmdom."[54] What it may have lost in a coherent image for Tierney, it gained in a remarkable adaptability with an image open to different reading strategies, meanings, and uses for the U.S. home front.

The decade of the 1940s was itself rife with contradictions, extending and modifying cultural changes in the United States that began in the first two decades of the twentieth century. McLean goes as far as to argue that for all of the "contradictions and ambiguities" attributed to the discourse on gender in the 1920s, "there are many more [. . .] marking the commercial discourse about Hollywood stars and their films in the late 1940s and the 1950s."[55] In her groundbreaking book, *Babel and Babylon*, a study in the shift from early to classical U.S. cinema between 1907 to 1917, Miriam Hansen posits that cinema served as an "alternative public sphere" in an era of late modernity. Then a new medium, cinema opened possibilities for marginalized social groups—the urban working class, immigrants, and, overlapping with both groups, women—that "had either no access to existing institutions of public life or, in the case of women, only in a highly regulated and dependent form; they had not previously been considered an audience in the sense of a 'viewing public.'"[56] Stars such as the male sex symbol Rudolph Valentino emerged from this new configuration of gender, desire, pleasure, and consumption in the public sphere.[57] As part of a burgeoning urban culture of consumerism, cinema's address to women was not unproblematic, ranging between "experimental differentiation (to satisfy as many diverse constituencies as possible) and long-term homogenization (predicated on a notion of 'woman' as white, heterosexual, and middle-class)."[58] But as a medium exhibited in public spaces, it established "a perceptual, experiential horizon" for women regardless of marital status, age, or background, articulating a new discourse on femininity.[59]

One of the major ways Hollywood responded to the war was through the patriotic values encoded in the films, which had a profound effect on film and female-audience relations at this time. Created in 1942, the Office of War Information (OWI) was the U.S. government agency in charge of regulating information about the war (i.e., propaganda) communicated to the U.S. home front through print, broadcast, and screen media. The OWI's Bureau of Motion Pictures (BMP) reviewed Hollywood scripts and made suggestions to ensure that films supported U.S. investments in the war, glorifying the promise and prosperity of life on the home front, depicting the strength and endurance of civilians eager to "do their bit" for the war effort, and promoting a democratic image of a nation where the ills of society are the result of individual failings—not systemic problems—and therefore both temporary and solvable. With its mostly female reviewing staff, the BMP urged studios to produce films that registered the rewarding experiences women found by adopting new roles in a public labor force in which they contributed to war work and occupied jobs previously held by men who were now fulfilling military service.[60] The quintessential example of this type of home-front "woman's film" was Selznick International Pictures' epic *Since You Went Away* (John Cromwell, 1944), a prestige production starring Claudette Colbert as an army wife, who trades the comforts of her midwestern home for a welding torch to work in a shipyard while holding her bourgeois family together during her husband's absence. Aimed at female audiences and driven by female stars, the so-called woman's film of the studio era provided female-centered narratives of women liberated from their marginalized and domesticated social roles (at least temporarily or in qualified ways) and depicted new possibilities for women to take action in their daily lives.[61]

Although the OWI could exert ideological pressure and go as far as to deny export licenses for films, which threatened studio profits, film scholar Philippa Gates points out that studios embraced "war messages" even without OWI intervention. For example, William Wyler directed *Mrs. Miniver* (1942) for MGM before the creation of the OWI in 1942, and Wyler finished *The Best Years of Our Lives* (1946) for Samuel Goldwyn Productions after the war, but both films concern women's home-front labor and sacrifice as wives, mothers, and war workers.[62] Both films, incidentally, won Oscars for Best Picture of their respective years, and Greer Garson won for Best Actress in *Mrs. Miniver*, playing the hero of this Dunkirk story—a British housewife. Home-front propaganda films were good business as much as they were good for morale and Hollywood's cultural value. Until the 1950s, studios targeted women more than any other moviegoing demographic, believing that its dominant audience was female, and although combat films were a mainstay of the Hollywood genre system, the war years turned the industry's attention to a new audience category: "the unescorted female." Wives and mothers who attended theaters alone were thought to prefer romantic melodramas to violent, all-male action films that reminded them of their husbands and sons away in battle.[63]

Representations of workingwomen were not exclusive to film but spanned wartime media, and they were both symptomatic and pedagogical, reflecting and helping to stimulate the influx of U.S. women's employment. In her book *Hollywood Heroines*, Helen Hanson explains, "Highly visible female icons of the working woman were key to wartime propaganda campaigns designed to encourage women to join the wartime workforce."[64] Rosie the Riveter was the most prominent of these "can-do" icons, popularized by the War Production Coordinating Committee's posters and Norman Rockwell's May 29, 1943, cover of the *Saturday Evening Post*. Notwithstanding the enormous attention to women in war plants, between 1940 and 1947 women held an average of 41.4 percent of all of the white-collar jobs in the United States. What is more is that women filled professional, managerial, and sales roles and took up the majority of all of the country's clerical positions.[65] The importance of this historical moment is not that women in the United States found jobs outside the home for the first time. From the Great Depression of the 1930s onward, Hanson reminds us, it was actually quite common for women to work temporary jobs after finishing their education and before getting married. Yet World War II brought greater numbers of women into the labor market, especially married women, and female employment "became particularly accented and visible during the war era." Mass media images of women at wartime helped reorganize U.S. cultural perceptions of women's roles in both the private and public sphere.[66] Whether playing workingwomen in patriotic films marketed to a female audience or engaging in publicized war work off the screen (e.g., selling war bonds), Hollywood stars put a recognizable face on home-front labor that made them appear more ordinary (they too are doing their part), just as it made ordinary home-front labor look more glamorous.

Wartime media's address to women was not this straightforward, though. Film historians have detailed how films from the 1940s presented a highly vexed discourse on gender and U.S. social life. Dana Polan, for example, argues that a dialectical relationship between power and paranoia structured film narratives that juxtaposed ideological affirmation (the unity of family and wartime commitment, optimism about scientific knowledge and progress) against threats to the stability of such affirmation (loss, death, disillusionment, the limits of vision, epistemological uncertainty).[67] Writing about films specifically made on the backdrop of World War II, Thomas Doherty claims that although the settings for women's stories may have moved from the home to a public workplace, their new occupations (e.g., factory workers, nurses, or servicewomen) coexisted with traditional, reassuring gender roles of girlfriend/wife or mother. Female characters often still relied on their "natural" domestic skills (e.g., sewing parachutes) and retained normative femininity (e.g., as glamorous gunnery girls).[68]

More recently, film history's turn to audience reception has shown how audiences do not interpret cinematic meaning from films alone but take interpretive cues from extratextual material available in a historical context of viewing. Tim Snelson's reception study of 1940s horror films makes the case that the "female monster cycle" was "both [a] mediation upon and response to women's shifting wartime roles and experiences," a topic of discussion in film reviews, social commentaries, and news articles at the time.[69] Women's bodies were discursively positioned as "the home-front battleground where the war would be won or lost," besieged by "dual demands of productivity and desirability."[70] In other words, women were simultaneously celebrated for doing men's jobs and condemned for ignoring their maternal responsibilities, encouraged to imitate pinup poses adored by servicemen and at the same time shamed for indulging in "promiscuous behavior" in the name of "misplaced patriotism."[71] According to Snelson, "Multiple voices vied for control in defining the meaning of female identity and the meaning of women's bodies specifically," but the home front also brought "possibilities for contestation whereby women could redefine their own identities."[72] Star images help mask and smooth over these sorts of tensions. While embodying and seeming to normalize social ideals, a star can simultaneously enact less traditional norms of behavior that certain social transformations enable. Tierney's buildup as a sex symbol from 1940 to 1942 gives us a concrete example of this dual function.

Gene Tierney's Star Buildup and Her "First Modern Role"

Laura was only one in a string of successful films Tierney made for Fox, but that work came after 1942. In the meantime, her image bifurcated along two promotional lines—"averageness" and "exoticism"—that were not reconciled until Fox's *Rings on Her Fingers* (Rouben Mamoulian, 1942), which fully exploited the iconography of Tierney as a pinup girl. When Tierney signed with Fox in 1940, the studio began promoting her through a discourse of Anglo-American authenticity (i.e., whiteness) that presumably intended for audiences to see her as ordinary. Born in Brooklyn on November 19, 1920, Tierney was "the average American girl with family advantages," who dreamed of becoming "a great actress some day." She was "really crazy about dogs and horses[,]" and "being sincere herself," she liked "sincere people."[73] Her father, Howard Tierney, was a Wall Street insurance broker and, shortly after her birth, moved the family to the Greens Farms neighborhood in Westport, Connecticut.

Between attending school at St. Margaret's in Waterbury and Miss Porter's in Farmington, she traveled to Lausanne, Switzerland, to study at Brillantmont International School, where she learned French and "such domestic things as would enable her to become a good wife." Stressing her "natural" star quality, her studio biography informed the press that her real name was Gene Eliza Tierney; Gene was "not short for Eugenia or anything else."[74] "There's nothing about the girl that is either an illusion or delusion," read her profile in *Silver Screen*, which cheered on the "wholesome, buoyant spirit of a girl eager for life and determined to get the most out of it."[75] The initials "G.E.T." were not lost on the press and became part of Tierney's star persona. As columnist Sidney Skolsky put it, she is "a positive gal who generally gets what she goes after."[76]

Tierney's studio biography also chronicled the "Cinderella story" of her discovery in Hollywood, a story she later retold in her autobiography. Just before her society debut in Fairfield, Connecticut, she took a sightseeing trip to Hollywood with her mother and sister in the summer of 1938. Warner Bros. producer Gordon Hollingshead was giving the Tierneys a private tour of the studio—as it turned out, he happened to be a cousin of her mother's—and Gene caught the eye of director Anatole Litvak. The story goes that Hollingshead arranged for a screen test and Warner Bros. quickly came back with an offer to put her under contract.[77]

After reluctance to see his daughter become an actress, Howard Tierney felt that stage work would make her both a more experienced actress and more qualified for a higher starting salary in Hollywood. Through his facilitations, she landed a role in George Abbott's *Mrs. O'Brien Entertains* (1939) (in preparation, Abbott gave her a walk-on part as a water carrier in *What a Life*, and she understudied for *The Primrose Path*, both 1938 productions). The play received poor reviews and closed after thirty-seven performances, but she earned favorable notices from critics. Columbia Pictures offered her a six-month contract that satisfied her father from a financial perspective. Without any success securing film parts at the studio, she returned to Broadway for another Abbott play, *Ring Two* (1939).[78]

It was the Elliott Nugent and James Thurber comedy *The Male Animal* (1940) that finally led to her contract with Fox in the midst of publicity from *Life*, *Harper's Bazaar*, and *Vogue*.[79] Fox was producing a sequel to *Jesse James* (Henry King, 1939) titled *The Return of Frank James*

(Fritz Lang, 1940), and Tierney made her screen debut as a newspaper reporter covering the Frank James story after his brother, Jesse, is killed. The *Harvard Lampoon* named her the "Worst Female Discovery of 1940."[80] Supporting roles followed with *Hudson's Bay* (Irving Pichel, 1941), a historical melodrama about fur trade in seventeenth-century Canada (she played a British aristocrat), and the earthier *Tobacco Road* (John Ford, 1941), a loose, comic adaptation of Erskine Caldwell's novel about Depression-era Georgia sharecroppers, which had already inspired the longest-running Broadway play at the time. The latter film gave Tierney a small part in a high-profile, moneymaking production, pitched as a follow-up to Fox's *The Grapes of Wrath* (John Ford, 1940), but it failed to generate the same level of acclaim. In *Belle Starr* (Irving Cummings, 1941), the first film in which she topped the bill, she portrayed a southern belle turned outlaw during the American Reconstruction (a character based on a historical figure). Critics panned her performance. Not until the early 1950s would she return to the Western genre, starring as a good woman who shelters an escaped convict (Glenn Ford) in *The Secret of Convict Lake* (Michael Gordon, 1951) and a Spanish lady in love with an outlaw "gaucho," or Argentine cowboy (Rory Calhoun), in the runaway production *Way of a Gaucho* (Jacques Tourneur, 1952), both Fox films. Whether Tierney was actually "bad" in these early films cannot be fairly assessed without accounting for her lack of experience, the degree to which she may have been miscast in her roles, and the weakness of the roles themselves, but in the absence of such considerations, her merits as an actress had been decided.

Tierney's proverbial "big break" came when Fox loaned her out to independent producers Walter Wanger and Arnold Pressburger, respectively, to star in *Sundown* (Henry Hathaway, 1941) and *The Shanghai Gesture* (Josef von Sternberg, 1941). United Artists distributed both films. The New England debutante traveled to the New Mexico desert to shoot the colonial adventure film *Sundown*, playing a European woman raised as an Arab named Zia, who runs the largest trading network in East Africa. In the film noir *The Shanghai Gesture*, she played a half-British, half-Chinese tourist in Shanghai, who loses herself in sex, liquor, and gambling at an underworld casino. Presented to the public as an "average American girl" and now also an "exotic" Other, Tierney was both a duplication of and a complement to Fox's other wartime pinup queen,

Betty Grable, who made female sexual expression and desirability more innocent as a "pure white" blonde.

The Orientalism of Tierney's star image will be a topic of further discussion later in chapter 1, but I raise it in relation to these early roles to show how her buildup as a sex symbol conditioned the eroticization of femininity through an exoticization of race. Initially undecided about whether to renew her contract, Fox admitted to keeping her on the payroll after the "notorious publicity" she suddenly attracted with the Wanger/ Pressburger films.[81] Reflecting on *Sundown* in her autobiography, Tierney tells us that her "harem girl" look was the result of a "veiled and scanty" costume that Wanger altered further with a pair of scissors to give her a low-slung skirt with an exposed midriff.[82] The costume landed her on the cover of *Life* in November of 1941. Wanger may have wanted to find ways to show off more of Tierney's skin, but *The Shanghai Gesture* takes the opposite approach by giving almost fetishistic attention to the wardrobe Cassini designed for Tierney. Off the screen, the costumes garnered attention in glamour photos, and *Photoplay* heralded the couple "March Mode-Makers" in a 1942 fashion layout.[83] An extensively censored adaptation of a successful Broadway play, *The Shanghai Gesture* was intended as a comeback film for director Josef von Sternberg, who helped launch German star Marlene Dietrich at Paramount, where she reigned as Hollywood's foremost international "exotic." Sternberg returned to the Chinese setting of *Shanghai Express* (1932), the biggest hit of his seven films with Dietrich, and infused *The Shanghai Gesture* with a similar eroticism at the level of mise-en-scène. The introduction of Tierney's character Poppy hints that the very atmosphere of the Shanghai casino might stimulate sexual arousal. "It smells so incredibly evil," she coos after entering for the first time. "I didn't think such a place existed except in my own imagination. It has a ghastly familiarity like a half-remembered dream. Anything could happen here. Any moment."

Casting Tierney in these Orientalist roles meant that her films needed to manage the taboo of "miscegenation," as the Hays Code referred to it. Whereas the tragic "half-caste" Poppy dies in *The Shanghai Gesture*, alleviating the threat of racial mixing, *Sundown* permits the white man to enter into a courtship with Zia after the film reveals her true identity as a white European and confirming her British and Christian assimilation in the final scene. The same is true of her next film at

Fox, the South Seas swashbuckler *Son of Fury: The Story of Benjamin Blake* (John Cromwell, 1942). Wearing two pieces and dancing in a leaf skirt, Tierney played a happy Polynesian islander whom Georgian fortune hunter Ben (Tyrone Power) names "Eve" and teaches to speak pidgin English. Eve's body is colonizable, and therefore the film allows the white man to reunite with her at the end. What all three films have in common is their use of Tierney to map race onto sex. Steven Dillon points out in his book *Wolf-Women and Phantom Ladies* that covering female stars with ethnic or racial masks during the 1940s served as a means of "sexual display and passionate expression," letting Hollywood remove (white) feminine constraint. Films such as *Sundown*, *The Shanghai Gesture*, and *Son of Fury* reflect the Hays Code's contradictory and inconsistently enforced guidelines on miscegenation throughout the decade, evincing both a U.S. cultural anxiety about and attraction to racial Otherness as a source of sexual desire.[84]

Following *Son of Fury*, Fox's screwball comedy *Rings on Her Fingers* was a transitional film in that it reconciled the studio's original conception of her as an "average American girl" with her new image as a symbol of unrestrained sexuality. Further, she had officially entered the ranks of the "Fox Girls," Zanuck's cohort of beautiful women who contributed to the studio's signature brand.[85] After Fox Film Corporation merged with Twentieth Century Pictures in 1935 to become Twentieth Century–Fox and Zanuck assumed his role as head of production, a position he held until 1956, he gained a reputation for discovering young talent he could groom for box-office star power.[86] Despite his "office bedroom," where casual sex with his aspiring female stars reportedly took place, Peter Lev's book on the studio describes a "kinder, gentler" relationship with Tierney in which Zanuck "looked out" for her during her struggles with mental illness and "tried to adjust her production schedule to her health needs."[87] "He was always fair, often generous to me," she confirmed in her autobiography.[88]

Paired with her *Frank James* costar Henry Fonda, Tierney now had her "first modern role," according to the language of the pressbook.[89] *Rings on Her Fingers* was Fox's answer to the Paramount hit *The Lady Eve* (Preston Sturges, 1941), with Tierney in Barbara Stanwyck's con-artist role and Fonda reprising the part of the lovable dupe. The studio attributed the "modernity" of Tierney's role to the contemporary settings and costumes after a string of period films, but Fox did more than simply update her image to the present. Differentiating *Sundown* and *The Shanghai Gesture* as period films (they were both set in the present) equated the Eastern world with an ostensibly primitive or premodern past. By capitalizing on the contemporary iconography of the wartime pinup, Fox squared Tierney's image with the "modern" feminine ideals of the U.S. home front without losing the overt appeals to sex in her last three films.

World War II had directly touched the production of *Rings on Her Fingers*. The Japanese bombing of Pearl Harbor interrupted shooting on Catalina Island, and the cast immediately sailed for San Pedro, listening to broken radio reports, afraid the water had been mined, and anxiously speculating about the possibilities of an attack on the California coast.[90] A publicity release claimed that Tierney wanted "to keep movie star–soldier boys alive in the memories of the fans" and requested that their pictures "be placed on her dressing table for several scenes in the film." Every other night of shooting, Fonda supposedly spent six hours as an air-raid warden, and no one complained when he showed up on set the next morning with circles under his eyes. Written before the United States entered the war, the script originally included a $32,000 wedding between Tierney and Fonda's characters, but director Rouben Mamoulian eliminated this scene "because he thought such pretentious rites would not be in keeping with the times." Mamoulian was quoted saying that the U.S. intervention in the war should motivate Hollywood to produce more comedies "so that we may escape realities at night and go about our defense work in the daytime with a fresh perspective."[91]

Implicitly disavowing Tierney's recent Orientalist associations, Fox announced her as its new "find" of 1942. The *Rings on Her Fingers* pressbook cited her status in two polls: out of 548 U.S. publications, *Film Daily* ranked her number one as the nation's "find of the year," beating Veronica Lake, Teresa Wright, and Joan Leslie, and the Royal Canadian Air Force Flyers poll voted her as "the most appealing girl in films." Marveling at how she finally "comes into her own" in *Rings on Her Fingers*, one story read, "Gene Tierney took the long way round to achieve the role she was most obviously suited for in films." Another story underscored Fox's "good investment" in Tierney as a star, itemizing the expenses involved with star hires (salaries, dramatic coaches, makeup and wardrobe tests, hairdressing, etc.). Allegedly beating out fourteen other young women for a contract with Fox, she went from "virtually an unknown at the beginning of 1941" to a star already in demand for loan outs to five other studios. Exhibitors could even blow up a standee of Tierney in a white swimsuit, mount it in theater lobbies, and award guest ticket prizes to patrons able to pitch three quoit rings through her outstretched arm in faux marriage proposals.[92]

Rings on Her Fingers stars Tierney as Brooklyn shopgirl Susie Miller, who abandons the girdle counter to join up with two swindlers, Warren (Laird Cregar) and Maybelle (Spring Byington), and seduce money out of millionaires. "My dear, in these ugly times, mere beauty alone achieves a great deal," says Warren, tutoring her on the part she will play as his daughter and Maybelle's niece named "Linda" (the Spanish and Portuguese word for "beautiful"). "Now, your role is just to be beautiful and unobtainable—nothing else," he instructs. The trio's latest victim, John Wheeler (Fonda), claims to be an investment banker from New York. Mistaking John's interest in buying a yacht off Catalina Island as an indication of his wealth, they scam him for $15,000. Susie/Linda lies on the beach in a white swimsuit to lure him in, suggestively writhing on a cushion in a series of different pinup poses (fig. 2). She bounces one leg on top of the other, crosses them from side to side with her toes pointed forward, and dangles one foot off the cushion, gently swaying it back and forth. Shots of John talking to the yacht captain over the phone alternate with close-ups of Susie/Linda's legs and long shots of her body as her sunbathing increasingly distracts him ("I like her topsides. Good sheer. Yes, nice and trim. Smooth and graceful." "A slender stern, hasn't she?" "What about her ankles—[*stammering*] anchors?"). Originally, the film was to feature Susie modeling girdles in several scenes, but Fox substituted swim and play clothes after determining that girdle material was too valuable during wartime. This comic scene provided the studio with inspiration for advertising illustrations of Tierney posing in bathing suits or lounging in poolwear, often with Fonda gawking from the sidelines as if to stand in for the heterosexual male moviegoers and fans of her pinup photos.[93]

The film also allowed the studio to mitigate Tierney's class privilege by unveiling the "average" girl from Brooklyn behind the debutante in a kind of reverse makeover of her star image. Warren transforms Susie

Fig. 2. Tierney poses like a pinup model in *Rings on Her Fingers* (Rouben Mamoulian, 1942).

into "unobtainable" society girl Linda, but the narrative requires Linda to learn to be Susie again in order to engineer a successful courtship with John. When they are coincidentally reunited later in the film, he confesses that he is only an accountant and his financial loss cost him his life savings (although he remains unaware of her deception). Having developed genuine feelings for John, and ridden with guilt over what she has done, Susie decides to run away with him and get married. She conspires a plan to return the money without giving away her involvement in the theft, but until then, she tries to perform the role of the perfect wife. On their first night in their new apartment together, John is impressed to find her cooking dinner, exclaiming, "Say, I've really got a triple-threat woman, haven't I? Class, beauty, now domesticity. You didn't tell me about this." Susie replies, "I couldn't very well go around wearing a neon sign on my bathing suit: 'I cook too.'"

The figure of pinup functions in two key ways for this film. As a semiotic calling card in the text, it can be easily extracted and reproduced in the advertising campaign to sell the film through a fetishistic attachment to the female star. Like other wartime pinup stars, though, Tierney also modeled behavior for women on the home front. Jeanine Basinger contends that if "women on the home front were in their own way serving in a militarized world," we might think of them as "home-front soldiers."[94] Pinups were young women who were not only sexy but also "feisty, independent, and patriotic." On the screen, they dominated the narrative of a film and initiated its action, while in photographs they "were living in military camps, in the barracks, alongside American soldiers," sometimes wearing military-inspired outfits, holding weapons, or sitting on rockets to convey "an 'I-am-in-the-military-alongside-you' quality." If their photographs boosted servicemen's morale, their films taught women serious and chaste practices of dating, such as not to toy with a soldier's affections before he is about to be sent to fight overseas.[95]

Female pinups were the products of new ideas about female sexual self-expression and women's roles in the labor force, and therefore quite popular with ordinary women on the U.S. home front during wartime. Advertisers used female pinups to sell women's fashions and consumer goods, both for women and the men for whom they may have shopped, but art historian Maria Elena Buszek stresses that female pinups were neither exclusively sources of heteronormative male visual pleasure nor symbols of heteronormative romance. The image of the female pinup was actually able to inspire emulation from women outside of those regimes. Buszek asserts that "by World War II the pin-up could serve as a model through which contemporary women on the home front could construct themselves: at once both conventionally feminine and subversively aware of her own power for sexual agency."[96] Susie is a woman in pursuit of socioeconomic independence and mobility, who possesses her own sexual subjectivity and desire. She wears her bathing suit not only for leverage in a system that has excluded her but also because it is *she* who wants John to look at her. After all, the game of deception is mutual at first (she is not a society girl, and he is not an investment banker), and Susie's sexuality gives her a kind of bargaining power. To be clear, *Rings on Her Fingers* was not a war-themed film, but its wartime reception conditions were such that audiences had different interpretive strategies available to them to read Tierney's role vis-à-vis the pinup photo. So strongly is Tierney still identified with pinups that when the Galerie Joseph in Paris advertised its 2017 pinup exposition *L'âge d'or du Balnéaire*

(The golden age of seaside), it selected Tierney as the logo for the event. Her pinups continue to circulate widely on social media fan pages.

The following chapters will further examine how Tierney personified ways of being on the home front, representing different types of women who negotiated their subjective positions within the social prescriptions of femininity. Chapter 1 turns to the development of Tierney's image from a pinup girl to workingwoman through the war films *Thunder Birds* (William A. Wellman, 1942) and *China Girl* (Henry Hathaway, 1942) and a film in which the war is conspicuously absent, *Laura*. We will see how *Laura* made female beautification compatible with women's wartime labor through Tierney's costumes that, as designed by Bonnie Cashin, inspired "ready-to-wear" fashions for white-collar women.

The next two chapters consider Tierney's related images as wife and mother. Chapter 2 looks at Tierney's roles as overly eager wives in *Leave Her to Heaven*, *The Razor's Edge* (Edmund Goulding, 1946), and *That Wonderful Urge*, which appeared concurrently with her off-screen marriage to Cassini and the postwar demobilization of women in the public workforce. While Tierney's publicity idealized heterosexual marriage and viewed her as a domestic "nurturer," these films either melodramatically or comically make this "real" image hyperbolic. Chapter 3 explicates ideals of motherhood in the United States during the 1940s and Tierney's star publicity as a real-life mother in this context before focusing on her maternal roles in *Heaven Can Wait* (Ernst Lubitsch, 1943), *Dragonwyck*, and *The Ghost and Mrs. Muir*. As works of fantasy or Gothic horror, they offset the presence of death that their genres required in the 1940s through the productive and reproductive capabilities of Tierney's maternal figures, managing larger anxieties about mortality.

The final chapter revisits all three of these types—workers, wives, and mothers—through the press coverage of Tierney's psychiatric treatments in the late 1950s and early 1960s. Tierney's release from the Menninger Clinic in 1958 was announced as a return to work, which newspapers and magazines reported as the rehabilitation Tierney needed after suffering personal disappointments as a wife and mother. Using this discursive material as an interpretive framework for films released before the public's knowledge of her mental illness, this chapter also reads *Whirlpool* through what Rebecca Bell-Metereau and Colleen Glenn call an "erotics of suffering."[97] Tierney plays a kleptomaniac housewife accused of murder in that film noir, which Fox advertised as "another *Laura*." Despite the studio's efforts to replicate the success of her earlier film, Tierney's star began to dim in the early 1950s, but as I hope readers will learn in this book, there is more to her work than what might have been, and ample evidence of what was.

1
Working It

Beautification and War Effort

Immediately after *Rings on Her Fingers* (Rouben Mamoulian, 1942), Tierney returned to the screen twice more the same year with the World War II propaganda films *Thunder Birds* (William A. Wellman) and *China Girl* (Henry Hathaway). Publicity did not try to hide her early films that critics "deplored" but instead reframed her as a star who rose above ill-suited projects unscathed, in part through a kind of transcendent beauty. An article in *Silver Screen* assured readers, "No matter how badly miscast, Gene always has been something delightfully nice to look at. [. . .] Lately, Gene has fared better with her roles. Particularly in *Thunder Birds* and *China Girl*. As a result, she is showing what a truly talented actress can accomplish when not handicapped with inferior screen material." Female beauty was cited as a limitation that a star had to overcome to prove herself as an actress, but romantic desirability was also expected of female stars such as Tierney and culturally prioritized as the source of their value. In one photograph she dines at the Hollywood nightclub the Mocambo next to husband Oleg Cassini (dressed in his military uniform), and in another she sits atop a motorcycle on the Fox lot, chatting intimately with her *Thunder Birds* costar Preston Foster (costumed in a flight cap and leather bomber jacket).[1] The article clearly equated her on-screen romance with her off-screen marriage to verify her investment in the war as no mere act, but real and personal.

References to her appearance also carried wartime implications, and not only for her status as a pinup girl. Through her marriage to Cassini, the renowned Hollywood costume designer responsible for her wardrobe on nine films, she was recognized as a member of fashion nobility. When Tierney played a model in *Where the Sidewalk Ends* (Otto Preminger, 1950), Cassini even showed up in a cameo as a designer named

Oleg working at her agency. He was the son of a Russian countess and a diplomat and eventually launched his own designer fashion label in New York to become one of the most influential designers of the postwar era (creating looks for Grace Kelly, to whom he was engaged after his 1952 divorce from Tierney, and later for Jacqueline Kennedy during her term as First Lady of the United States). During World War II, however, he joined the coast guard before transferring to the U.S. Army Cavalry. Fan magazines featured Tierney wearing Cassini's designs in fashion layouts, but studio promotion and publicity also went to great lengths to portray them as a relatively average American couple: serviceman and army wife. Tierney wrote in the *Hollywood Reporter* that she preferred his new title of "Lieutenant Cassini," insisting that he "discarded the title of 'Count' in favor of becoming an American citizen."[2] Before leaving home for the coast guard, he supposedly created all of Tierney's clothes.[3] A fashion layout in *Silver Screen* illustrated Tierney modeling five of Cassini's designs from her "personal wardrobe," which "shows the feminine morale trend of war, conservation of fabric with no sacrifice of beauty or glamour."[4] By 1943, she was teaching *Modern Screen* readers how a movie star goes shopping for spring wear on a war-conscious budget.[5]

Like many of her contemporaries, she participated in bond drive tours and entertained troops at the Hollywood Canteen, but there was also the sense that acting for the camera (particularly in morale-building films about the war) was another form of home-front labor—itself a service to the country analogous to enlisting in the military. Promotion for *China Girl*, for example, purported that Tierney was in the middle of shooting when Cassini said goodbye before leaving home: "Cassini waited for the end of the scene. Husband and wife embraced. He went off to the wars, this new nephew of Uncle Sam. She returned to the cameras."[6] Tierney was therefore not simply playing "home-front soldiers" but was herself part of the mobilization of U.S. women during World War II. Writing in her autobiography, she described the war years "as a time when we were united in a way known only to that generation. At home we worked hard, believed in what we were doing, and felt we belonged to a common cause. In one way or another, everyone went to war."[7] Perhaps Hollywood stars were not too different from the women whom Tierney remembered baking, organizing sewing teams, collecting scrap and wastepaper, and wishing their husbands farewell,[8] at least according to wartime star promotion. At the dawn of the postwar era, when Tierney and Cassini had settled in their house in Beverly Hills, she was just a "Countess from Brooklyn" with modest tastes. A *Photoplay* cover story professed that she wore "very simple clothes," disliked coffee, liquor, and desserts, and would rather visit with friends at home instead of going out to nightclubs.[9]

The demystification of Tierney's haute couture beauty was not exclusively the project of such publicity stories. Over the course of three films, *Thunder Birds*, *China Girl*, and *Laura*, Fox sought to make her beauty accessible to the U.S. home front at wartime by foregrounding Tierney as a worker rather than a consumer. This chapter first looks at *Thunder Birds* and *China Girl*, films in which Tierney's characters explicitly aided the war effort (with the latter film, Fox even attempted to turn Tierney's Chinese character into the "all-American girl"). In the second half of this chapter, we will see how Tierney's makeover in *Laura* (Otto Preminger, 1944) combined her image as a fashionista with her image as a workingwoman. Although quite different from one another, these three films cumulatively secured Tierney's status as a wartime star at Fox by attempting to coordinate the star system's process of female beautification with an endorsement of women's labor and austerity coded as "American."

Gene Tierney Goes to War: *Thunder Birds* and *China Girl*

Cowritten by Fox veteran Lamar Trotti and "Melville Crossman" (Zanuck's pseudonym), *Thunder Birds* was the product of the studio's especially strong ties to wartime propaganda.[10] Zanuck served in the U.S. Army during World War I and since 1939 had been a part-time lieutenant-colonel in the Army Signal Corps. Following the U.S. intervention in World War II, he was commissioned full-time and traveled to North Africa, where he produced a forty-minute color documentary about the Battle of Tunisia. Thanks to Zanuck's service and the influential connections he made, the studio enjoyed a cooperative relationship with the U.S. military in the war and immediate postwar years.[11] The director of *Thunder Birds*, William A. Wellman, was a combat veteran who flew for France during World War I.[12] After the war, he worked as a stunt pilot and taught at the Rockwell Field flight school in San Diego.[13]

Among the films in his long line of directorial credits was the aviation classic *Wings* (1927), the first Academy Award winner for Best Picture. Peter Lev notes how *Thunder Birds* came out of a cycle of war-themed productions at the studio that "combined military training with love stories and other familiar themes," including *To the Shores of Tripoli* (H. Bruce Humberstone, 1942), *Crash Dive* (Archie Mayo, 1943), and *Wing and a Prayer* (Henry Hathaway, 1944).[14]

Shot in Technicolor at Arizona locations Thunderbird Field (Glendale) and Falcon Field (Mesa), the film stars Tierney as Kay Saunders, a young woman living with her grandfather, a retired air force colonel, on a ranch next door to Thunderbird. When her old flame Steve Britt (Preston Foster) arrives as the new flight instructor, he must compete for her affections against one of his trainees, Peter Stackhouse (John Sutton, Tierney's love interest from Irving Pichel's 1941 *Hudson's Bay*), an intern with the British medical corps. Peter wants to honor his family's tradition and fly in the Royal Air Force—if he can overcome his fear of flying. It turns out that Steve was an ace pilot in World War I and knew Peter's father before he was killed. The film's alternate title, "A Tommy in the U.S.A.," telegraphed its national reversal of an earlier Crossman/Zanuck story, *A Yank in the R.A.F.* (1941), directed by Fox workhorse Henry King while the United States was still adhering to an isolationist policy. Tyrone Power and Betty Grable starred with Sutton as the triangulated lovers in that hit for the studio.

Literally playing a "girl next door," Kay exemplifies the "Extraordinary Ordinariness" or "hyperbolic ordinariness" that David M. Lugowski and Adrienne L. McLean have identified, respectively, in the wife-mother and pinup girl of the 1940s.[15] More precisely, Kay is the type of "home-front soldier" that Jeanine Basinger dubs the "All-American Girl," a World War II–era update of the "girl next door," who represents "what our boys—the unmarried soldiers—are fighting for." She is "the image of American youth: fresh, clear-eyed and clear-skinned, desirable but decent, honest, and wholesome."[16] The "tomboy" nature of the all-American girl "reflected the new emergence of dominant women by being a character with strength to draw on in difficult times," and if "the Pin-Up Girl is the soldier of love, the All-American Girl is the soldier of companionship and partnership."[17] Kay is definitely a tomboy (just look at her red, white, and blue cowgirl ensemble with boots), but according to her publicity, so was Tierney. As one article commented, "She gets furious when casual acquaintances call her 'honey' or 'baby.' She detests makeup and off the screen likes to go around with her face shiny. She loves the smell of gasoline and has a tomboy's interest of taking motors apart. She can never get them back together, but enjoys getting greasy."[18] Tierney's supposed inability to reassemble motors still implies a dependence on masculine "know-how," but her preference for mechanics over makeup implies a desire to work alongside men or in roles they may have performed prior to their military service.

After the release of *Thunder Birds*, Tierney christened a B-25 bomber with the name "Thunder Bird," an event that followed heavy studio promotion for the film. Fox even featured her prominently in a full-color comic strip summarizing the premise, a marketing strategy the studio previously exploited for *To the Shores of Tripoli*. The pressbook encouraged the use of her photos in advertising campaigns and referred to her as "Hollywood's fastest rising star." According to one bit of studio-planted publicity, Tierney became friends with real cadets while shooting in Glendale, and this "typical American young lady" acclimatized young British and Chinese men to "some good old-fashioned American institutions"—the barbecue, the square dance, the rodeo—and left them "pretty much on their way to being Westernized."[19]

Tierney fulfilled the utopian promise of the U.S. Army articulated in the film's opening sequence, shot and edited in the style of an educational film (with voice-over narration by journalist John Gunther). In the "melting pot" of the Thunderbird base, U.S. flyers and their international allies come together with a common goal: "Here are Chinese boys. They learn to fly well, these Chinese. They have something to fight for. They remember the smoking ruins of their villages back home. They remember the 'Rape of Nanking.' And here are British boys. They fly well too. They fly with a will to win. They too remember. They remember the battle of London—the wanton destruction of life and property." All these men, the film seems to say, are Americans at the end of the day. Gunther continues over a montage of white U.S. trainees: "And here are American boys. Boys from Kansas and the coast of Maine. Boys who never saw a plane close up till yesterday. Boys who were soda jerks, law school students, dry-goods salesmen, high school athletes. Here they are. Here they come! Watch 'em fly." This opening sequence tells us that Thunderbird unites not only nations but also regions, classes, ages, and occupations within the United States.

The anecdote about Tierney's "Westernization" of Thunderbird cadets also reinforces Kay's role in the film as Peter's American ambassador. Kay hosts a Fourth of July party at her grandfather's ranch that includes square dancing, bronco riding, and fireworks, and she introduces him to the "great American delicacy" of hot dogs roasted over a campfire. "Hope you don't like women who pretend to be delicate eaters," she remarks after taking a big bite into four hot dogs sandwiched between a hamburger bun in an appetitive assertion of her all-American tomboyishness. For the campfire scene, alleged one promotional item, Tierney ate nine meals of hot dogs, "six too many" even for the star with "probably the most robust feminine appetite in Hollywood."[20]

Kay's courtship of Peter is not exclusively a private or domestic matter, though. We learn early in the film that Steve never got over Kay, but she still resents him for treating her as an auxiliary to his first true love: planes. While Kay initially tries to make Steve jealous by pursuing his handsome student, a young man much closer to her own age, she is also attracted to Peter's cultural difference. "I've never really known an Englishman before," she says, asking, "You typical? Don't have a title, do you?" Better yet, Peter believes that the United States is a fundamentally philanthropic nation. "I traveled around the world once," he informs her. "Everywhere I went, I saw churches and schools and hospitals—even in the jungles—all built with American money for somebody else to use. I never saw any German or Japanese philanthropies." His endearing awkwardness also conceals a vulnerability that Steve refuses to accept in himself. Through the course of the film, it is apparent that what Kay most desires is a romantic future in which she can share equal partnership.

The film's romance angle partly allowed Fox to capitalize on Tierney's pinup image and create continuity with *Rings on Her Fingers* at a time when almost every major studio had its own pinup queen (Betty Grable at Fox, Veronica Lake at Paramount, Ann Sheridan at Warner Bros., and Lana Turner at MGM). Ernest Palmer, the cinematographer of *Thunder Birds*, is quoted in the pressbook with the proclamation that "legs are back to stay!" Conservation of textiles ostensibly motivated this trend in shorter skirts.²¹ Indeed, Peter's introduction to Kay begins in a women's clothing store when he spies her ankles as he shops for stockings to send home to his grandmother. Kay's earlier reunion with Steve on her grandfather's ranch is even more sexually overt. Swimming in an elevated tank above a phallic cactus, she pops her head above the water (red lipstick still firmly applied) and discovers that a low-flying plane has blown her towel to the ground. The pilot then shows off some aerial stunts and drops down his flight coveralls for her to wear before he lands the plane and reveals himself—to Kay's exasperation—as Steve. When he asks for his coveralls back in response to her dismissal, she unzips them to expose a tight, skin-colored bathing suit, a sexually provocative but also tauntingly defiant gesture. "I won't have you at Thunderbird—I won't *have you* anywhere around here," she declares (emphasis mine).

Both the clothing store and swimming scenes redirect Kay's significance, shifting her from a visual object of heterosexual male desire to a desiring subject in a wartime context. Even her grandfather is surprised by women's wartime empowerment: "Darned women! It's gettin' so that a fella can't even spit [*spitting*] unless they say so." A Red Cross volunteer, she drags Peter and his buddy George Lockwood (Richard Haydn) from the clothing store to a local first-aid station, sarcastically thwarting Peter's clumsy attempt at a pickup and coercing them into spending their afternoon of leave as test patients for the "angels of mercy." Practicing her tourniquet on Peter, she learns that he is a medical doctor and grows more interested in him, perhaps as a more compatible partner than Steve. When Steve shows up looking for Kay and sees her interaction with Peter, he breaks them apart and asks why she was not home at the ranch where he planned to meet her. In response, Kay asks him to lie on the table, and she ties his leg to a splint, then leaves with Peter (fig. 3). Although this sequence is played mostly for broad comedy, it emphasizes Kay's public role as a war worker, whose life exists beyond her grandfather's domestic environment and who seeks control of her own future (neither as Peter's pickup nor Steve's standby).

The clothing store / first-aid sequence also reflects back on Tierney's extradiegetic war work as a Hollywood star for the home front. Her presence in a World War II aviation film may have been a draw for heterosexual male audiences, but Fox also saw opportunities to address female audiences, making posters available for local chapters of the Red

Fig. 3. Red Cross volunteer Kay Saunders (Tierney) makes ex-boyfriend Steve Britt (Preston Foster) her test patient at a first-aid station in *Thunder Birds* (William A. Wellman, 1942).

Cross that read, "Get behind our 'Thunder Birds.' Join the Red Cross Volunteer Workers Today!" Store tie-ins included tagging the film's title to "military-styled clothing for women" and featuring Tierney's likeness on window displays and counter cards to advertise House of Westmore cosmetics. The pressbook highlighted her wardrobe in the film, as well, such as her poinsettia-print "date dress" and matching purse in the clothing store / first-aid sequence.²² I would add that her "urban sombrero" is an appropriation of a Latin American cultural symbol, implicitly acknowledging Tierney's earlier star image associated with "exotic" foreignness but also allying her with a "Good Neighbor" to the United States during World War II.

Labeled "Time out for fun," her "date dress" appears in the pressbook between two more stereotypically masculine ensembles. Tierney's "snug 'dude-ranch' outfit, complete with jodhpurs, while nice for riding the range, can be just as convenient on the vital home front—whether you're spot-welding, plane spotting or just walking the beat of the air raid warden." Another outfit, although never worn in the film itself, "combines style with ease in trim-suspender slacks of smooth wool gabardine, with Tyrolean touches of gray embroidery." Advertising copy specifically identified Tierney as a model for home-front femininity: "charming young Gene Tierney shows modern girls how to be pert yet practical. Young America is on the march. While the uniformed men go into battle, the women are tending to those 'home fires'—keeping them burning all night, in defense factories."[23]

In the swimming scene, Tierney literally wears a military uniform (Steve's flight coveralls), and her confrontation with Steve establishes the new romantic terms she has set. "You were marvelous, Steve, really superb," she says with a pat on his shoulder, mocking his showboating in the plane. To whatever degree Kay still maintains affection for Steve in this scene, she knows he is unable or unwilling to provide her with the companionate relationship she seeks. "I've stood all I'm going to from you," she tells him, gently but confidently, suggesting she reached this decision well before his arrival. Grasping Kay (and, ironically, failing to grasp why they have "fizzled," in her words), Steve tries to convince her that they belong together:

> STEVE: I never tried to kid you. I'm not a bank clerk or a
> night watchman punching a time clock. You knew that
> from the beginning. Well?
> KAY: It's no use, Steve. Your kind of life and mine just
> don't mix.
> STEVE: Of course they do. [*pulling her in for a kiss*] What is all
> this talk? My kind of life is your kind of life. You can't get
> away from that any more than I can. Isn't that right?
> KAY [*shaking her head*]: Sorry, Steve. [*She pats his shoulder, this
> time almost with pity, and walks out of his grasp.*] You see,
> the trouble is, I came off the line a woman and not a P-38.

Kay traces lines in the air with her finger, playfully imitating the buzzing sounds of a propeller, and she jabs his chest, pushing him into a water trough as payback for blowing off her towel moments earlier.

Toward the end of the film, Kay's story recedes in the interest of dramatizing Steve's mentorship of (and rivalry with) Peter, a dynamic that leads to some exciting aerial action sequences, but she takes on a more symbolic significance for the film's ideological project. Although Peter holds enormous respect for Steve as both his instructor and a war hero, he declares his intentions to pursue Kay. Steve nevertheless agrees to continue training him, willing to sacrifice his chances with Kay for a greater good. The commanding officer at Thunderbird, Colonel MacDonald (Jack Holt), and R.A.F. squadron leader Barrett (Reginald Denny) insist that Steve "wash out" any cadet "not up to scratch," but Steve feels Peter will make a great flyer like Peter's father, and Steve puts his job on the line to prove it. Meanwhile, Kay does not want to hurt either Steve or Peter (she tells Peter as much, explaining that she may still be in love Steve), and her relationship with both men inadvertently strengthens their homosocial bond in the service of wartime unity.

Kay/Tierney's personification of home-front femininity becomes a mediator for "international solidarity," a term Kay even uses when Peter invites her to tea, but by confining her romantic involvements to white men, Kay avoids the taboo of miscegenation. It is Steve and Peter's mutual love for her that catalyzes their duties and values as Allied servicemen. Peter finally earns his wings during a flight in which Steve parachutes out of the plane, forcing Peter to conquer his fear by flying solo and leaving him to land the plane in an unexpected sandstorm. The wind catches Steve's chute, dragging him across the ground, but Peter lands the plane and comes to his rescue (the plane, on the other hand, does not survive the storm). MacDonald and Barrett assume the accident was the result of Steve's recklessness and Peter's inability to fly. When they threaten to fire Steve and transfer Peter back to the medical corps, Kay persuades them to give Peter one more chance.

In the film's closing scenes, Peter makes his successful flight and Kay admits her love for him; she now has a partner in whose military life she can actively participate. Steve stays at Thunderbird but only at Kay's behest: "Look what you've done for Peter and the other boys. And this is only the beginning. Why, there'll be hundreds of others just like them, with kinks to be ironed out. You said yourself that this war will be won on fields like this, by boys like these. But they can't win it unless they know their jobs, and how are they going to learn unless men like you stay here and teach them?" The war work Kay performs in the film exceeds the Red Cross and ultimately serves to guide home-front norms of gender, labor, and heterosexual romance. Tierney, in turn, helps shape the "idea" of the all-American home front for wartime audiences.

From *Thunder Birds*, Tierney continued on her wartime trajectory with *China Girl*, although at first glance it seems more like a regression to her pre-1942 Orientalist roles. Produced by Ben Hecht, who wrote the script from a Crossman/Zanuck story, the film reunited Tierney with director Henry Hathaway, the action-film metteur-en-scène who had previously worked with her on *Sundown* in 1941.[24] Another takeoff on *A Yank in the R.A.F.*, *China Girl* was even given the working title "A Yank in Burma" at one point. The Yank this time is a photojournalist in Mandalay, Johnny Williams (George Montgomery), attempting the first complete filming of the Burma Road. Johnny is interested only in the money he will earn and refuses his friend's plea to help fight the Japanese as a volunteer for the "Flying Tigers" ("When I die, I ain't dyin' for China. I'm dyin' for Johnny Williams"). After he meets Haoli Young (Tierney), a noble Chinese woman dedicated to her father's war work, Johnny's isolationist position proves dubious.[25] *China Girl* opens with the following prologue: "An American will fight for three things—for a woman, for himself, and for a better world. He was fighting for only two of these when the story begins, November 1941." Fox created its own airfield for its war productions and this film was shot entirely at the studio, with the Bradbury Building in downtown Los Angeles doubling for the Hotel Royale Mandalay. According to the pressbook, the production required a small army of Asian cast members (two hundred men and forty women), but the wartime shortage of actors and extras in Hollywood necessitated making up the disparity with other nationalities.[26] Regardless of the truth in the studio's claim, presumably a white star would still have been cast in Tierney's role. Fox promoted her identification with Eastern roles as a sign of her "versatility."[27]

Although the film shifts her on-screen war work from the U.S. home front to Japanese-occupied China just before the bombing of Pearl Harbor, she once again facilitates "international solidarity." And as a member of an Allied Nation, the film problematically suggests, Haoli is *almost* American (she speaks English fluently without an accent and even attended Vassar!). Steven Dillon explains that viewing this beautiful woman as an incarnation of modern China, Johnny comes to believe the country is worth fighting for. Yet at the same time, the film's desexualization of Haoli makes their sexually restrained relationship compatible with the way "wartime ideals asked waiting wives and fighting soldiers to put sexual desire on hold."[28] This idealized "China girl" is thus a variation on the all-American girl, a good and chaste worker for the Allied war effort played by a white Hollywood star, alleviating potential concerns the film might raise during wartime about the racial Other as a sexual competitor with white women on the U.S. home front.

As Johnny and Haoli's feelings for each other progress over the course of the film, Johnny grows frustrated at the impasse the war has created in their relationship. Whereas he wants to move back to the States with her, she plans to return to China with her father, Dr. Kai Young (played by Korean American actor Philip Ahn), and reopen a school for orphans he established in Kunming. Haoli's commitment to a larger political cause is incomprehensible to Johnny, who understands China only as a mere "rival" for her attention. Invoking the sort of mysticism stereotypical of Asian characters in Hollywood films, she tells him, "Whatever I do, my spirit will belong to you," to which he responds, "I don't want your spirit." After walking her home, he asks, "Can I come in?" Haoli tells him she "must work," and again Johnny fails to comprehend, responding, "I'll just sit and look at you." Dillon observes that after their first meeting, Haoli rebuffs Johnny for giving her an unwanted kiss, but rather than developing a physical relationship with him, she advocates for a "contemplative, abstract love." By contrast, the "dangerous white woman" Fifi (Lynn Bari), a spy for the Japanese, makes herself sexually available to Johnny.[29] Only after he follows Haoli to Kunming does he learn to appreciate the value of her work and a relationship beyond the physical realm.

The Kunming sequence conveys the film's blatantly propagandistic intent. Dr. Young teaches his students about the war, with his assistant Haoli sitting behind him dutifully, hands folded, and his lesson also serves the film's pro-China message: "For many years, our people have been fighting and dying for something. We are poor people. We have barely anything to defend or to lose. And for what do we die?" A student replies, "Our country," and others equate China with "goodness" and "justice." When bombs start dropping around the school, Dr. Young asks the class to sit quietly with the knowledge that the "good in [their] hearts" cannot be destroyed, and Haoli rushes to comfort a crying student. No sooner than Dr. Young begins reading a poem to the class does the roof collapse over his head, killing him under the fallen rubble. Tearfully, Haoli takes up her father's position as the instructor. Standing before the class with pride, she resumes reading aloud as light streams in from the window beside her, illuminating her in an angelic glow (fig. 4). The poem, written "for all who stand against evil and darkness," concludes: "Above the graves where heroes live, there gleams the light of victory. For freedom's soldiers when they die hand down their spirit to the free."[30] Johnny enters the school just as Haoli finishes reading, and he now sees her as one of "freedom's soldiers" instead of simply someone to "look at."

Japanese dive-bombers interrupt their reunion, laying waste to the school, and Johnny finally takes action, first by freeing the students trapped in the burning debris. The students run to Haoli, who awaits outside and lifts them out of her father's ruined school. Before Johnny can join them, a bomb drops near Haoli, leaving her fatally injured. Johnny carries her in his arms until he realizes is unable to save her, but he believes that she has handed her "spirit" to him so that he may fight for China's freedom. With their love never physically consummated,

Fig. 4. Haoli Young (Tierney) takes over teaching her father's class at a school for orphans in *China Girl* (Henry Hathaway, 1942).

Peter Lev concludes, "the film's romance across racial lines is never completed—and since Gene Tierney is Caucasian, the romance isn't really biracial, anyway."[31] Yet Johnny's ongoing love for Haoli moves him to continue her work so that she does not die in vain. Spying an unmanned machine gun, he asks a Chinese boy to load the ammunition belt while he takes aim at Japanese planes with the fire of newly converted patriotism. "We got that one, China girl," he says after shooting down a plane, and the film ends with a medium shot of him firing directly into the camera with his sights set on the next target.

In turning Tierney into a Chinese character, the studio had to find ways to re-Americanize her for a home-front audience. Kay in *Thunder Birds* is a more active character than the almost saint-like Haoli, whom *China Girl* sacrifices to ensure Johnny's redemption and subsequent agency in the war effort, but both women represent the "goodness" and "justice" of their respective Allied countries (i.e., what unmarried soldiers were fighting for). The print advertisements for *China Girl* sought to draw explicit parallels between Haoli and white "home-front soldiers." Advertising copy referred to her as a "Flying Tigress!" and "A girl who wouldn't say die!" Although the illustrations never exactly indicate what Haoli's war work entails, her love for an American in wartime is enough to make her the titular hero of the film. As one tagline read, "In her heart . . . cold hate that defied the terror of the Japs . . . warm love for a fighting, flying Yank!"[32]

The most obvious way the studio connected Haoli to the U.S. home front was through a suggested exploitation campaign that awarded a woman for her war effort in a local community. Newspapers would advertise their search for an "American Girl," or "the worthy American counterpart of Gene Tierney's 'China Girl.'" Contestants would then submit letters of no more than one hundred words describing their work, along with a photograph of themselves, all of which newspapers published for readers and theater patrons to judge. Exhibitors would finally crown the winners on the film's opening night, awarding what else but war bonds and stamps. The ad copy read, "Right in your community girls are working shoulder to shoulder with men towards the same objective as the 'China Girl,'" and solicited "ALL girls who are WORKING toward victory," among them WAACs (Women's Army Auxiliary Corps) and WAVES (Women Accepted for Volunteer Emergency Service), nurse's aides, war plant workers, drive volunteers, and air raid wardens. As if to make Haoli's "patriotic" work more legible to U.S. moviegoers, she is identified not as a teacher's assistant at a Chinese mission but as a nurse who "boldly faces danger, intrigue, and death!" The promotion art included a still of her wearing a nurse's smock, sitting at the bed-side of a bandaged child and holding their hand (a scene never shown in the film).[33]

Tierney's agility in crossing racial lines was merely one such example in the Hollywood star system. During the silent era, actresses with darker features were often cast as dangerous vamps, but by the end of the 1930s Hollywood promoted certain stars who represented an "exotic" racial or ethnic difference. In the first decade of film sound, racist and ethnocentric stereotypes were instead modified to accommodate "the glamour of exoticism," to borrow Sarah Berry's phrase in her book *Screen Style*.[34] Love goddesses such as Dolores del Río and Lupe Vélez (both RKO stars from Mexico) showed that the "pure white" blonde no longer monopolized U.S. beauty culture.[35] Berry finds that Hollywood deployed stars with darker features in order to satisfy Anglo-American audiences attracted to the "exoticism" of cultures outside the United States while also seeking to reach both a global market and immigrant moviegoers at home.[36] Even if the Hollywood blonde experienced a comeback in the 1940s and 1950s, brunettes such as RKO's Jane Russell and MGM's Ava Gardner, not to mention Warner's "dirty blonde" Lauren Bacall, were among the most popular sex symbols of the era (although all three of these stars were white and born in the United States). It was also common to cast Anglo-American stars with darker features as foreigners, "Orientalizing" them through costume and makeup.[37] Casting privileged European ancestry (Spanish ancestry in particular) as the ideal Hollywood ethnicity in that it was the most "assimilable form of nonwhiteness possible."[38] A non-white star could therefore be used interchangeably between characters of different races and ethnicities, but rarely was she allowed to play a white character. Opening space for more diverse star images therefore created new stereotypes by adhering to this racial hierarchy.

Aside from Tierney's conical fashion hats in *China Girl*, neither her costumes nor her makeup in the film immediately marks her as a racial Other. "That suit makes me homesick," says Johnny when he first meets her. "Fifth Avenue?" To emphasize this point, promotion contrasted

Tierney in "the typical Chinese wardrobe, with its high-braid-trimmed collar and slit skirt" against the version she wears in the film, which "retains the charming Oriental touches" but "may be worn anywhere." Fox announced that the war against Japan has "emancipated" Chinese women, who have adopted "modern, practical clothes" and "emerged as trim as a WAAC, yet smooth and polished as a Rockette." Moreover, the studio added that "no tape was required to slant [Tierney's] slumberous eyes, no paint to widen her full lips," and that as "the most cosmopolitan actress in Hollywood," she can "pass on the screen for almost any national type." Exhibitors, audiences, and the press needed to see Tierney as more American than Chinese but also, paradoxically, more Chinese than a Chinese woman; her stand-in reportedly had to wear makeup to look the part despite being Chinese herself.[39]

Even without makeup, the casting of Tierney as a Chinese woman is consistent with Hollywood's historically biased representation of Asian characters on-screen. We might add Tierney to the group of studio-era stars Karla Rae Fuller cites in her book *Hollywood Goes Oriental*, whose faces "provide the physically normative standard onto which an ethnic inscription can take place."[40] By mediating the Chinese experience of World War II through a white star and keeping audience at a remove from the subject, *China Girl* undermines its claims to a "positive" representation and reinscribes whiteness as a universal norm. Fuller's examination of star discourse shows how "going Oriental clearly suggests both a displacement and an adaptation that allow Caucasian stars [. . .] to delight film audiences with their skills of impersonation through the embodiment of people whom they are not."[41] Although Tierney did not rely on the sort of makeup that earlier stars such as Myrna Loy or Loretta Young used to impersonate Asian women, Fox followed similar rhetorical strategies in promoting and publicizing Tierney's role. As Fuller explains, "Part of the process in the objectification of racial/cultural groups foregrounds certain qualities while effacing others. One of the elements routinely effaced is the process of training and acculturation required to become a member of any cultural group. The specific qualities ascribed to the objectified group are usually defined as intrinsic and biologically based."[42] Fox justified casting Tierney in the role by invoking her physical appearance and "versatility." Audiences knew that Tierney was white and that playing a non-white character was only temporary.

Performing across racial lines put her "skills of impersonation" on display as an actress, which a performer of color would not have the opportunity to demonstrate. This promotional logic for Tierney and others reinforced the racist assumption that white stars were more qualified to play any role.

Tierney was allowed to move between white and non-white roles through two avenues: discourse on ethnicity and codes of dress, the latter of which will be discussed in the next section. Publicity was quick to remark about Tierney's "de-lovely" appearance "in the best Irish tradition," citing the reddish-brown color of her hair, the green in her eyes, and "the essentially Irish contour" of her oval face.[43] Establishing her Irish heritage in the press as early as 1940, Fox was able to promote her as an "ethnic" star who could play "exotic" parts, without threatening her "ordinary" whiteness. Sean Griffin's work on Fox musicals set in the turn-of-the-century United States has shown how the performance of Irishness functioned metaphorically to negotiate ideologies of race and national identity in the 1940s. The "nostalgically American" appeal of Betty Grable musicals such as *Coney Island* (Walter Lang, 1943) and *Sweet Rosie O'Grady* (Irving Cummings, 1943) relied on a construction of Irishness that was both ethnic and white. Such films promoted multicultural diversity in the United States during World War II through the ethnic heritage of Grable's Irish American characters at the same time as they allowed her characters to assimilate into the white mainstream so as not to challenge the power structure of white dominance.[44]

While the Irishness of Grable's characters did not extend to her star persona outside of her films, the assertion of Tierney's ethnic heritage is more similar to the promotion of the redheaded, green-eyed tomboy Maureen O'Hara, an Irish-born star. Eventually nicknamed "the Queen of Technicolor," O'Hara worked under contract at RKO, but Fox acquired her for a film a year.[45] Tierney was actually Zanuck's first choice for the role that made O'Hara a major star—the Morgan daughter in *How Green Was My Valley* (1941)—and began her collaborations with director John Ford. Based on the acclaimed novel of the same name by British author Richard Llewellyn, this family melodrama about coal miners in nineteenth-century Wales also won the Academy Award for Best Picture.[46] Although Tierney's career followed a different direction with *Sundown, The Shanghai Gesture,* and *Son of Fury,* the adaptability of her image as a star discursively framed by ethnicity and whiteness allowed the studio to make (and then remake) that image in accord with changing fashions into the war years. *China Girl* was the last of her "whitewashed" roles until *The Egyptian* (Michael Curtiz, 1954), but *Laura* was the film that completed her transformation into the all-American girl with the uniform of the white-collar war worker.

Office Politics: The Making of *Laura* and Tierney's Image Makeover

Creating the character of Laura Hunt proved particularly difficult for Zanuck, director Otto Preminger, and the series of script contributors. *Laura* was known around Fox as a "hard luck picture."[47] As Sheri Chinen Biesen explains in her book *Blackout: World War II and the Origins of Film Noir*, "Laura's character is, in fact, manufactured not only by the men in the narrative but also by the male production executives in making the film."[48] The film's production history exposes the ways both the authorial projections at Fox and the feminine idealizations in the diegesis contributed to a malleable and contradictory character. Both diegetic and extradiegetic negotiations of Laura's identity, in turn, managed Tierney's star image. Vera Caspary wrote the film's source novel—first serialized in *Collier's* magazine from October to November 1942 as *Ring Twice for Laura* and then published as the hardcover *Laura* in 1943. Having originally conceived the story as a stage play, Caspary tried to adapt it for Broadway before it became a Hollywood property. Preminger was producing for Broadway after his mid-1930s stint as a Fox contract director culminated in a falling-out with Zanuck, and he pursued Caspary to collaborate on a revised version of the original script. According to Caspary, Preminger "wanted to make it a conventional detective story," whereas she envisioned it as "a psychological drama about people involved in a murder."[49] Their collaboration on the play did not go further. Instead, when Preminger returned to Fox as a producer in 1943 and learned of the studio's interest in the novel, he pressured Fox to buy the book rights and let Caspary keep the rights to her play with coauthor George Sklar.[50] Not until after the release of the film adaptation did Caspary and Sklar bring *Laura* to the stage (their play opened in London in 1945 and on Broadway in 1947).

The novel unfolds in five parts, each told from the perspective of one of the principal characters. Narrating the first section is Waldo Lydecker, an acerbic, well-connected gossip columnist, who helps facilitate Laura's ascension in the cafe society of New York City. Next comes Det. Lt. Mark McPherson, whose investigation of Laura's presumed murder turns into a personal obsession with the mystery woman. We learn that a shotgun blast has rendered the victim's face unrecognizable, a detail made pertinent by Mark's eventual discovery that Laura is actually alive and unaware of the attempt on her life. The murderer had killed another woman by mistake; it turns out that the dead woman, model Diane Redfern, had been wooing Laura's fiancé, Shelby Carpenter, whose statement to Mark is presented in a stenographic report that comprises the novel's third section. Laura, now a suspect herself, narrates the fourth section before Mark's voice returns for the summation and conclusion in part five.[51]

Writing the first draft of the continuity script, Jay Dratler kept faithful to Caspary's unique structure—telling the story from multiple points of view—through the use of voice-over narration. This device remained in the script through Ring Lardner Jr.'s two subsequent drafts.[52] Originally planned for Bryan Foy's B-unit at Fox, *Laura* rose in production status when Foy complained about the script to Zanuck; Zanuck liked the script and decided to make the film for his A-unit instead.[53] He allowed Preminger to produce the film but forbade him to direct—there was still bad blood between them—and hired Rouben Mamoulian instead. Mamoulian brought on screenwriters Samuel Hoffenstein and Betty Reinhardt, and a new revision to the script was under way.[54]

The character of Laura presented difficulties even prior to shooting. In response to Dratler's first draft of the script, Zanuck wrote a memo to Preminger on November 1, 1943, with the following concerns: "Laura is a mess. She is neither interesting nor attractive, and I doubt if any first-rate actress would ever play her. As it is now, she seems terribly naive—a complete sucker. [. . .] She does no thinking in the picture at all. She has no decisions to make. She doesn't try to solve anything or really think in any situation. She just acts as the scenario writer wants her to act." Zanuck continued, "Unless you work hard on Laura she will continue to be a nonentity. This is the most difficult problem you have to overcome. You have to make her just as much a character as Waldo and Mark. She has to become a distinct, definite personality."[55] The memo ended with his most serious demand for revision: "The only place I did not like the [voice-over] at all was when Laura starts to tell her own story. There is no reason for her to tell her own story. [. . .] It was good with the other people because you had to explain what they were thinking about, but for Laura you do not need it because then it becomes straight action."[56] Before Hoffenstein and Reinhardt began their version, Zanuck held a story conference on March 20, 1944, and wrote to Preminger, Mamoulian, and Hoffenstein with the instructions that "Laura's charm should be in her frankness and honesty. Where the others are Park Avenue cutthroats, she should be as fresh as a child. She should be witty but never mean."[57] The actress cast as Laura would be faced with the seemingly impossible task of portraying a female character who exists in the diegesis as a construction of competing male fantasies and whose own voice would be denied in the film.[58]

Treating her story as "straight action" in the script meant that the performance would have to articulate her subjectivity as a character, which was still taking shape at the extradiegetic level through negotiations over who she is and who she should be. Laura also had to be an accessible character rather than an inscrutable object of mystery. With Hoffenstein and Reinhardt attending to final revisions, Fox began casting the film. Hedy Lamarr rejected Preminger's offer to play Laura, and David O. Selznick's new star Jennifer Jones dropped out due to a legal dispute between Selznick and Fox over the terms of her contract.[59] The studio then turned to the twenty-four-year-old Tierney. Although she resented being an alternate, the film would give her the opportunity to establish herself as a romantic leading lady. Upon reading the script, she was disappointed with her amount of screen time, but with Cassini serving in the army and their daughter Daria only a year old, she felt she could not afford to be overly selective. *Laura* would be her first suspense film, and her first film of any kind in a year.[60] The role of Mark went to Dana Andrews, who had previously appeared in Tierney's films *Tobacco Road* (John Ford, 1941) and *Belle Starr* (Irving Cummings, 1941). Four years later, Tierney and Andrews would reunite in the anti-communist espionage film *The Iron Curtain* (William A. Wellman, 1948), part of Fox's postwar cycle of "semidocumentary" investigative dramas.[61]

Imagining the character of Laura for the screen also led to disagreements between Preminger and Caspary. When Preminger offered Caspary the first draft of the script, she found Laura "a flat, conventional movie heroine" and asked, "Why don't you give her the character she has in the book?" Preminger replied, "Laura has no character," and assuming Shelby was not a lover but a gigolo, he added, "Laura has no sex" (Vincent Price played Shelby in the film). By contrast, Caspary viewed Laura as a woman who "was adored by every man in the story" but who also enjoyed her lovers, who "gives everything with her love." Caspary described Laura as "too kind for caution, too bright-eyed about a man's virtues to see his flaws clearly."[62] In her book *Settling the Score*, Kathryn Kalinak mentions that composer David Raksin shared Caspary's view of Laura as "a sensitive romantic" and used the theme music "to suggest both Laura's spirit [. . .] and her naivete," with a waltz variation titled the "Tierney Waltz" to convey the latter.[63] When George and Ira Gershwin refused Preminger permission to use "Summertime" as the film's theme song, he opted for Duke Ellington's "Sophisticated Lady." Raksin objected because he felt the piece reflected "the usual Hollywood approach to a woman of relatively easy virtue," while the frustrated Preminger told him Laura was "a whore," so Raksin composed an original theme melody.[64] Even if Preminger and Caspary could not agree on Laura, Caspary later acknowledged that Hoffenstein and Reinhardt's version of the script better understood the character's "generosity and romantic short-sightedness."[65] Hoffenstein and Reinhardt dropped her voice-over in the shooting script, but Mark's voice-over narration remained (Andrews even recorded it) only to be abandoned postproduction.[66]

After shooting began on April 27, 1944, creative differences escalated between Preminger and Mamoulian until Zanuck instated Preminger as director. Preminger took over on May 15, scrapped Mamoulian's costumes and sets, replaced director of photography Lucien Ballard with Joseph LaShelle, hired costume designer Bonnie Cashin from the Fox wardrobe department, and eventually reshot all of Mamoulian's scenes. The original *Laura* portrait had been painted by Mamoulian's wife, Azadia Newman, but it was Preminger's idea to use Frank Powolny's glamour photograph of Tierney instead.[67] Recalling her visit to the set, Caspary commended Preminger's direction of a scene where Laura dines at Sardi's, which re-created "not only the appearance of the restaurant, but the sense of gossip and phony charm."[68] (Ironically, this scene would later be cut from the theatrical release print.) Despite the shuffling of creative personnel, *Laura* received Academy Award nominations in the categories of Art Direction (Black-and-White), Directing, Cinematography (Black-and-White), and Writing (Screenplay). LaShelle won for the film's cinematography.

The conceptualization of Laura continued to evolve through shooting the film's ending. Fans of the film will remember that concealed in Laura's antique longcase clock is the shotgun used in the murder. Consumed by jealousy, the Svengali-like Waldo (Clifton Webb) had attempted to shoot Laura; if he could not possess her and those qualities he attributed to himself, he would rather see her dead. Having murdered the wrong woman, he stowed the weapon in the secret compartment of the clock he had given to Laura as a gift. In the first cut of the film, Laura discovers the shotgun, realizes Waldo killed Diane, and tries to persuade him to flee. After hiding the weapon in a storage room, Waldo returns to Laura's apartment with the intention of murdering her at last, but Mark thwarts his efforts and takes him into custody. Dissatisfied with the ending, Zanuck assigned staff writer Jerome Cady to make changes. In this revised version, Mark finds the gun in Laura's clock, and Laura offers a larger backstory for her sense of indebtedness to Waldo. She had been unable to find a job after moving to New York City. One night, locked out of her apartment, she was picked up for vagrancy. Laura explains to Mark that Waldo paid her fine and secured a position for her at a Manhattan advertising agency. In other words, this twist asked audiences to reread Waldo as an unreliable narrator: his version of their first meeting, recounted in an earlier flashback, was a story he dreamed up. Waldo has been hiding in her building during her conversation with Mark, and after Mark leaves, he sneaks into her apartment. Before Waldo can shoot Laura, Mark returns with the police and guns him down. The theatrically released ending reflects these changes, but the additions to Laura's backstory were jettisoned after Zanuck's friend (and real-life gossip commentator) Walter Winchell saw the new cut and confessed he did not understand it.[69]

While Preminger chose the other main cast members, Tierney was Zanuck's decision. After screening the first cut of the film, Zanuck was still unhappy with Laura as a character and suggested an alternative ending.

"I don't think we can save the picture," he said, "but at least we can save Gene Tierney. She's an extra in this picture; you've made an extra out of my new star."[70] Zanuck's suggestion and his anxiety about Tierney proved unnecessary; hitching Tierney's star to *Laura* confirmed her arrival in the Fox firmament. The film also began a career-long collaboration with Preminger that included *Whirlpool* (1950) and *Where the Sidewalk Ends*, the latter of which reteamed her with Andrews before Joseph LaShelle's camera once again in another New York noir (her fifth and final film with the actor). When she returned to theater screens after a seven-year absence due to her psychiatric treatments, it was in Preminger's *Advise & Consent* (1962). Writing in her autobiography, she described him as "a gentleman," remarking, "Unlike certain other directors of that period, he had no insecurity and did not feel obligated to attempt the seduction of his leading ladies."[71]

Tierney was an unusual star for the studio in that she did not conform to what film scholar Shari Roberts calls its "golden blonde" policy during World War II. Reigning stars such as Alice Faye and Betty Grable represented "the feminine, all-American 'norm,'" as the studio defined it: the wartime antithesis of the Japanese, German, and Italian stereotypes that pervaded popular culture and linked dark eyes and dark skin to the Axis powers.[72] A notable exception was Carmen Miranda, the Brazilian samba singer and film star, born in Portugal, whom Fox turned into its fruit-hatted mascot for the Good Neighbor policy in a cycle of popular wartime musicals. Roberts argues that by assigning Miranda to films with Faye or Grable, Fox accommodated her into its blonde policy to make her "the allowable cultural Other for wartime Hollywood, playing the dark but comic and, therefore, unthreatening foil to all the gilded war-time female musical stars."[73] The long line of Fox blondes included Sonja Henie, Carole Landis, June Haver, Vivian Blaine, and Mitzi Gaynor, and later Marilyn Monroe and Jayne Mansfield. More of a counterpart to Tierney was the Fox brunette Linda Darnell (three years her junior). The studio cast them each in their first big films around the same time, struggled to type them, paired them with Tyrone Power in period-adventure movies, and put them to work in the war effort. A white North American also celebrated for her "dark" beauty, Darnell played Native American, Asian, and Latina characters. Preminger even directed her opposite Andrews in the film noir *Fallen Angel* (1945) (as the trailer pledged, "The creator of

Laura has done it again!"). Before Darnell replaced Peggy Cummins as the blonde Amber St. Clair in *Forever Amber* (Otto Preminger, 1947), Fox had originally considered Tierney for the coveted role.[74]

However, the two stars ultimately followed different paths. Darnell was never Zanuck's first choice, and, deprived of his continued interest, her career waned after the success of *Blood and Sand* (Rouben Mamoulian, 1941), which starred Power as a romantic bullfighter and Darnell as his childhood sweetheart. By 1943, she had been relegated to second or third leads and starring roles in programmers, partly Zanuck's way of censuring her for marrying the much older cinematographer Peverell Marley.[75] Loaning her out to play a sultry Russian peasant in *Summer Storm* (Douglas Sirk, 1944) began to change her image from "good girl" to sex symbol, but not until topping the bill in the scandalous British Restoration melodrama *Forever Amber* did she enjoy a bona fide (if belated) star status. Despite its negative critical reception, the multimillion-dollar production triumphed at the box office. Behind the scenes, Darnell hated working with the autocratic Preminger again.[76] The "woman's film" *A Letter to Three Wives* (Joseph L. Mankiewicz, 1949) followed, giving her the role for which she is best remembered. When the studios began cutting back on long-term contracts during Hollywood's postwar economic slump, Fox released her in 1952.[77] Then divorced from Marley and suffering from alcoholism, the twenty-nine-year-old Darnell languished in financial trouble as a result of poor investments and her fraudulent business management. Her career never recovered, and she died in 1965 from burns caused by an accidental house fire.

Conversely, Tierney's star was on the rise between 1942 and 1944. Until 1951, Fox's habit of recycling previously successful story properties even gave the studio opportunities to swap out its biggest blonde stars for Tierney, who replaced Grable when *A Yank in the R.A.F.* became *Thunder Birds* and later when *Sweet Rosie O'Grady* became *That Wonderful Urge* (Robert B. Sinclair, 1948). As we will see in this book's conclusion, Tierney also replaced Alice Faye when Fox remade *That Night in Rio* (Irving Cummings, 1941) as *On the Riviera* (Walter Lang, 1951). With the studio's competing interpretations of Laura (the character), *Laura* (the film) provided Tierney with a vehicle that could accommodate the contradictions in her image. The *Los Angeles Times* reported that the film "not only persuaded both studio and public to regard her seriously for the first time as an actress, but in a kind of delayed take got her an Academy nomination for *Leave Her to Heaven* [John M. Stahl, 1945]," making her "the most sought after star on the [Fox] lot."[78] Tierney reprised the role twice on *Lux Radio Theatre*, first in 1945 and again in 1954 (Andrews and Price both joined her for the first adaptation, but she was the only member of the film's cast to return the second time). As we will see, the film reconceived Laura from an "exotically" sophisticated socialite into an all-American workingwoman, affording coherence to the character, in the same way that the film makes over Tierney to conform with the U.S. home front's class politics of consumption and dress. This dual makeover is evident from Bonnie Cashin's work fashions and a montage sequence that contains footage excised from the theatrical release print but included in the trailer.

The trailer promises that audiences have rarely met a woman like its title character. "Few women have been so beautiful, so exotic, so dangerous to know," the announcer intones. As the trailer boasts that everyone is talking about both the film and the woman, it baits viewers with rhetorical questions—"Who is Laura? What is *Laura*?"—and offers a partial (though misleading) account of Laura's origins from Waldo. "She was always quick to seize upon anything that would improve her mind," he says, "or her appearance. Laura had innate breeding." Waldo continues, "I selected a more attractive hair dress for her. I taught her what clothes were more becoming to her." Shots of her hairdressing and outfitting—presumably shots from the film—accompany his narration and culminate in the fully made over Laura Hunt meeting new acquaintances for dinner at Sardi's (figs. 5, 6, and 7). The trailer supports Waldo's romanticized portrait while adding a threat of danger: "Every woman will feel that when it comes to men, Laura gets by with murder. Every man will feel that when it comes to murder, it couldn't involve a more enticing girl." Of course, we will see Laura cast as both murder victim and suspect during the film.

Contemporary audiences familiar with film noir, and with *Laura*'s reputation as a canonical example, may not be surprised by the trailer's connection between luxurious female style and dangerous femininity. Fashion scholar Ula Lukszo notes that the sexual iconography of classical film noir includes "any articles of clothing that are conspicuous for their excessive luxury, such as evening gowns, exotic hats, long gloves, high heels,

Figs. 5, 6, and 7. Fox deleted the makeover montage from the original the-atrical release print of *Laura* (Otto Preminger, 1944).

and furs." She explains, "Women of excess" are coded as "in some way or another dangerous to the male protagonist."[79] More surprising is that the montage recounting Laura's transformation was absent from the theatrical release print, qualifying the origins of Laura and Waldo's relationship. The *Hollywood Reporter* uncovered that Fox excised one minute fifteen seconds of footage from the flashback sequence due to concerns that the film would "offend World War II soldiers overseas with its depiction of decadent luxury and non-military obsessions happening on the home front."[80]

With the "decadent luxury" of Laura's makeover removed from the film's theatrical release print, Cashin's ready-to-wear wardrobe signifies women's work as the source of Laura's upward mobility and, by extension, endows Tierney with those same values. Quoting Sheri Chinen Biesen, Tierney's Laura is as much "otherworldly" as she is an "everywoman," mir-roring "issues important to home-front working women." Biesen insists that if Laura is "a sweet, warm, and earnest all-American girl-next-door," she also "demonstrates that she is secretive and capable of duplicity," thus appearing as "bad girl, good girl, working woman, and male fantasy" all at once.[81] In the context of the truncated montage, Laura's "otherworld-liness" derives from the way the film codes the character as a kind of "classless" nobility through her inconspicuous consumption.

The flashback in the film's theatrical release print introduces Laura as a youthful, awkwardly earnest stenographer for the fictional Manhattan advertising agency Bullitt and Company. Seeking Waldo's endorsement for a fountain pen the agency hopes to promote, she encounters him having lunch at the Algonquin Hotel. Waldo initially dismisses her, but he finds himself fascinated by "something about her" and decides to endorse the pen after all. He describes in voice-over how his endorsement helped launch Laura's career, but he acknowledges that "it was her own talent and imagination that enabled her to rise to the top of her profession and stay there." We see Laura meeting with new clients, overseeing the work of designers, and enthusiastically participating in board meetings, showing this "talent and imagination" at work (figs. 8, 9, and 10). "But Tuesday and Friday nights we stayed home, dining quietly, listening to my records," Waldo reflects over a cozy two-shot of them mixing a salad together. A dissolve to Tierney in medium shot shows Laura seated to his left, about a foot taller than him, staring ahead with

Figs. 8, 9, and 10. As a Madison Avenue advertising executive, Laura Hunt meets with new clients, oversees the work of designers, and participates in board meetings.

elegant composure, and we know her transformation into a Madison Avenue executive is complete. The camera tracks into a close-up, and she gracefully takes a long, cool drag on her cigarette as Waldo reads his articles to her.

A curious bump in the editing and problems of narrative continuity reveal a disjuncture in this sequence. Where are Laura and Waldo on nights other than Tuesday and Friday? Waldo's remarks about Tuesday and Friday evenings seem to refer to something other than Laura's daytime professional activities. Fox answered these long-standing questions in 1990 when it restored the original, full-length montage for the laserdisc release (contemporary DVD and Blu-ray versions allow audiences to play the "extended version" or simply the "deleted scene"). While Laura may be a successful career woman, here she also defers to Waldo's "judgment and taste." He tells us, "Through me, she met everyone: the famous and the infamous. Her beauty and charm of manner captivated them all. She had warmth, vitality. She had authentic magnetism. Wherever we went, she stood out." Attributing her glamour to his own design, he muses, "She became as well known as Waldo Lydecker's walking stick and his white carnation." Laura is not simply fashionable but, in fact, is a fashion accessory for Waldo to show off at Sardi's and El Morocco, at the theater, and on the dance floor. She is, in effect, an extension of his own queer self-presentation.

This missing footage points to the shifting function of Tierney's star image in the film. Like Laura, she was the subject of a female image-making project. Film scholar Donna Peberdy finds in *Laura* "a self-conscious critique of 'performance' within the diegesis," with Andrews playing "the role of detective as an identity to be acted out" and Webb as a narrator "calling attention to the various diegetic performances and vocalizing the audience's questions."[82] With Waldo reconstructing Laura's femininity and fashioning her into his escort, the film also "foregrounds gendered and sexual identity as performance."[83] What I would add is that the film also calls attention to the emergence of Tierney as a major Fox star, performing a particular construction of femininity via Laura's diegetic performance.

Privileged both in the film's plot and its mise-en-scène, Tierney is a significant locus of the film's ideological meaning. As Kristin Thompson observes, "Time and again, a scene will favor our view of her by turning her out away from the person she is conversing with, toward the camera. She is lit far more attractively than any other character, with glowing three-point glamour lighting. (The portrait itself contains a depiction of such lighting, with a 'halo' effect around the body.)" Formal techniques of this sort were standard practices in studio-era Hollywood, but *Laura* makes them especially apparent through the use of the portrait and what Thompson calls an "emphatic depiction of the obsessive and fetishistic treatment of the heroine." In short, Thompson remarks, "a film about a man who falls in love with a portrait [. . .] also offers Gene Tierney as an object of contemplation for the cinema spectator."[84] Fox capitalized on both Tierney's stardom and wartime ideas about feminine beauty in creating this character. At the same time, wartime beautification concealed the very cosmetic process of female self-adornment—what we might call the labor of beauty—in the service of propagating beauty as labor.

Laura as War(drobe) Film: Bonnie Cashin's Costumes

The trade press announced Tierney's new look in *Laura* using the star's own words to promote her image and signal a new direction in her career. In a November 1945 *Hollywood Reporter* article titled "Farewell to the Orient," she expressed her frustration over getting repeatedly cast as Asian Pacific characters, describing herself as "an average American girl" from Brooklyn "who threatened to become Hollywood's perennial Asiatic." Not only did *Laura* offer "an escape from the Pacific," followed by roles in *A Bell for Adano* (Henry King, 1945) and *Dragonwyck* (Joseph L. Mankiewicz, 1946), but it also provided a more "varied character 'wardrobe'" and "a role more demanding in its emotional delineation."[85] A second article published the following month in the *Hollywood Reporter* reiterated that she never resorted to "eye make-up or taping" for *China Girl*. With the exception of the makeup that aged her thirty years in *Heaven Can Wait* (Ernst Lubitsch, 1943), she claimed, "[T]he truth of the matter is I have never used make-up, other than lipstick" in either films or publicity photos. Tierney cited her "mixed ancestry"—Irish and English on her father's side; French, Spanish, and Swedish on her mother's—for her ability to "look like any nationality."[86] Regardless of whether these articles were written by Tierney (as the bylines indicate) or Fox's publicity department, they both make clear Fox's strategic efforts to align Tierney with an all-American and all-natural image of feminine beauty.

Disavowing cosmetic beautification speaks to an unornamented star quality (i.e., she is an "average" girl and therefore a "real" actress instead of a "made-up" celebrity). Just as Fox attempted to erase the "decadent luxury" involved in Laura's makeover by crediting her upward mobility exclusively to hard work, the studio sought to present Tierney's makeover as simply lifting the veil off a naturally beautiful, Anglo-American face. This inconspicuous framing of the process of creating a female character and star, however, does not preclude contributions from designers. Costume affixes Tierney to the wartime beauty ideal and makes Laura a model for home-front women.

Before examining Cashin's contributions to the film's costumes, some historical context is necessary to understand the relationship between ornamentation and gendered, raced, and classed bodies. In her book *Pretty: Film and the Decorative Image*, Rosalind Galt reminds us, "The popularity of non-European bodies in film—especially in cinema's first decades—demonstrates a dynamic market for an image that could be enjoyed as colorful (in all senses), sensual, and foreign, but that was clearly marked off from the nobility and beauty that was reserved for the white subject." The colonial politics of modernist visual culture dictated an aesthetic regime whereby the gendered and raced body was the object of a "dangerous primitive desire," desirable because of a spectacular "ornamental aesthetic," or what Galt defines as "the interleaving of the non-European primitive, the erotic body, and the decorative detail."[87] Yet ornamentation was thought to be unnatural in its cosmetic appearance and stylized artifice, making this desire also "dangerous" for the Western male who bears the gaze; he risks misrecognizing the "correct" image of beauty and thus falling short of his proper role in modern civilization.[88] Galt turns to Josephine Baker as a representative example, but this racializing discourse similarly intersected the decorative images of the many "dangerous" women played by white Hollywood stars.

The influence of Orientalism on U.S. modernity in the twentieth century was also evident off cinema screens. White stars posed against chinoiserie backgrounds in promotional photos. Imported Orientalist art was on display in bedrooms and drawing rooms. Orientalist style suffused mass culture. Such images and objects circulating in the Western world may have signified "an excess of pleasure in material things," but according to Galt they were also valued as "markers of modern cosmopolitanism that offered mass market access to cultural capital and fashionable design."[89] Waldo has decorated his apartment with Asian masks and statuettes, which we see in the long take that opens the film (the first clue to his queer taste). We also see an Asian figurine table lamp in Laura's office, a racialized signifier no longer marked on the body but projected onto props and decor. Displacing race onto class in the film, Fox freed Tierney from her stereotypical roles but made her over into a culturally correct image of white nobility. This so-called purification of primitive beauty via Anglo-American modernism allowed the studio to maintain continuity with the high style of Tierney's earlier films, adding to *Laura*'s mystery with the danger and "exoticism" that imbued colonial constructions of non-Western femininity. Zanuck's memos even include a suggestion for a scene in which Mark watches a newsreel and the woman on the screen, Madame Chiang Kai-Shek, dissolves into Laura to show how she has possessed his mind (the scene never made it into the script).[90]

The film also displaces sexuality onto class in its construction of the Wildean dandy Waldo, a holdover from the Decadent movement, played by real-life gay actor Webb, whose performance earned him an Academy Award nomination for Best Actor in a Supporting Role. Recall that Laird Cregar, another gay actor, played a similar character in *Rings on Her Fingers*. Zanuck wanted Cregar to play Waldo, but Preminger was afraid his associations with screen villains would spoil the twist ending. Only a few years earlier in Fox's first noir production, *I Wake Up Screaming* (H. Bruce Humberstone, 1941), Cregar played a psychotic police inspector obsessed with a murdered made-over society woman (Carole Landis). Betty Grable starred as the victim's sister and roommate, a "working-girl investigator," in her onetime noir role.[91] Set in New York City and told in flashbacks with a memorable theme melody by Alfred Newman, *I Wake Up Screaming* anticipated *Laura* in a number of ways and also started Cregar on course as a Hollywood "heavy."[92] By turns, Zanuck was worried Webb would come across as too effeminate and explicitly identify the character as gay, breaking the taboo on homosexuality under the Hays Code.[93] Critic Alexander Woollcott of the *New Yorker* and Algonquin Round Table fame (also gay) has been credited as Caspary's inspiration for Waldo, although she claims to have been influenced only by his writing style.[94] This influence seems most obvious in Waldo's dialogue, replete with ornamental literary flourishes.

Managing ornamentation in *Laura* was paramount to Tierney's all-American makeover. Audiences would have been aware of her socioeconomic background at the time of Laura's release, which received copious attention in studio biographies and fan magazine coverage. But publicity could elide her class privilege by playing up her educational opportunities (Brillantmont, Miss Porter's) and bookish interests, such as starting a diary after shooting *Hudson's Bay*, "the kind of secret day-by-day record that a boarding school girl might have dashed off between house parties at Yale and Princeton or Texas Christian and Southern Methodist."[95] Similarly, the studio translated a discourse of affluence into a discourse of labor by disseminating the details of Tierney's work regimen to the public. Tierney was said to have demanded a contract with the studio that provided she "work for her money and be given very little lay-off time" and "that she be permitted six months of each year, upon demand, to return to the New York stage," where she began her acting career. Contract stipulations demonstrated her desire to manage her own star image: the right to keep the natural length and color of her hair; the right to keep her teeth lest the studio wanted to correct her overbite; and a clause preventing the studio from changing her height, posture, or figure.[96] A 1941 article in *Modern Screen* characterized Tierney as a "lovable renegade who ran away from doting parents, gorgeous clothes and prosperous swains—because she'd much rather work for a living!"[97]

Rejecting class privilege, respecting live theater, and owning her physical appearance and "imperfections" echo the claims to "naturalism" and "authenticity" that framed her stardom in the 1940s. While we have seen these claims marshaled to promote a traditional North American beauty devoid of ornamentation, here they also underscore the drive and determination of a young star eager to work, not to indulge in gratuitous leisure activities or to flaunt the wealth of Hollywood's celebrity culture. This image of Tierney as a hard worker continued even after World War II when she was already an established star. For instance, Fox circulated a publicity story informing audiences that she broke a small bone in her left foot while shooting *The Ghost and Mrs. Muir* (Joseph L. Mankiewicz, 1947), but after ten days at home while her foot healed in a plaster cast, she insisted on coming back to work—not wanting to delay production further. Her cast was replaced with a splint in high-laced shoes that her long period costume hid from view, and she used a studio-rented jeep for transportation on location at Pebble Beach in Monterey, California. Between takes, she relied on the aid of crutches and a wheelchair, but to keep her feet on firm ground for her scenes on the beach, Fox built a smooth boardwalk for her and covered it with sand.[98]

For *Laura* to keep Tierney on course as a star with "authentic magnetism," her stylish clothes could not signify material excess consumed by an elite for the purpose of displaying wealth to improve social standing, the phenomenon Thorstein Veblen famously identifies as "conspicuous consumption."[99] Rather, they eschewed ostentation for a mass-market appeal. After shooting *Laura*, *Photoplay* averred that she visited Manhattan and lunched at the Algonquin Hotel, the "[b]iggest thrill" of her trip since she had only sat in Fox's replica. Less of a star descended from the Hollywood heavens than a down-to-earth movie fan, Tierney "sat near the table at which she sat in the scene" and was amazed to see the real "movie-scene table."[100]

Fox costume designer Bonnie Cashin provided her with a wardrobe remarkably dissimilar from the strapless black evening gown that Laura wears in her portrait, turning to face the spectator as a lacy shawl drips off her ivory shoulders. The portrait of Laura as a passive, exhibitionist woman is the painter's fantasy of Laura as an image to be looked at. After all, it was painted and given to her by one of her suitors. Cashin's obituary in the *Guardian* describes her approach to Tierney's wardrobe in the film: "Gene Tierney's wardrobe in the 1944 Hollywood film noir, *Laura*, is like no other of the period. She wore, not costumes for an actress's part, but real clothes that could have been owned by a real woman: separates, a witty raincoat and hat [fig. 11]. They, more than the script or playing, suggest Laura chooses what she wears: not to advertise nubility or family wealth but to please herself."[101] Film costumes conceived as full clothing collections, Cashin's designs for Tierney attracted fans and manufacturers alike, inspiring retail adaptations. (Tierney even borrowed some of the costumes to wear during the press junket.) The costumes for *Laura* earned Cashin a five-year contract at Fox, where she rose through the ranks to become top costume designer. In 1949, she left Hollywood and developed commercially successful ready-to-wear women's fashions in

Fig. 11. Wearing a raincoat, hat, and separates, Tierney models Bonnie Cashin's wartime costume designs for women.

New York, where she turned into a trendsetting fashion celebrity in her own right. Tierney's wardrobe from *Laura* reemerged in one of her later collections.[102]

One cannot fully appreciate Cashin's designs without looking back at the previous generation of women's costumes. Gilbert Adrian was the quintessential women's costume designer of the 1940s, known for broad-shouldered, slim-hipped suits that connoted masculine power but exuded modernist abstraction and sophistication with their clean lines and severe angles. Adrian designed costumes for MGM's signature stars from 1928 to 1941 before opening his own salon and supplying the most expensive retailers in the country. Given the amount of fabric and labor required for their geometric, high-fashion designs, Adrian's suits were incompatible with the needs of middle-class U.S. women who worked outside the home during World War II.[103] At one point in *Laura*, the Adrian-esque "coat-hanger look" is explicitly contrasted with Tierney's costume, juxtaposed in medium long shot. Like two actors from different generations preparing themselves in a dressing room, Laura sits in front of a mirror dressed in a peasant blouse with drawstring neck and matching skirt while her wealthy aunt (Judith Anderson) stands behind her retouching her makeup and pulling down the veil of her pillbox hat (fig. 12).

Remembered for her democratic and American style, off the rack rather than tailor made, Cashin is celebrated for asserting an alternative to the midcentury fashion industry of Paris. Underlying this alternative style are two historical precedents. First, the manufacture of U.S. military uniforms and, later, "sports and hardwork wear" involved mass production and the standardization of sizes. Second, the women who entered the U.S. labor force during World War II were spending disposable income on "quality casual wear" that was both practical and affordable at a time when austerity programs limited the types and amounts of material in clothing.[104] Cashin's innovations included her use of organic materials such as leather and mohair; her incorporation of East Asian

Fig. 12. The Adrian-esque "coat-hanger look" of Judith Anderson's costume (*right*) contrasts with Tierney's peasant blouse with drawstring neck and matching skirt (*left*).

design traditions through objects like kimonos and Noh coats; the introduction of layers, purse pockets, and carriables; and, to quote her biographer Stephanie Lake, the combination of luxury with utility "when she elevated a workaday garment or object to high-fashion use," as when she used industrial fastenings—zippers, harness buckles, brass toggles—as design solutions.[105] The Eastern influences of her designs were well suited to Tierney's performance in *Laura* in light of her prior roles, as seen in the striped kimono jacket and palazzo pants Tierney wears in one scene (fig. 13) or the mandarin-collar dress in another (fig. 14). More to the point, Cashin's feminine sensibility and functional approach helped naturalize Tierney's image as a workingwoman from high society.

A 1945 feature in the fan magazine *Screenland* offers a salient example of how Cashin's costumes for *Laura* helped promote that image. Written by Cashin, these "Notes from a Designer's Diary" authenticated Hollywood's commitment to storytelling above ornamentation for its own sake, instructing moviegoers on how a costumer contributes to a story by designing a wardrobe to fit each character.[106] "If the average American girl could be the heroine of her own life story," wrote Cashin, "and *dress accordingly!*" Alongside the article appeared a photo of Tierney in one of Cashin's "dreamy dresses" from *Laura*—the strapless, floral-print evening gown she wears in footage that Fox excised from the montage.[107] In the context of a shopping spree and makeover, luxurious vehicles for ornamental transformation, it is perhaps not the sort of dress the average American girl would wear, but repurposed in Cashin's "Notes," it might be. The same issue of *Screenland* includes "Personal Notes on Bonnie Cashin" informing us that the "casual air" of her designs—"essentially young with just a touch of sophistication tossed in"—achieves the "essence of chic." The costumes look "wearable, and in no way delegated just to some picturesque setting in a motion picture."[108] Laura exercises her own agency, autonomy, and pleasure in selecting what she wears. Female audiences across class lines could not only fantasize about dressing like Laura but also potentially buy their own Cashin-inspired ensemble or at least learn from her fashion advice.

Cashin's "Personal Notes" illustrate the narrative and social functions of costume in the studio era—the relationship between costume and characterization, on the one hand, and fashion and consumption, on the other—that together construct Tierney's wartime star image. In her

Fig. 13. Tierney's striped kimono jacket reflects the Eastern influences of Bonnie Cashin's designs.

Fig. 14. Tierney's mandarin-collar dress refashions her from Orientalist "exotic" to "the average American girl."

foundational analysis of film costuming, Jane Gaines observes that "costumes are fitted to characters as a second skin, working in this capacity for the cause of narrative by relaying information to the viewer about a 'person.'"[109] The better the costume fits the character, the more the costume is read as the character's "natural" clothing rather than exclusively an element of production design.[110] While a skillfully designed wardrobe for a film collapses the boundaries between costume and clothing, it also fuses character to star, expressing a personality that is ascribed to the actor playing the role.[111] The studios are then able to market a film's costumes as consumable fashions through star-driven promotional campaigns and publicity stories. Film historian Mary Desjardins elucidates how stars advertised both costume (the wardrobe from their films) and fashion (their personal wardrobe that influenced, or was influenced by, costume). Articles and photo spreads, she suggests, "strengthened the symbiotic relations among studios, female fans, and consumer industries that relied on star testimony and a visualized glamour to sell their products."[112] Cashin's insistence upon fitting characters to costumes reinforced the idea of Laura as "the average American girl," which her "wearable" and "casual" attire made visible. The costumes guaranteed that the "real" Tierney, revealed through Laura, embodied Cashin's everywoman style. If, in the context of film narrative, costume becomes inseparable from a character's clothing, it also becomes inseparable from fashion in the context of film stardom.

Films may inspire fashion or exploit current trends most explicitly when they are *about* fashion at the diegetic level. *Laura* is not such a film—nor is it about World War II, for that matter—but it is preoccupied with fashioning the home front. Laura's/Tierney's wardrobe, therefore, should not be taken for granted. Consider the flashback scene in which Laura prepares to leave her office with Shelby for an evening of dinner and dancing. Wearing a black poor-boy sweater and pencil skirt, she sits at her desk and inspects Shelby's design for a bath product advertisement (fig. 15). Laura asks about the model—Diane Redfern, who bears a passing resemblance to Laura and who will be murdered instead of Laura by mistake—and Shelby responds, "You hired her yourself last week, don't you remember?" Before leaving the office, she checks herself in the mirror as she puts on a floppy hat, and Shelby helps her slip into a bolero jacket with tie front. "I approve of that hat," Shelby tells her, "and the girl in it, too."

Fig. 15. Laura wears a black poor-boy sweater to the office.

Of course, Laura does not need Shelby's approval. Continuing his flirtations at the restaurant, he insists, "What about lunch? Beautiful lunches day after day after day after—." Laura interrupts him with a gentle rebuttal: "What about work? Beautiful work, day after day after day" (fig. 16). We have already seen Laura's "talent and imagination" carry her to the top of Bullitt and Company, and we understand that she has an eye for design both in terms of her smart fashion sense and the advertising her agency produces. ("It's excellent," she assures Shelby about the artwork, adding with a hint of jealousy over Diane, "It's really very good.") The irony of Laura forgetting she hired Diane lies in the eventual realization that Diane's relationship with Shelby threatens his engagement to Laura and leads to Diane's murder. Diane also acts as a double for Laura. Seen only in photographs and illustrations, Diane's modeling is never more than a function of Laura's "beautiful work" on the advertising campaign. Meanwhile, the costumes that Tierney models for the audience in these office scenes indicate Laura's professional labor. Soft-looking, informal, even sporty, her clothes are anything but purely

Fig. 16. For a night out of dinner and dancing, Laura wears a floppy hat and bolero jacket with tie front.

ornamental. She is outfitted for action and needs to be able to move in what she wears.

The foregrounding of costumes is not uncommon in the Cinderella or Pygmalion narratives of transformation that feed Hollywood star vehicles. One waits in anticipation for a favorite star, concealed in body suits or frumpy attire, to return to the star image she is assumed to embody. This revelation of the star's normative self often occurs over a makeover sequence or an invisible process implied by "before" and "after" moments. In her book *Hollywood Catwalk*, Tamar Jeffers McDonald regards the shopping sequence as key to a female character's metamorphosis in such films, contending that the shopping sequence displays a spectacle of commodities to the audience, through either montage or musical interlude, to suggest that "shopping is the labor that will accomplish the desired change."[113] Female characters often transform from a "sexual innocent to a more poised and seemingly experienced incarnation of the woman," she claims.[114] Furthermore, "films that use the shopping montage encourage viewers to feel better about themselves by spending."[115] New clothes and accessories are presented as the ingredients for a magical alteration of personal style, but *Laura* sets different parameters for its trajectory of female self-improvement. Laura's transformation does not restore Tierney to her more familiar Orientalist image of beauty—the transformation narrative instead posits a new look for the star. With the makeover montage excised from the film, a work montage takes its place, as if to say that a woman's work outside the home is the means by which she can accomplish a desired change. Thus by virtue of her wardrobe and its connotations of labor, Laura shares little with women in other Hollywood films about fashion transformations and belongs more in the company of "home-front soldiers."

Laura is considerably different from other "woman's films" about war work. Take, for example, RKO's *Tender Comrade* (Edward Dmytryk, 1943) in which Ginger Rogers plays a factory worker, who learns how to live communally with other women while their husbands are away. Fox's own *In the Meantime, Darling*, also directed by Preminger and released in the same year as *Laura*, features Cashin's costumes and stars Jeanne Crain as the spoiled new bride of an army lieutenant, who cultivates a wartime work ethic by sharing a military boardinghouse with the wives of the other officers stationed nearby.[116] Although the war is never mentioned in *Laura*, it takes on an absent presence in the historical context of 1944, especially through the professional opportunities traditionally reserved for men that Laura navigates in her position as an advertising executive.

Compared to Tierney's previous characters Kay and Haoli, Laura is a more ambitious and independent woman whose work occurs entirely on the home front. "I never have been and I never will be bound by anything I don't do with my own free will," she says to Mark, defying the attempts of the men in the film to determine her future. These attempts at control are conveyed on the levels of plot and mise-en-scène both; in five of Tierney's major scenes, Preminger frames her between two male actors, containing her in spaces of action. Preminger's characteristically observational and detached visual style gives these characters an opaque quality, making it difficult to identify with either Waldo or Mark, who jockey for discursive authority as writer/narrator and investigator, respectively, but whose motivations are never entirely clear.

Playing a handheld dexterity game to keep calm, Mark's desire to manipulate and control his environment appears innocuous enough, but as his hallucinatory investigation continues, these tendencies manifest in an unconscious desire (voyeuristic, if not necrophilic) to possess Laura for himself. Under the impression that Laura is dead, Mark bids on her portrait, reads her letters, rummages through her drawers (including the nightstand drawers where she keeps her delicates), sniffs her perfume, peers into her closet, drinks her Scotch, and finally sleeps in her apartment. After Laura becomes a suspect in his case, Mark finally arrests her for Diane's murder. Laura retroactively interprets his interrogation at the police station as a smokescreen. If Mark believes she is innocent, his presumption of guilt was only an attempt to solicit an official statement, confirm her alibi, and clear her name—or so it would seem to Laura at a time when no one trusts her, nor she them. What the audience knows is that Mark's questions are not purely motivated by altruism, as he is really driving at whether she still loves Shelby. Even with the ostensible closure of the film's ending, Laura's "romantic shortsightedness" and Mark's perversely obsessive qualities cast doubt on what kind of romantic future is realistically possible for this couple.

While in certain respects the film draws visual and narrative comparisons between Mark and the other men in Laura's life, it also reminds us that he presents an alternative to them. References to Mark's working-class status as a police detective help explain his fascination with Laura (whose world he can only imagine or, at best, observe) and possibly her ultimate attraction to him, not only as a "white knight" (however naive that may be) but also as socially different. If Laura's maid Bessie (Dorothy Adams) is any indication, Laura has already engaged in an intimate relationship across class lines. Writer Barry Gifford wonders whether Bessie's "hysterical defense" of Laura to Mark suggests yet another queer subtext in the film.[117] In contradistinction to Mark and Bessie, both Waldo and Shelby, respectively, are archetypes of the leisure class: an aristocratic writer who types his articles while soaking in a marble bathtub and an idle playboy from southern gentility who has found a patron in Laura's aunt.

Although Laura is part of Waldo's and Shelby's world among the glitterati of the Upper East Side, her clothing marks her as a woman who came by financial rewards honestly. When Laura first meets Shelby at her aunt's penthouse party, she chides him for living off his family's inheritance, only to take pity on him after he admits to the foreclosure of the estate. Incredulous over his pretense of wealth, she asks, "Why maintain the fiction? Why not work?" After Shelby admits further that a friend reneged on a job offer, she offers him a position at Bullitt and Company. Much in the way Laura turns her aunt's party into a job interview, the film turns a fashion style into a performative articulation of integrity. According to the film's aesthetic value system, even the outfits she wears outside of work distinguish her from a lady of leisure, as with the striped tunic peplum top, skirt, and cloche hat when she confronts Shelby about his philandering, and the peasant blouse outfit with added shawl when she defends herself during Mark's interrogation (figs. 17 and 18). Jewelry is kept to a minimum throughout, save for a broach, a belt ornament, and the occasional rings and cuffs. Laura believes in the value of work. The codes and contexts of fashion are constant reminders of her labor, showing her financial independence from men.

That the film ultimately condemns Waldo's and Shelby's extravagant lifestyles is in some ways at odds with its lavish production design. *Variety* reported that a "total of 43 sets, the highest number since pre-war days, will be used in the filming of *Laura*."[118] Furnished and decorated with antiques and shimmering with mirrors, Laura's apartment is the home of an aesthete more than an executive. While the mise-en-scène highlights wealth, status, and vanity, recall that Waldo was the designer. Seeing Waldo's more palatial apartment, it comes as no surprise that he loaned Laura the longcase clock, vase, and fire screen from his collection of ornate objects—of which he imagines Laura as his most prized piece. Laura's apartment evokes Waldo's efforts to possess and control her private life, as well as her feelings of indebtedness to him for her career. Given the way the film associates her more with spaces of her work than her home, to fashion herself for work is Laura's most unmediated form of self-expression. As much as clothing may reinforce hegemonic assumptions about gender, it also constitutes the social fabric by which one may reconstruct a symbolic identity. Through Tierney and her costumes, *Laura* promotes a fantasy of class mobility enabled by professional labor that the audience may experience vicariously with Laura, who satisfies her girlhood "dreams of a career."

Figs. 17 and 18. *Top*: Standing between Shelby (Vincent Price, *left*) and Waldo (Clifton Webb, *right*), Laura wears a striped tunic peplum top, skirt, and cloche hat. *Bottom*: During Mark's interrogation, she adds a shawl to her peasant blouse outfit.

Between the making of *Laura* and the making over of Tierney, we have access to period discourses of female beautification during World War II that affected the promotion of the film by way of its star—and vice versa. Repackaging Tierney as an all-American girl instead of an "exotic" Other while reframing her socioeconomic background as the source of her work ethic, Fox updated Tierney's star image to coincide with wartime ideologies at the intersections of race, class, and gender. A reflexive star vehicle for Tierney's new, unornamented look, *Laura* thematized Tierney's transformation and upheld female labor on the home front, giving her the opportunity to model an emerging trend in female work fashions. Of course, other female stars have undergone similar "Americanizations"—Myrna Loy is the most famous example of an Orientalist beauty turned "good girl"—but Fox gave Tierney's image special context in the "natural," inconspicuous beauty of the home front. While *Thunder Birds* and *China Girl* are World War II propaganda films in the most obviously deliberate ways, *Laura* demonstrates how Hollywood participated in the war effort on-screen almost exclusively through mise-en-scène, without relying on plots or characters that explicitly acknowledged the war.

Coda: *A Bell for Adano*

The year 1945 was a banner one for Tierney. She starred in two films, first *A Bell for Adano* and then *Leave Her to Heaven*, earning an Academy Award nomination for the latter, and won the annual award for "Hollywood's Best Dressed Star" from *Screen Stars* (a gold bracelet with her initials inlayed with pearls). Judges based their decision on her "innate good taste in the selection and ensembling of her personal wardrobe, and also on her all-around exquisitely groomed appearance." The issue of *Screen Stars* that announced her recognition featured a publicity still for *Adano* with Tierney, now a blonde (like Betty Grable), in her Tina Tomasino costume.[119] Certain fan magazines speculated that she was "[s]tudying to be a blonde" to star in the upcoming *Forever Amber*,[120] while others promised readers that she was only a "Temporary Blonde" and that she would return to her "natural coloring" in *Dragonwyck* (i.e., her "natural" star image).[121] Although Fox had essentially cast her in a secondary role in *Adano* (and miscast her at that), she received top billing—a testament to her star power in the middle of the decade. "Gene is now the hottest star on the Twentieth Century lot since the release of *Laura*," as an article in *Screenland* put it.[122]

Set in a small town on the Sicilian coast just after the Allied invasion (Licata served as the basis for the fictional Adano), the film was not exactly World War II propaganda like *Thunder Birds* and *China Girl* but instead a prestige production for Fox, shot in the Santa Monica Mountains at Brent's Crags, near Malibu, the same location the studio used for *How Green Was My Valley*. The war was nearing its close during filming. Director Henry King learned that his son, an air force pilot, went missing in action after a combat mission; it was later confirmed that he was a prisoner of war, but he returned home after the war's end.[123] In some respects, *Adano* was a precursor to Fox's cycle of realist films about the effects of the war and the escalation of the Cold War, including *Twelve O'Clock High* (Henry King, 1949), *The Big Lift* (George Seaton, 1950), and, finally, *The Longest Day* (Ken Annakin, Andrew Marton, and Bernhard Wicki, 1962).[124] Screenwriters Lamar Trotti (also a coproducer) and Norman Reilly Raine had adapted the 1944 novel of the same name by John Hersey, a former war correspondent in Italy, which immediately inspired a Broadway play by Paul Osborn and won the Pulitzer Prize the following year.

Maj. Victor Joppolo, the Italian American protagonist played by Fredric March on stage and John Hodiak in the film, was based on former senior civil affairs officer Lt. Col. Frank E. Toscani. Asserting that the story "damaged his reputation as a civil affairs officer and a husband" and, in his words, "recklessly, maliciously and falsely states certain defamatory matters," Toscani issued a $250,000 libel suit against Hersey (the author of the novel), Alfred A. Knopf (the novel's publisher), Osborn (the playwright), Leland Hayward and the Playwrights Producing Company, Inc. (the play's producers), and Fox. Of chief concern was the depiction of Joppolo's relationship with Tina while he was still married—a subplot that "emotionally upset" Toscani's wife—and Joppolo's countermanding an order, which led to his transfer from Adano. In real life, Toscani was commended for his work in Licata and promoted.[125] A New York Appellate Division ruling "barred recovery for characters resembling living persons unless the work used either the name or the portrait of the complaining party."[126] The court threw out the suit, but as the *New York Times* quipped in Toscani's obituary, "It might not have helped Mr. Hersey's case that the alluring Gene Tierney had her hair dyed blond to play Tina."[127] The public implications of an affair would be upsetting enough. With a woman played by Tierney, it would be a *cause célèbre*.

Laura's Oscar-winning director of photography Joseph LaShelle gives Tierney a few ethereal close-ups in "butterfly lighting," accentuating her high cheekbones and halo of golden curls, but despite the mutual attraction between Tina and Joppolo evident in some longing looks, they never do more than peck each other on the lips and share a hug the night before Joppolo leaves Adano. After interviewing Toscani over a week in Licata, Hersey concluded that like Joppolo, he was "a good man." Hersey expressed this sentiment to Toscani when he sent him an autographed copy of the novel, "With thanks for a very good time in Licata."[128] For whatever unpleasantness Toscani may have experienced from the novel and its adaptations, the film encourages audiences to view Tina and Joppolo not as a lustful couple on the verge of an affair but as two young people forging a platonic relationship out of wartime loneliness. A soldier in the U.S. Army, Joppolo has left his wife back on the home front as he helps Adano rebuild after fascist rule and the recent invasion. The daughter of the head fisherman in town, Tina was engaged to an antifascist soldier in the Italian army who has gone missing (eventually, she discovers he was killed trying to control a drunken riot that broke out among his fellow troops). Tina and Joppolo remind each other of their absent partners whom they still love. Just as she learns to heal through his companionship and he gains strength of resolve from her affections, so too does Adano begin its postwar recovery.

Tina recognizes what Joppolo feels for her because "sometimes a woman's loneliness is just like a man's loneliness," and the film characterizes her as a surrogate for women on the U.S. home front awaiting soldiers' return. As she assures him when he shows up at her home one night, "You are only doing what most men do when they are lonely. You are a long way from home. You think of someone you love back there, and you miss her terribly. Then you think of someone here—of me, perhaps—who reminds you of her. You try not to, but you cannot help it." She also identifies with his restlessness and dissatisfaction growing up in the Bronx, wanting "a little more," and she explains that she dyed her hair blonde because she "wanted something different" in the dark-haired region of southern Italy ("My dark hair was my Bronx," she says, surely one of the most awkward lines of dialogue Tierney ever had to deliver). Understanding that he and Tina are more similar than the war would have them believe, Joppolo tells her that his parents were poor and emigrated from a small town near Florence. His father was able to make good in the United States as a waiter, and his parents can now afford a washing machine and an automobile, which leads Tina to assume that "in the Bronx, everyone is rich." This midcentury American dream story, the film suggests, bodes well for the poor townspeople of Adano, as the Allied occupation brings democracy to Sicily.

Adano was Tierney's last film released during the war. Playing a white, blonde European, she was less "exotic" than in *China Girl* and more safely closer to home. The parallels between Tina and Joppolo establish another example of "international solidarity," now looking toward the postwar era of European assistance and the consolidation of U.S. power in the world order. Joppolo's investment in the people of Adano deepens the more he sees Tina; as if beholding a spiritual vision, he first notices her in his pew at Sunday mass. Next, he catches the chief of the Carabinieri fighting with Tina over her spot in the breadline and orders that all town officials must henceforth govern as "servants of the people," not "masters of the people" (taking special liberties will be grounds for removal from office). Joppolo then convinces her father to resume fishing in order to help feed the town, vowing that he will not demand a tribute or impose a tax. When Joppolo negotiates with the U.S. Navy lieutenant in charge of the port, he is able to cut through the military bureaucracy that grants fishing permission. To repay him for coming to the town's aid, Tina's father invites Joppolo to a dinner she plans to make at their home. Finally, Joppolo countermands an order banning carts and civilian vehicles from the town's main roads. The order would leave the roads open for military vehicles but prohibit transportation of water and food into town.

Before the army transfers Joppolo for his insubordination, he acquires a replacement for the seven-hundred-year-old town bell that the fascists had melted down for ammunition (the navy finds a bell off the African coast that used to hang in a monastery and installs it for the town). The tolls of the bell had alerted the people of news, offered them a source of morale, and kept their everyday lives running on schedule. In celebration, they throw a party that allows Joppolo a last dance with Tina, and the next morning he departs for Algiers with the new bell ringing behind him, symbolizing the rebirth of the community and validating his heroic work for Adano. Tina is the most passive character Tierney played during the war years: not a beautiful workingwoman but a woman whose beauty inspires a man's service in the war effort. The films that followed after the war took a far less idealistic approach to male–female relationships, shifting perspective from the symbolic space of a home front to the literal space of the U.S. home, where feminine beauty is not a restorative quality and marriage does not guarantee unity.

2
Women on the Edge

Demobilization and Domesticity

Historical sociologist Andrea S. Walsh reports that six months after the end of World War II, at a time when 11 million veterans returned home, production in U.S. government and industry was reduced by half and unemployment increased to 2.7 million. The majority of those unemployed were women: 4 million were fired or quit their jobs as the public female labor force fell from 19.5 million to the approximate prewar figure of 15.5 million.[1] Even while 50 percent of prewar homemakers wanted to keep working after the war and approximately 90 percent of those women wanted to keep their war jobs, "the dominant ideology was that women, although to be commended, should 'step down' for returning soldiers."[2] Walsh explains, "The dominant culture supported female demobilization by stressing the importance of traditional femininity," and traditional femininity was understood both in terms of physical appearance and social roles.[3] As she goes on to make clear, "Postwar women were encouraged to return to their 'place' as 'nurturers'" not only in the home as wives and mothers but also in the "pink-collar ghetto" of the labor force, where they were reemployed. With the shrinkage of women in skilled blue-collar, business, and professional positions, as well as the decline in women's average weekly wages from $50 to $37, the United States witnessed an expansion of the service and clerical sector. Walsh's data bears repeating: "By late 1946, 80 percent of wartime women workers were still employed but only 40 percent occupied their wartime positions. [. . .] By 1950, half of all female workers and 66 percent of white women workers were employed as clericals."[4]

Despite the wartime propaganda campaigns described in the introduction and first chapter of this book, it is important to note that even by late 1944, government agencies began referring to women's war work as "excess labor," and workingwomen came under scrutiny in media and popular culture almost as quickly as they were publicly valorized. Opinion forums and editorials in newspapers and magazines, for example, encouraged women to withdraw voluntarily from the U.S. home front's public labor force.[5] According to Michael Renov, "This climate of animosity, functioning as a negation of female achievement, was never entirely absent during the war years and was preserved within the minds and hearts of women themselves."[6] On the screen in the United States, the emergence of what would be termed film noir from 1941 to 1946 gave recurring visibility to the so-called femme fatale, popularly recognized as the seductively "fatal" woman, with memorable performances by major stars such as Barbara Stanwyck, Lana Turner, and Joan Bennett. Of course, this archetype has a much longer history in literature and film, but it received particular and recurrent attention during the 1940s with contemporary female characters of noir who are driven by career ambition, sexual desire, money (or at least financial security and independence), the prospect of escape from loveless marriages and domestic confinement, or seemingly unknowable motives through which these women are presumed "evil."[7] For Renov, "The moral ambivalence and double binds which confronted the newly recruited female worker [. . .] instilled the shards of self-doubt and fostered the neurosis which animate the bleak moral landscapes of *Double Indemnity* [Billy Wilder, 1944], *The Postman Always Rings Twice* [Tay Garnett, 1946], *Mildred Pierce* [Michael Curtiz, 1945], and *The Woman in the Window* [Fritz Lang, 1944]."[8]

Alongside concerns over the "excess labor" of women, sexual tensions escalated with the rising divorce rates and numbers of single women in the United States. Among those who divorced at this time were Tierney and Cassini, in 1952, following a separation from 1946 to 1948 (while temporarily reconciled, Tierney gave birth to their second daughter, Christina). Both their separation and divorce received enormous media coverage.[9] "Many times I contemplated giving up my career to be with my husband," she admitted in her divorce testimony.[10] Renov points out that "single men outnumbered single women three to two in 1940, but by 1944 there were two and one-half times more single women than men living in America," during which time divorces nearly doubled as a result of hasty wartime weddings. Greater competition among women for available men, more dissatisfied couples, and growing disillusionment over marriage itself are among the additional factors Renov cites that contributed to the postwar backlash against working-women.[11] As we will see, Fox attempted to mitigate Tierney's war work (and at the same time affirm its value) with a more domestic image as a devoted "war bride."

Following the success of *Laura* (Otto Preminger, 1944), Tierney starred in *Leave Her to Heaven* (John M. Stahl, 1945), *The Razor's Edge* (Edmund Goulding, 1946), and *That Wonderful Urge* (Robert B. Sinclair, 1948), three films that, respectively, focused on three domestic contexts in the cultural redefinition of women's roles after the war: the home, the adjustment of returning veterans, and marriage. In all three of these films, however, Tierney plays women who do not so much acquiesce to or resist the social prescriptions of their postwar roles but *overinvest* in them to fulfill those roles on their own terms within limited possibilities for agency and control (in each case to the detriment of the film's patriarchal authority figure). To whatever degree the films endorse, condemn, or equivocate about the actions of Tierney's characters, they disrupt the normative image of the feminine domestic—the white, middle-class wife and "nurturer"—used to promote and publicize Tierney's star image by rendering it hyperbolic. This chapter argues that the dialectical tensions between different constructions of her domesticity make women's "natural" domestic place untenable for Tierney at a time when historical women experienced frustration and internalized misogyny over cultural expectations to demobilize in multiple ways. What follows does not necessarily aim to determine historical causalities of production, accounting for the films' intended meanings on the part of the studio, the filmmakers, or Tierney herself, but interprets possible meanings available in the historical context of Tierney's stardom. To begin, we need to return to World War II from the perspective of Tierney at home, where her war work could be viewed in terms of an army wife's domestic obligations.

The Dark Side of the Moon: *Leave Her to Heaven*

The space and idea of the home has long been central to the themes, narratives, and mise-en-scène of Hollywood cinema, but what the home meant in the context of World War II is historically and culturally specific. Philippa Gates claims, "The American Home was inextricably linked to the female body: literally, the woman kept the home running in the absence of a male head of the household financially as well as domestically and, metaphorically, as her body was also a fortress to be defended against unsanctioned (i.e., extramarital) entry."[12] Cultural critic Elisabeth Bronfen makes a similar point when she observes that as wartime propaganda established a "fluid boundary between the home front and front lines," Hollywood films conceived of the U.S. home "both as an actual place and a persistent idea in the name of which troops fight."[13] If Rosie the Riveter sponsored the strength of a newly mobilized female workforce in a wartime industry, the "self-sacrificing home-keeper" coexisted as "a counter-icon of feminine fortitude, for whom the base for her war effort is first and foremost the domestic home itself."[14] What Tierney's wartime films lacked in traditional domestic settings, fan magazines compensated for in stories about her marriage to Cassini while he served in the U.S. Army Cavalry as a first lieutenant. In 1942, the couple moved into a house in Beverly Hills overlooking Franklin Canyon, but while it was being renovated, they lived in the guest cottage on the property.

The first tendency in publicity pieces was to emphasize the ordinariness of their temporary home, characterizing Tierney and Cassini as an average middle-class U.S. couple in wartime. A March 1942 article in *Silver Screen* described a "three-room cottage, sans tile baths and hardwood floors, gleaming fixtures, a furnace, or the comforts and luxuries to which both had been accustomed."[15] Complete with interior and exterior photographs of this secluded "Honeymoon Home," a March 1942 article in *Screenland* assured readers "that you and you and even you live in a much better, and bigger, house than does Hollywood's most promising actress. Cozy is the word for it." Readers were also informed that the drapes did not fit, and rooms were still not fully furnished.[16] A *Silver Screen* article from September 1942 titled "Mister Cassini's War Bride" takes readers off Mulholland Drive "to a wide, old-fashioned wooden farm gate" and then "down a tree-lined lane, which looks like something out of the back country of Connecticut," before arriving at "a small-frame cottage, which has been there long enough for bougainvillea vine to clamber all over it."[17] By this point, Tierney and Cassini had moved out of the guest cottage and into a "small, two-story Dutch Colonial," their permanent but not-yet-finished home, which the author calls "Early American in its simplicity."[18] Most of the furniture supposedly came "straight from old New England—picked up here and there, piece by piece, wherever a good buy presented itself."[19]

The second way that publicity linked Tierney to the home was through repeated allusions to her wartime domestic labor. In an August 1943 article in *Screenland* titled "My Problems as a War Wife," Tierney advocated that army wives visit their husbands in camp, as she did when she joined Cassini in Fort Riley, Kansas, and they rented an apartment together in town (after she weathered the cold, gave up her privacy, and contended with infestation while staying in "a boarding house, barracks, an auto court, and rooms for rent"). If a soldier need not worry about the health, safety, and loving commitment of his wife, she felt, "he can concentrate entirely on his work."[20] An August 1945 article in *Screenland* detailed the "civilian problems" Tierney encountered back in Beverly Hills, keeping up the new house during Cassini's absence,[21] such as a broken furnace (soot that collected in pipes caused fires on two different occasions), a leaking roof, an overgrown garden, and the threat of prowlers.[22] Yet these articles ultimately reinforced her willingness and ability to balance her domestic and professional life, aiming to resolve this contradiction in her star image by presenting the army wife and movie star as complementary roles for Tierney. "I'd come on the set with circles down to my chin and my nerves twitching like Mexican jumping beans," she told the magazine but added that she "just accepted the fact that everybody has troubles these days and there's no point crying about it."[23] When she appeared in *Silver Screen* as "Mister Cassini's War Bride," side-by-side photographs of Tierney at home and at work illustrated this dual logic explicitly. The first page paired a photo of Tierney sporting a garrison cap to promote *Thunder Birds* (William A. Wellman, 1942) with a photo of her and Cassini standing in front of their living-room fireplace, their arms around each other. Another page included a promotional photo of Tierney hand-propping a Thunder Bird next to a photo of her tending a Victory garden.[24]

Tierney's advice to her fans on the home front supported women's work in and outside the home as essential contributions to the war effort, but as per the domestic ideology of wartime, it was therefore equally in the service of upholding traditional marriage norms. As she declared in one quote, "It's up to women to be pioneer women again. Men's partners, not men's pampered pets. Completely feminine, but calm and courageous and untiring, no matter what crisis comes along. Women whose strength of courage is a bulwark to men, and an influence on children." But just as she urged women to "have something to occupy her mind while her husband's away," she reminded them that it "shouldn't be another man." She felt women should volunteer for war work, not simply return to their parents, and also bear their husbands children. For her own purposes, she said she has decided to follow Cassini wherever he is stationed in the country (regardless of her career).[25]

Leave Her to Heaven pushed Tierney's idealized-homemaker image to its breaking point, showing the cracks in the hegemonic domestic ideology. Tierney plays Ellen Berent, an affluent woman newly married to an author of some renown, Richard Harland (Cornel Wilde). The couple meet on a train en route to New Mexico, where Ellen is attending her father's funeral to scatter his cremated ashes and Richard plans to write his next novel. Coincidentally, they are both staying at the Rancho Jacinto, the vacation home of Richard's friend Glen Robie (Ray Collins), who happens to be the Berents' attorney. Joining them are Ellen's mother (Mary Philips) and her cousin Ruth (Jeanne Crain), the latter of whom Mrs. Berent adopted as a child. Ellen is engaged to attorney Russell Quinton (Vincent Price) but calls off the engagement when she and Richard immediately develop a mutual infatuation. After their whirlwind marriage, they move to Warm Springs, Georgia, so that Richard can be near his younger brother, Danny (Darryl Hickman), while he recovers from polio. Eager to start her new life with Richard at his fishing lodge in Deer Lake, Maine, which he has named "Back of the Moon," Ellen secretly works with Danny to help him walk again using crutches, but her honeymoon plans are dashed when Danny's doctor (Reed Hadley) encourages her and Richard to bring Danny with them to the lodge. As Richard divides his attention between Danny and his writing, life at Back of the Moon bores Ellen, and her need for Richard's validation intensifies to the point that she allows Danny to drown while teaching him to swim.[26]

The couple relocates to the Berents' seaside home in Bar Harbor, Maine, where Richard (believing Danny's death was an accident) sinks into a depression. When Ellen announces that she is pregnant, she hopes the expectant child will renew her relationship with Richard, but instead he grows closer with Ruth as she tries to help the Harlands prepare for starting their family. Ellen comes to resent her unborn child as another possible competitor for Richard's love and attention, not unlike Danny. In one of the film's most famous scenes, she throws herself down the stairs to cause a miscarriage.[27] The publication of Richard's new novel confirms Ellen's suspicions that he has fallen in love with Ruth—he dedicates the book to her—and she confesses that she deliberately let Danny drown. Inspired to visit the book's setting and escape Ellen's destructive influence on the family, Ruth decides to leave for a trip to Mexico but not before Ellen poisons herself and frames Ruth for murder. Ellen has arranged for the trial to be prosecuted by her ex-fiancé, whom she knows still carries a torch for her. Earlier comments seem to have portended Richard and Ruth's fate ("Nothing ever happens to Ellen," Mrs. Berent tells Richard, attesting to her self-reliance, and Glen assures him that "Ellen always wins," musing on her competitiveness). On the stand, Ruth admits her love for Richard, which appears to provide her with a motive for murdering Ellen. To clear her name, Richard delivers a testimony that implicates Ellen in Danny's death, establishing the jealousy that would drive her to commit suicide and falsely accuse her cousin. Although Ruth is acquitted, Richard is sentenced to two years in prison as an accessory to murder for withholding knowledge about the drowning. The film is told as an extended flashback when Richard returns to Deer Lake after his sentence, with Glen recounting the events on the shore as Richard paddles a canoe to Back of the Moon, where he reunites with Ruth in the final scene.

Presented as a cautionary tale about jealousy, personified by a literally green-eyed woman, *Leave Her to Heaven* capitalized on Freudian notions popular at the time such as the "Electra complex." The film partly attributes Ellen's competition for and possessiveness over Richard to a displacement of her attachment to her late father whom she insists Richard resembles and whose death she may have caused. A memo from Zanuck to producer William A. Bacher puts this idea in no uncertain terms: "Ellen is a girl with a possession complex. She captures and marries Richard because he represents somehow the attraction she had for her father."[28] Or, as Mrs. Berent says to Richard, "It's just that she loves too much." If Ruth is the nominal "good woman," who takes after her surrogate mother by occupying a nurturing, domestic position in Richard's life, Ellen would be the "femme fatale," a woman unable to sever her bond with a masculine figure (her father, the source of her jealousy) and fulfill a properly feminine domestic role. The provocative psychosexual themes lent ample opportunities for sensationalistic marketing for an adult audience. Fox's production notes called the film "the uncompromising story of a girl who wanted a monopoly on the thoughts and interests of the man she loved; the story of a girl guilty of 'the deadliest of the seven deadly sins: jealousy'—and the effect on the people close to her."[29] Borrowed from a line in *Hamlet*, the title refers to Ellen's judgment via the ghost of Hamlet's father, who instructs the prince of Denmark to avenge his murder. Hamlet is told to take action against his uncle Claudius, who poisoned his father and succeeded to the throne, but to spare his mother, Gertrude, whom Claudius marries: "Leave her to heaven / And to those thorns that in her bosom lodge / To prick and sting her" (act 1, scene 5, lines 86–87).

The film's literary origins have deeper roots and stem from Ben Ames Williams—not quite Shakespeare but a popular author whose novel *Leave Her to Heaven* was an enticing property for Fox. At the princely sum of $100,000, Zanuck won a bidding war for the film rights in 1944, before the novel was even published.[30] Adapting the novel was the job of Jo Swerling, a prolific screenwriter fresh off *Lifeboat* (Alfred Hitchcock, 1944), but remembered most for his collaborations with Frank Capra and the Oscar-nominated script he cowrote for *The Pride of the Yankees* (Sam Wood, 1942).[31] John M. Stahl was one of three directors at Fox who, along with Otto Preminger and Joseph L. Mankiewicz, had recommended that Zanuck buy the rights to the novel; he became the film's director.[32] A founding member of the Academy of Motion Picture Arts and Sciences, Stahl had been making films in Hollywood since 1914 and gained a reputation for "woman's films" such as *Imitation of Life* (1934) and *Magnificent Obsession* (1935) (both adaptations of novels and both remade in the 1950s by Stahl's more widely celebrated Hollywood heir Douglas Sirk).[33] After its publication later in 1944, the novel *Leave Her to Heaven* proved to be one of Williams's best sellers.[34]

Bacher determined that in order to emphasize the novel's settings and level of realism, the film should be shot in three-strip Technicolor,[35] which also gave Fox the opportunity to make Tierney into an even greater spectacle. Although Fox conceded that "a tense psychological drama in Technicolor was a daring experiment" (in the 1940s, color was primarily associated with musicals, period-costume films, and animation), the studio promised that the film will open "new horizons to Hollywood."[36] The studio made good on the unsure bet as the film earned $5,750,000 at the box office, an amount equivalent to $72 million to $76 million today. By 1946, *Leave Her to Heaven* was the highest-grossing film Fox had produced, responsible for one quarter of Fox's $22.6 million profit that year (its largest total yet), and the seventh most profitable film for any studio.[37]

Of the film's four Oscar nominations, which included Best Art Direction (Color), Best Cinematography (Color), Best Sound Recording, and Best Actress for Tierney, its only winner was Leon Shamroy, the director of photography, whose exquisite achievements in cinematography give the film the seemingly contradictory status of a "film noir in color."[38] Shamroy had won an Oscar the previous year for *Wilson* (Henry King, 1944), Fox's biopic of former U.S. president Woodrow Wilson, and the studio promoted *Leave Her to Heaven* with the prediction that Shamroy's cinematography would make him "a certain candidate for another Academy Award."[39] Garnering a total of eighteen Oscar nominations over his career, Shamroy tied with Charles Lang as the most nominated director of photography in Hollywood (Lang incidentally shot *The Ghost and Mrs. Muir* [Joseph L. Mankiewicz, 1947]), and after taking home the trophy for four films, he tied with Joseph Ruttenberg as the director of photography with the most wins. The color cinematography was optimal for shooting at the five exterior locations that provided authentic geographic places for the film's diegetic settings: the sequences set in New Mexico were shot in Arizona at Sedona Basin and Granite Dells; Busch Gardens in Pasadena, California, doubled for Warm Springs; Bass Lake in the Sierra Nevada region of California substituted for Deer Lake; and Monterey, California, stood in for Bar Harbor.[40] According to Fox's production notes, Sedona Basin was never before filmed in Technicolor, and Bass Lake had not yet been used as a shooting location. Craftworkers built a large platform for the camera and camera crew to float on Bass Lake, but to generate power for the camera and sound equipment, they strung eight hundred feet of cable from the shore to the platform without getting it wet, a job that earned them the nickname "the 20th Century-Fox Seabees."[41]

Fox's message to the public was clear: after *Laura*, Tierney was worthy of the hottest properties, biggest artistic talents, and latest trends in studio filmmaking, no matter how risky those choices may have seemed. Focusing on the film's landscape representations, film historian Jennifer Peterson locates *Leave Her to Heaven* at the intersections of multiple postwar developments related to Hollywood mise-en-scène and cinematography. If *Leave Her to Heaven* might be classified as a film noir today, in 1945 it would have been seen as a "woman's film," but as Peterson claims (following film scholar Linda Williams), both film noir and the "woman's film" are more specific varieties of melodrama: the basic expressive mode of popular U.S. cinema.[42] After World War II, with the emergence of domestic and global tourism as an industry, outdoor locations in melodrama functioned "as leisure destinations for the main characters," while simultaneously "serving as implicit promotion for actual tourism."[43] The circulation of wartime documentaries and Italian neorealism also fostered a "new taste for realism" in the moviegoing public.[44] Production on *Leave Her to Heaven* began in the last year of the war and the film came out in December of 1945, four months after the war's end.[45] During wartime, shooting on location was less expensive than building sets in studios, and for Stahl's purposes, relying on natural environments in California was cheaper than traveling cross-country to Maine.[46] At the time of the film's production, though, location filming had not yet become the norm for Hollywood.[47]

The studios were even more selective about shooting in Technicolor than shooting on location. Between 1935 and 1953, Technicolor practically held a monopoly on three-strip color cinematography and the studios reserved this costly process for A-films with the preeminent stars, directors of photography, costume designers, and production designers in the business.[48] Technicolor cameras were in high demand and short supply; instead of buying their own cameras, studios were contractually required to rent them from the company and hire its "color consultants" to oversee production.[49] Nevertheless, Zanuck was committed to the technologically innovative possibilities of Technicolor, which existed on a continuum between realism (recall that his service in the U.S. Army Signal Corps gave him experience working in documentary cinema) and a sense of showmanship based on artifice. Fox produced nearly two-thirds of the Technicolor films made in Hollywood from 1936 to 1954.[50] Thus, the location shooting of *Leave Her to Heaven* in three-strip Technicolor marks it as a production that looks ahead to the conventional artistic decisions of postwar Hollywood cinema, as Peterson shows, but also distinguishes it as a special-event film for Fox in 1945.

Turning more closely to Fox's production notes on the film, we can see that the studio viewed Tierney as an exploitable attraction justifying the use of color as much as any of the outdoor locations. The notes highlighted the film's "tempestuous [. . .] love scenes" and her twenty-eight "ultra-smart outfits, all of which help her defend her title as 'the best-dressed screen star.'" Among those outfits was the "one-piece, aqua blue bathing suit" she wore under her white robe in the drowning scene, which Fox called "probably the most dramatic scene any actress has ever had to play in a bathing suit." Quoting a "G.I. visitor," the notes boasted that "[n]o movie 'bad girl' ever looked better." And in the words of Tierney's costar Vincent Price, "audiences will also get the full force of those Tierney eyes."[51]

When it came to the selection of costumes, the primary colors of light (red, green, and blue) were used for Tierney exclusively. Film scholar Marshall Deutelbaum has observed that in each of the film's settings "the sequencing of Ellen's costumes suggest the separation and recombination of light primaries, as her costumes begin in white, progress through the light primaries, and return to white as she concludes her stay." Through this sequencing, the film "mimics the physical process of the three-strip Technicolor camera which [. . .] employed a prism to split light into separate photographic records on emulsions sensitive to red, green, and blue light."[52] The popularity of the film notwithstanding, some reviewers at the time complained that *Leave Her to Heaven* was too "feminine" in its aesthetics. Film historian Mark Jancovich cites critics who derided the film "for being pretty, attractive and decorative, terms that were claimed to imply superficiality," basing their evaluation on the expensive production values (including the Technicolor cinematography) and Tierney's starring role as the radiantly beautiful Ellen.[53] Vis-à-vis Tierney, Ellen is more than just the main character; she *is* the film itself. Like Tierney/Laura in *Laura*, Tierney/Ellen consumes *Leave Her to Heaven* such that she seems to possess even the film, affecting the story while both on and off the screen. This time, we understand the character's omnipresence through color and setting rather than a single prop. Tierney never had this kind of status in any of her other films, and it is no wonder *Laura* and *Leave Her to Heaven* remain her best-known films.

Ironically for a film so invested in color, Richard is color-blind. Peterson reminds us that his color blindness "would have rendered him 4—F, or ineligible for the draft for medical reasons," accounting for his presence on the home front.[54] This detail, which Richard mentions on the train to New Mexico, "is also a heavy-handed signal that he will ultimately be unable to appreciate Ellen's passionate, colorful nature (or, from a different perspective, that he cannot perceive what others can plainly see)."[55] Upon first laying eyes on Ellen in the club car of the train, he resorts to the sort of vague Orientalist clichés one might expect to see unironically stated in promotion for one of Tierney's earlier films:

> **RICHARD:** While I was watching you, exotic words
>   drifted across the mirror of my mind as summer
>   clouds drift across the sky.
> **ELLEN:** Couldn't you be a bit more specific?
> **RICHARD:** I'll try. Watching you, I thought of tales of the
>   Arabian nights, of myrrh and frankincense and—
> **ELLEN:** And patchouli?
> **RICHARD:** Patchouli. That's it.

Nobody's fool, Ellen finds Richard's pickup lines lifted right from the book she is reading—his novel *Time without End*—and it is clear that Richard is less interested in her than her recognition of *him* as the author.[56] Whereas Richard fails to "see" Ellen even while looking directly at her, she is able to "read" him even if his novel puts her to sleep. The pine-green color of at least three different settings also matches the color of Tierney's eyes, as if Ellen has dominated her environment through the overwhelming power of her sublimated emotions: the interior of the train, the woods at Back of the Moon, and (even after her death) the courtroom where Russell prosecutes the murder trial. To Richard's horror, Ellen's remark after her father's funeral that "people you love don't really die" proves to some degree true.

References to the character in the production notes reflect Fox's conception of the film as a lurid drama about the destructive pathology of jealousy. For example, Ellen is identified as "a subtly psychopathic young wife who will stop at nothing, even murder, in her desire to be loved as completely as she loves." Yet the studio's conception of Ellen was never entirely coherent, leaving her open to different interpretations beyond simply a psychotically jealous woman. Consider the following: "She was young, American, beautiful and lovable; and, at the same time, she was a psychopathic demon. She could be both passionately warm and murderously cold."[57] A humorous memo from Zanuck to writer Jules Furthman in 1947 slips between describing Ellen as "a vicious woman" and confessing to an ambivalence about the character. Zanuck wrote, "The woman in *Leave Her to Heaven* deliberately kills her own unborn child, drowns the crippled brother of her husband and endeavors to send her adopted sister to the electric chair. And yet despite all this, there are certain things about her you rather like."[58] Even when James Agee panned the film in his review for *Time*, he inadvertently betrayed an almost sympathetic (if perhaps unconscious) understanding of Ellen when he quipped, "Audiences will probably side with the murderess, who spends all of the early reels trying to manage five minutes alone with her husband."[59] Ellen's unruliness does not run afoul of the "woman's film" in the 1940s; it is consistent with how critics defined the genre at the time. The reviewer for the *New York Daily News* wrote, "The movie is made of the stuff women go for—love, hate, sex."[60]

Equally incoherent was the discourse on Tierney herself. As much as Fox wanted to advertise the film as a Technicolor vehicle for her beauty, the production notes also seek to clarify how Tierney was a star "who first found fame as a glamour girl but has made a determined and successful fight to become a versatile actress." *Leave Her to Heaven* would be "her big opportunity to prove herself."[61] The trailer advertised her star turn with the announcement that "she gives one of the truly great dramatic performances of our time." Publicity attempted to distance Tierney from the character of Ellen in order to show how this role demanded she play someone truly different from her "natural" self, protecting her image as the all-American girl that the studio had built up during the war years.[62] Shortly after the film's release, when the *Los Angeles Times* asked her how she felt playing such a character, Tierney replied, "Mentally unbalanced!" "In a world of sick human beings," she said, "it's a full time job trying to get inside these people and finding what makes them the way they are." Although she described the experience as "fascinating," she explained that she is "naturally a happy person" and would like to star in another comedy.[63] Yet her versatility as an actress (i.e., more than a "glamour girl") was only further obscured as the studio asked audiences to view her within the narrow parameters of another social type. Fox labeled her "a *femme fatale*" opposite contract player Vincent Price: "In *Laura*, he became first her fiancé, then her suspected murderer. In *Dragonwyck* [Joseph L. Mankiewicz, 1946], for love of her, he committed murder. Now, in *Leave Her to Heaven*, he is the disappointed suitor who tries to avenge her death."[64]

What exactly qualifies Tierney as a femme fatale here? This use of the term in the production notes tacitly acknowledges its prescriptive function. Women are misread as "bad" within patriarchal regimes in order to preserve those very regimes of cultural power. In her book *Rethinking the Femme Fatale in Film Noir*, Julie Grossman argues that "patriarchal culture projects images onto women that perpetuate a binary opposition of good girl versus 'femme fatale.' Attempts to assert independent existence and live beyond or to escape such projected gender fantasies then upset patriarchal order and cause it to redouble its efforts to categorize these women as deviant."[65] If Tierney is a femme fatale because her characters pose a danger to the men in her films, what actually proves dangerous are the ideations of women that these men project onto the women she plays. Suspected of murdering Laura Hunt, Shelby was one of several men entranced by her beauty, but unable to control her life, and while she prioritized her professional career, he played gigolo to her rich aunt and began seeing a model on the side. By turns, in *Dragonwyck*, Nicholas Van Ryn (Price) sees the possibility of replacing his wife with a younger, more fertile bride (Tierney), so he murders the former to marry the latter. And in *Leave Her to Heaven*, the opportunity for Russell to avenge the death of his ex-fiancé offers him a chance to regain his masculine potency even as it means prosecuting an innocent woman. Each case derives from a crisis of patriarchal masculinity and, in particular, patriarchal marriage.

Tierney was incredibly proud of her role in the film and reprised the character of Ellen Berent in a *Lux Radio Theatre* adaptation that aired March 17, 1947, with Wilde returning as Richard Harland. Commenting in her autobiography on the experience of playing Ellen, she wrote, "I had developed a difficult character and not just a pretty face on the screen."[66] When producer David O. Selznick and his wife, Jennifer Jones, saw the film at a private screening, they phoned Tierney to compliment her on her performance. Tierney appreciated their call as a moment of uncommonly genuine support in Hollywood. Further, she cathected with Ellen as a more complicated character than the "psychopathic demon" of Fox's production notes: "As much as any part I played, Ellen had meaning for me as a woman. She was jealous and sad and destructive. Jealousy is, I think, the worst of all faults because it makes a victim of both parties. Although treated subtly in the book, and the movie, Ellen was without a doubt insane. She believed herself to be normal and worked at convincing her friends she was. Most emotionally disturbed people go through such a stage, the equivalent of an alcoholic hiding the bottle."[67] The mental health struggles Tierney endured (see chapter 4) would indicate that she knew whereof she spoke and found a personal connection with Ellen beyond what the filmmakers or studio publicity department may have envisioned for the character. Ellen is less a femme fatale in Tierney's assessment than a woman suffering both psychologically and emotionally, who alternately wants to deny and conceal a disorder from public view.

While the film may tell us that Ellen's problem is her jealousy (Glen's narration introduces this thesis in the opening scene), such a rationale does not fully account for her fasciation as a character. As we have seen, Ellen exceeds Fox's promotional discourse, containment within the mise-en-scène, and Glen's authoritative narration. Indeed, even within the somewhat limited critical writing on gender and *Leave Her to Heaven*, scholars have considered how Ellen's actions point not to jealousy or a fundamental badness but to the psychologically debilitating effects of women's social conditioning. Reading the film in relation to genre (as a film noir), Grossman sees it as "a portrait of female power as perverse, when it is forced into a conventional mold of social roles and expectations." She elaborates, "My point here is not that Ellen is a positive role model for women, or even that she is herself feminist, or that she isn't crazy. My point is, rather, that the film, like most film noir movies, provides a context for her action that complicates a simple reading of Ellen as 'femme fatale.'"[68] Working in a theory from psychological anthropology, Renov understands this context as "a process of double binding [. . .] by which a profusion of contradictory cultural messages had produced a confusion, a self-distortion rich with the possibilities of schizophrenia."[69] The film therefore cannot be neatly interpreted as "a foisting of misogyny upon a viewing audience nor a backlash of popular resentment after years of valorization of the self-sacrificing female."[70] I agree with both Grossman and Renov, but I want to expand on their claims to show how Tierney specifically functions in the film—how star image, performance, character, narrative, and mise-en-scène interact—and problematizes Ellen's status as a femme fatale. For the second half of this section on *Leave Her to Heaven*, I will look more closely at how Ellen's placement in different home spaces gives visibility to an alternative performance of feminine domesticity based on the limits of Tierney's normatively "domestic" star image.

Fox apparently intended for audiences to draw connections between Tierney's off-screen (albeit still public) life married to Cassini and her on-screen role as a homemaker in *Leave Her to Heaven*. An item in the production notes reads as follows: "Gene's experiences as an Army wife came in handy during *Leave Her to Heaven*. When her husband, Lieut. Oleg Cassini, was stationed at Ft. Riley, Kansas, she spent all of her time there between pictures, keeping house in a three-room bungalow. So, when the honeymoon sequences of the picture called for her to do her own housework, she 'felt natural.'"[71] What Fox likely did not intend was to undermine her "natural" role as an army wife, but reading it against the film's domestic scenes inevitably calls the hegemonic domestic ideology into question.

The Warm Springs scene is the first moment we see Ellen and Richard at home together as a married couple. An open pair of green curtains separating the dining and living rooms flank their dinner table, which Ellen and Richard approach holding hands in a tableau shot. Stahl's mise-en-scène brings a theatrical quality to their dinner as traditional middle-class domestic roles are exaggerated and acted out, but the couple's teasing banter hints at a latently abusive marriage. Sitting down to bowls of soup that Ellen has prepared, Richard plays the part of her employer ("Well, Mrs. Harland, I think I can feel safe in saying the job is permanent") and she responds by affecting servility ("Thank you, sir, I always does my best"). Ellen believes that maintaining exclusive domesticity will be necessary to keep Richard's love, and therefore her domestic role must be consciously performed in the film, but her desires also reflect an attempt to set the domestic terms of their relationship in which she is able to exert control of her life:

> **ELLEN:** I have no intention of hiring a cook, housekeeper, or any other servants.
> **RICHARD:** You mean for the present.
> **ELLEN:** I mean ever.
> **RICHARD** [*snickering*]: Idiot.
> **ELLEN:** I don't want anybody else but me to do anything for you. I want to keep your house and wash your clothes and cook your food.
> **RICHARD:** A born slavey.
> **ELLEN:** Besides, I don't want anybody in the house but us.

Coming from a wealthy family, Ellen's refusal of hired help is not a financially motivated decision. In fact, she later volunteers to support Richard were he to give up writing. The Warm Springs scene ends with Richard asking about whether their home might one day include children or even Danny, to which Ellen responds ambiguously, "That's different." Over this short exchange, the film establishes Ellen's masochistic, single-minded fixation on romantic love as expressed through domesticity and Richard's commitment to conservative family values, but the characters' goals remain incompatible.

Within the film's heterosexual domestic settings, the pursuit of romantic love and constitution of a larger family unit become twin structures of domination that strengthen each other as Ellen and Richard trade roles of victim and oppressor. Ellen's breakup with Russell shows how a declaration of love may be at once a tribute and a threat:

> **RUSSELL:** I loved you, and I'm still in love with you.
> **ELLEN:** That's a tribute.
> **RUSSELL:** And I always will be. Remember that.
> **ELLEN:** Russ, is that a threat?

The question might well be asked of her when she pledges eternal love to Richard in three of the film's four domestic settings:

And I'll never let you go. Never, never, never. (at Rancho Jacinto)

It's only because I love you so. I love you, so I can't bear to share you with anybody. (at Back of the Moon)

Richard! I'll never let you go, Richard. Never . . . never . . . (on her deathbed in the Berent home)

Meanwhile, Richard's codependence on family puts unreasonable demands on Ellen as his wife, first in the homosocial environment of Back of the Moon with adoring brother, Danny, and the avuncular groundskeeper, Leick Thorne (Chill Wills). "Not that I mind chaperones, not in the least," she tells Richard in a particularly juicy line of dialogue, "but there's Danny's room on one side of us and Thorne's room on the other side, and the walls as thin as paper and the acoustics disgustingly perfect." Unbeknownst to Ellen, Richard has invited Mrs. Berent and Ruth to stay at the lodge. As Ellen voices her exasperation over the surprise guests, Richard shushes her, fearing Ruth will overhear through their bedroom wall, and Ellen retorts that they change the name Back of the Moon to Goldfish Manor. Richard dismisses her outcry as "a fit of hysterics," accusing her of "acting like a shrew" on the assumption that she is simply in "a rotten mood."

Later in Bar Harbor, living with Ruth, Richard, and her mother leaves Ellen at an impasse where she must fully inhabit her domestic role while her domestic tasks are simultaneously being taken from her. When Ellen is expecting, she talks of feeling like a "prisoner" in her own home, complaining to her doctor (Gene Lockhart), "I can't do anything, I can't go anyplace, I can't even see my husband." Ellen fears that the pregnancy has made her physically unattractive to Richard, venting to Ruth privately, "Look at me. I hate the little beast. I wish it would die." Yet again, Richard attempts to surprise her, this time by redesigning her father's laboratory—her former childhood playroom—into a nursery for the new baby. Richard paints a grotesque clown on the wall while Ruth models for him in a folded-newspaper hat, transforming the room into an absurd space of mockery for Ellen, although when Ruth playfully dons him with her clown hat, the mise-en-scène singles him out as the fool. The costumes by Kay Nelson are coordinated with the interior decor of the home, creating the sense that Ellen has subsumed her identity into the Berent home, a new space of domestic entrapment. Ellen's white mandarin jacket and slacks match the white curtains, walls, and fireplace mantel on the ground floor, just as her green robe with red trim matches the green color and red floral print on the living-room sofa and window valences. In the feticide scene, when Ellen leaps from the top of the staircase pretending to have tripped while sleepwalking, her baby-blue nightgown matches the hallway wallpaper.

From the beginning of the film, Richard's "blindness" to Ellen has been a source of humor within the diegesis, but at an extradiegetic level, it also seriously underscores his inability to satisfy Ellen's desires for romantic love within a traditional family-domestic relationship. After the funeral at Rancho Jacinto, Richard is amazed that Ellen already knows his life story, failing to realize it was written on the dust jacket of his own novel ("You know, if you lived in Salem a hundred years ago, they would have burned you," he exclaims). Introducing her to Danny at Warm Springs, Richard jokes that he will "send her right back" if Danny disapproves. When Ellen amorously awakens Richard on their first morning together at Back of the Moon, he is more excited by Danny's knock on their shared wall and (to Ellen's incredulity) invites him to go swimming in the lake. What is more, Richard does not appear to comprehend romantic relationships from a novelist's perspective, writing a banal proposal scene in which his male character asks, "Will you marry me?" Ellen explains that even when men think they propose to women, it is usually women who propose to men, as she did to him, adding, "And if men do propose, they never say, 'Will you marry me?'" Unable to see (or at least admit) that he loves Ruth until they are each put on the witness stand, Richard demonstrates a blindness bordering on denial in his gradual rejection of his wife for her more conventional cousin, who will make a more subordinate domestic partner. The dictates of the Classical Hollywood style and the Hays Code may ensure the narrative closure that gives Richard and Ruth a "happy ending," but as film critic Michael Walker reads it, the ending also partially vindicates Ellen. Just as the trial proves Ruth's innocence of murder, it also proves how Ellen's "'paranoid' conviction that Richard and Ruth loved each other was in fact the truth."[72]

Tierney's flatness in the film—her still and sometimes silent performance—masks an emotional intensity that runs below Ellen's exterior self. This decidedly impassive approach is unusual for the "woman's film" melodrama of 1940s and 1950s Hollywood, which relies on scenes of heightened emotion to produce a melodramatic affect. In certain respects, Tierney's acting style contributes to Ellen's psychological mystery, such as in the club car scene that introduces her through a series of portrait-like shots reminiscent of Tierney's star/character introduction in *Laura* through an actual portrait. Beginning with a master shot of Tierney and Wilde across from each other, Ellen stares at Richard for nearly a full minute of screen time (edited in a shot / reverse-shot pattern) over the course of ten medium shots.

However, Tierney's acting later in the film implies an excess of private emotion that Ellen controls in an attempt to manage her less-than-private domestic life, wrought with pressures both self-imposed and thrust upon her. Ellen's nightmare that she recounts to Leick says as much about her fear of losing Richard as her unconscious resentment toward him for his "blindness." In the dream, Richard swims in the lake while she rows in a skiff, but she discovers that she has no voice when she tries to call out to him. As Richard drowns, she cannot move to save him.[73] Danny's drowning at Back of the Moon realizes Ellen's nightmare, with Danny replacing Richard as she slowly rows behind him (she later tells Richard that the paralysis was "like a nightmare"). Once Danny starts bobbing below the surface and calling for help, she tensely holds each paddle above the water and sits practically frozen in the boat, her lips tight as she watches him drown from behind her sunglasses. We know Ellen is a skilled swimmer; at Rancho Jacinto, she quietly sneaks up on Richard while he his writing next to the pond and then she laps the Robie children in a race to the other side. Tierney's monotone line delivery makes Ellen's occasional words of encouragement ring false, and her stark costume (white robe and sunglasses) adds to the glacial, inexpressive quality of her performance (fig. 19). For the feticide scene, Tierney uses mainly her eyes to communicate, staring down the staircase in the Berent home. She first looks concerned, furrowing her eyebrows slightly (perhaps Ellen is second-guessing her decision out of fear). After sticking one foot under the carpet to leave her shoe as evidence of tripping, she then sets her gaze in determination. Finally,

Fig. 19. Ellen (Tierney) watches her brother-in-law, Danny (Darryl Hickman), drown in *Leave Her to Heaven* (John M. Stahl, 1945).

she widens her eyes as she mentally prepares to jump, convinced of her plan's success.

To be clear, Ellen is not devoid of emotion but rather suppressing a flood of emotion, and Tierney conveys Ellen's depth of feeling in other scenes when her facade cracks, unable to bear the emotional weight. Her deathbed farewell to Richard provides the most extreme example, as Tierney utters Ellen's last words—panting, her mouth widely agape—before expiring with a final, dramatic exhale. But the film establishes Ellen's emotional vulnerability much earlier in the domestic conditions that regulate her life married to Richard. Toward the end of the argument in their bedroom at Back of the Moon, Ellen suddenly pauses after fuming about the surprise visit from her mother and Ruth. A close-up on Tierney shows her eyebrows slightly raised, eyes widened, and lips parted. Ellen appears to have frightened herself. When Richard asks what has happened, she responds, "I don't know," gasping quietly and shaking her head. "I don't know," she repeats, sobbing and kneeling on the floor.

The redesign of her father's laboratory brings Ellen to a similar point of desperation. As soon as she enters the room, Ellen immediately begins questioning Richard: "What have you done with father's lab?"; "What have you done with his things?"; "Why didn't you consult me?" Wringing her hands and looking around the room in panicked confusion, unable to speak, Tierney plays Ellen not as a "bad" wife or mother here but as a woman angered by her family's refusal to involve her in decisions about her child and their ignorance of her wishes ("But I didn't want the room changed, ever, I wanted it left just as it was," she pleas). Ellen's maternity top serves as a reminder of her unwanted pregnancy that has determined the body and now the domestic space in which she lives. The green color of the top is also consistent with Ellen's dominant color throughout the film, pointing to her unborn child as another source of her jealousy (she already must compete with it for Richard's attention).

Few Hollywood films of the era seem as wickedly committed to flouting the sacred tenets of marital domesticity, but as Ellen says to Ruth, "Sometimes the truth is wicked." Apart from its box-office success and delirious visual style, *Leave Her to Heaven* remains significant for Tierney's stardom in the 1940s as a negative afterimage of the home-maker she personified in promotion and publicity, which had become integral to her star-making in the first half of the decade. This inversion of the feminine-domestic ideal gave Tierney one of the most difficult, complex characters of her career and the greatest emotional range she performed on-screen. Paradoxically, the image of the workingwoman we saw in the previous chapter existed alongside the army wife in her star discourse, but in the second half of the decade, Tierney was increasingly linked to wife and mother roles. At the beginning of the 1950s, when Fox loaned her to Paramount, this trend reached its apex with films such as the touching romantic comedy *The Mating Season* (Mitchell Leisen, 1951), starring Tierney and John Lund as newlyweds from different social classes and Miriam Hopkins and Thelma Ritter as their respective mothers. Between 1946 and 1948, as the public watched her marriage to Cassini strain through their separation, her connection to Fox's matinée idol Tyrone Power shored up her standing as a perennial bride.

Gene & Ty: *The Razor's Edge* and *That Wonderful Urge*

Suddenly single, Tierney's marital separation brought at least three other men into her life. When she started out in Hollywood, Howard Hughes briefly courted the young star, and she began seeing him again socially during her time apart from Cassini. By this point, Hughes was a friend of the Tierney family.[74] The press later revealed that she also had a relationship with former naval lieutenant and congressional hopeful John F. Kennedy.[75] Yet at this time neither Hughes nor Kennedy substantially influenced the perception of her star image. It was "Ty" Power, her costar in *The Razor's Edge* and *That Wonderful Urge*, who traded places with Cassini as her romantic partner in the public eye before she and her husband reconciled in 1948.

Recall that Fox cast Power with Tierney in the swashbuckler *Son of Fury* (John Cromwell, 1942), but *The Razor's Edge* brought them together in a multimillion-dollar drama that conveyed great self-importance with a long running time (146 minutes), prestigious source material (the novel of the same name by British author W. Somerset Maugham), and a star-studded cast (Power, Tierney, John Payne, Anne Baxter, Clifton Webb, and Herbert Marshall).[76] After its serialization in *Redbook* from 1943 to 1944, Maugham's novel was published in hardcover 1944. Painter and illustrator Norman Rockwell designed the promotional art for the film, aligning the adaptation with middlebrow aesthetic value.[77] Zanuck wanted to make another Fox "masterpiece" in the tradition of *The Grapes of Wrath* (John Ford, 1940) and *How Green Was My Valley* (John Ford, 1941), but he also conceived of the project as a vehicle for Power's return to Hollywood after he was honorably discharged from the U.S. Marine Corps as a first lieutenant.[78] One of Fox's most popular leading men, Power was part of a cohort of handsome, dark-haired stars that included Cornel Wilde (Richard from *Leave Her to Heaven*), Don Ameche, John Payne, and Victor Mature, whom the studio paired with its signature blondes such as Betty Grable and Alice Faye (see chapter 1).[79] While Power served in World War II as a pilot, Wilde filled his absence back at Fox, but the studio was keen to reconnect Power with his fans, just as Power was hoping to reestablish his career in more serious and dramatically realistic roles than what his swashbucklers and light comedies provided in the past.[80] Power's character Larry Darrell was himself a U.S.

war veteran, a World War I pilot who returns home and, suffering from survivor's guilt, bravely undertakes a quest for enlightenment. Drawing analogies between actor and character, Fox was able to promote *The Razor's Edge* as a film with post–World War II significance even if it was set after World War I.[81]

Zanuck maintained a strong track record with literary adaptations, banking on the built-in audience for a presold property, and he purchased the rights to Maugham's best seller after the other major studios turned it down. A memo stated his interest in the project as "an adventure picture," or "a melodramatic adventure, wherein a man searches the face of the earth for the hidden key to contentment." The story's postwar themes of trauma and adjustment made it culturally relevant for Zanuck, who deduced, "There must be a reason why the American public at this moment is reading this book more than any other book. The answer, I think, is simple: Millions of people today are searching for contentment and peace in the same manner that Larry searches in the book."[82] Also a character in the novel who narrates the events as a kind of participant-observer, Maugham is portrayed in the film by Herbert Marshall. Lamar Trotti wrote the adapted screenplay, and when Zanuck began securing a director in 1945, he first pitched the film to George Cukor before the job went to Edmund Goulding, who also directed *Of Human Bondage* (1946) for Warner Bros. (an adaptation of Maugham's 1915 novel). In many ways Goulding was an ideal choice, given his experience working with large casts (*Grand Hotel* [1932]) and high melodrama (*That Certain Woman* [1937], *Dark Victory* [1939], *The Old Maid* [1939], *The Great Lie* [1941], and *Old Acquaintance* [1943], all starring Bette Davis), but the directorial assignment may have been partly a result of a scheduling conflict between Zanuck and Cukor. Zanuck was committed to shooting around both Power's and Tierney's availabilities. Believing that Tierney would win an Oscar for *Leave Her to Heaven*, he told Cukor, "I want her name badly in our film."[83] The other reason for Goulding's assignment may have been the evident disagreements between Zanuck and Cukor over Larry's character.[84]

The Razor's Edge was the only film Fox released in 1946 that Zanuck selected for sole producing credit. "I feel justified in saying that if something goes wrong with it," he pledged, "I will be primarily the one who is left holding the bag."[85] This decision was not entirely a selfless one.

Zanuck also told Cukor, "[I]f I cannot make *The Razor's Edge* my way, I would rather not make it at all, as it is too big a gamble and there are too many chances for it to come a cropper."[86] According to the production notes, the film required eighty-nine sets and took a hundred days to shoot (the longest shooting schedule in the Fox's history up to that point).[87] Once again, Zanuck's gamble paid off with a huge winning for the studio; the film grossed $5 million domestically.[88] Tierney later described the film's November 1946 opening at the Roxy Theater in New York City, writing the following in her autobiography: "In those days a New York premiere was as close to heaven as an actor could expect to get, and a great boost to the pictures selected for such treatment. [. . .] This was to be the first great postwar splash of Hollywood-made razzle-dazzle."[89] Rave reviews succeeded this much-ballyhooed premiere.[90] The *Hollywood Reporter* proclaimed, "Nothing could be more timely than Darryl Zanuck's production of W. Somerset Maugham's *The Razor's Edge*, which tells how an ex-soldier resolves his own spiritual unrest following the ending of the war."[91] In addition, the film received Academy Award nominations for Best Picture, Best Actor in a Supporting Role for Clifton Webb, and Best Art Direction (Black-and-White), and Best Actress in a Supporting Role for Anne Baxter, who won the Oscar.[92]

Tierney plays Larry's spoiled fiancé, Isabel Bradley, an expatriate socialite living in France, whose family in Chicago enjoys some cultural capital through her uncle Elliott Templeton (Webb).[93] After Larry returns home from the war, Isabel urges him to settle down and take a job that will support her at a time of presumed economic opportunity in the United States. Meanwhile, he has declined a lucrative offer to work as a stockbroker, preferring instead to "loaf." A fellow combatant died saving Larry instead of saving himself, and Larry, afraid of wasting his "second chance," wants to find a way to give his life meaning. On the eve of their wedding, he appeals to Isabel to prolong their engagement so he can study in Paris, where he will live off his modest inheritance. Isabel reunites with Larry a year later when she and her mother come to France to visit Elliott, but she realizes that Larry will never give up his bohemian lifestyle and they decide to call off the wedding. Eager for status that Larry will never be able to offer, she marries family friend Gray Maturin (John Payne), the son of a Chicago millionaire, who has always pined for her.

Promotion and publicity for Tierney concentrated heavily on the white Alençon lace bridal gown and veiled roundlet-style headdress that she wears in the wedding reception scene, which Cassini designed (fig. 20). Tierney and Cassini had not yet publicly separated, and the conspicuous absence of Payne in this extratextual material allowed the role of the groom to be transferred onto her real-life husband who worked as her costume designer behind the scenes. The film's production notes alleged that Cassini originally designed the gown for their own wedding five years earlier, but that he never fabricated it for her to wear it since they decided to elope.[94] *Photoplay* ran an article with a photo of Tierney modeling the gown in long shot and told readers that her "dream came true" now that she could finally wear it and preserve the ersatz white wedding in pictures for her daughter.[95] The article rehearsed the events of Tierney and Cassini's marriage when Tierney "put off lipstick" and "put on apron and sunbonnet of Kansas housewife" to stay with her husband at Ft. Riley, again communicating to readers that being a housewife was not natural for Tierney but required hard work. Quoting

Fig. 20. As the just-married Isabel in *The Razor's Edge* (Edmund Goulding, 1946), Tierney wears an Oleg Cassini wedding dress.

Cassini, "Gene had little experience but she became an excellent house-wife because she is methodical. She stuck the cook book on a shelf in front of her nose and followed its instructions meticulously."[96] At the risk of deromanticizing married life, the article also distinguishes this domestic labor from Tierney's more nerve-wracking professional labor as a movie star, positioning Cassini as her caretaker in an almost ther-apeutic marriage. When starring in her first film, *The Return of Frank James* (Fritz Lang, 1940), Tierney's "eyes became puffed and inflamed, and she had the jumps," but Cassini "assumed the care of the afflicted Miss Tierney. Diagnosis: Nerves. Prescription: Marriage. They eloped to Las Vegas. Result: Cured."[97]

Other stories presented the dress as a symbol of Tierney and Cassi-ni's mutually reinforcing style and taste as a married couple. For exam-ple, an article in *Movies* reproduced a medium-shot photo of Tierney posed in the dress, suggesting that if Tierney is "a man's idea of glamour," her glamour is "partly due to her gorgeous gown."[98] Detailing her vari-ous fashions off the set, the article concluded that glamour "runs in the Tierney-Cassini family!"[99] Tierney also reportedly supplied her stand-in, Kay Adell, with the $2,000 dress for her marriage to a U.S. Army Air Forces flight officer, making headlines such as "Gene Tierney's Wedding Gown Finally Gets to Real Wedding."[100] As a fashion designer, Cassini's name would not coincidentally become synonymous with bridal gowns later in his career.[101]

The very same year, Tierney's public separation from Cassini meant that this star discourse was not sustainable, and rumors started spread-ing of a romance between Tierney and Power. Tierney later confirmed in her autobiography that they "became great friends" making *The Razor's Edge*, but that their "romance was only happening on the screen." The platonic level of their relationship did not stop the studio from plant-ing gossip in the press or her family and friends from encouraging her to pursue her dashing costar. "Everyone on the set thought he had a crush on me and was rooting for us," she recalled.[102] Power was then married to French star Annabella, but supposedly they too had begun a separation. One story averred that "Gene and Ty were not in love when they were assigned to *The Razor's Edge*. But before long their screen love turned into the real thing."[103] In actuality, Tierney was dating Kennedy at the time, and the pressures surrounding the rumored romance with

Power exacerbated the difficulty she already experienced negotiating her relationship with Cassini (to whom she was still married). Reflecting on this period of her career, she wrote in her autobiography, "I have always known that I do not handle confusion well. I was tugged now in many ways; still trying to sort out my feelings about Oleg, drawn to Jack Kennedy and he to me, he said. But we were both unsure of where that road would lead."[104] Regardless of whether the rumors were true, Power discursively served a dual function as Tierney's romantic partner: a temporary public replacement for Cassini (in the same way she replaced Annabella) and, indirectly, a cover for Kennedy.

The Razor's Edge tie-ins made use of Tierney's and Power's images for cross-promotional purposes. When the Blakiston Company (a now-defunct Philadelphia press) published its Triangle Books edition of Maugham's novel in October of 1946 by arrangement with his original publisher Doubleday & Company, both stars graced the dust jacket. A photo-illustrated novelization of the film appeared in an issue of *Screen Romances* the following month, with both stars on the cover. From the rebranded novel that inspired the film to the magazine story adapted from the film, Tierney and Power organize a circuit of meaning that fuses source and derivative texts with the illusion of romantic love they perform in the film.

Released just prior to Tierney's public separation from Cassini, *The Razor's Edge* both reinscribed Cassini's position as her husband through attention to her bridal gown at the same time as it reintroduced Power as a romantic partner, securing Tierney's postwar image in an idealized (if alternating) heterosexual couple—lest she be left to singlehood. This image also papers over the film's ultimately incongruous attitude toward male–female relationships in the postwar era. Thomas Schatz groups the film under "a distinctive form of prestige-level 'male melodrama'" that emerged in 1946, including other Oscar nominees for Best Picture, *It's a Wonderful Life* (Frank Capra) and *The Yearling* (Clarence Brown), as well as the year's winner, *The Best Years of Our Lives* (William Wyler). What constituted this production trend were films "invariably centering on the efforts of a vaguely despondent male beset by postwar angst to 'find himself.' This search often took place in a dark and alienating milieu and clearly was related to the postwar *film noir* and social problem trends. At the same time, certain themes and concerns of the war film were displaced onto these melodramas."[105] Even as the promotion and publicity apparatus for *The Razor's Edge* ensured that Tierney was safely coupled with either Cassini or Power, in the film Larry "finds himself" by learning to live independently from women.

Integral to the film's sense of masculine self-discovery is a global mobility in which women cannot participate. Larry's journey takes him from Paris to India, where he spends ten years at a monastery in the Himalayas. A holy man there cautions him that "the road to salvation" is as difficult to pass "as the sharp edge of a razor," paraphrasing a translated verse from the Katha-Upanishad, but also teaches him that salvation can be achieved through faith and worship, good works, and the pursuit of wisdom through gaining knowledge. Empowered with this new spiritual guidance, Larry sets out to follow "the way of calmness, forbearance, compassion, selflessness, and everlasting peace." As soon as he returns to Paris, he finds Isabel and Gray raising children but living with Elliott. Gray has lost his fortune in the stock market crash and suffered a "nervous breakdown." Also living in Paris is Larry's childhood friend Sophie (Baxter), who has turned to alcohol, opium, and prostitution following the death of her husband and child in a car accident. Larry cures Gray through hypnosis and helps Sophie overcome her addictions through his love and care for her, but he also rekindles Isabel's feelings for him now that Gray represents no socioeconomic advantage. After succumbing to temptation and taking a drink, Sophie quickly falls back into the Parisian underworld. When Larry discovers that she has been murdered and that Isabel was responsible for tempting her out of jealousy and spite, he leaves France to work on a tramp steamer sailing to the United States. The film's representation of the East ranges from a place of pseudo-religious mysticism divorced from any cultural specificity (e.g., the Indian monastery), therefore easily appropriated by "enlightened" Western visitors, to corrupting influences on the West (e.g., Parisian opium dens).[106] For Larry to fulfill his unknown but promising destiny, he must return home.

While Isabel is materialistic and status conscious, Sophie is a victim of her own weakness, vices, and self-pity. By contrast, Larry's virtue makes him the unproblematic male hero—the film is his story. He attends lectures at the Sorbonne, travels, and reads (he can even quote Keats), but he also works in a French coal mine and tries to use his knowledge in the service of others. The film bifurcates the two main characters along the lines of the active male vs. the passive female, his "high" culture vs. her consumer mass culture, and his intellect vs. her emotional excess.[107]

Annoyed with Larry's restlessness and confusion when he returns from the war, Isabel considers his dissatisfaction with accepted capitalist values a shirking of a work ethic and personal responsibility. "Look, Larry, let's be sensible," she reasons with him, "a man must work. It's a matter of self-respect. This is a young country and it's a man's duty to take part in its activities." Gray's father has convinced her that the United States "is beginning an era that will make the past look like thirty cents" and that by 1930 it will be "the greatest and richest country in the whole world." In light of contemporary knowledge about the stock market crash and Great Depression, the film presents Isabel's belief in unlimited national progress as utterly naive. When Larry tells her that he wants more from life than "sitting in an office and making a lot of money," she replies, "Oh, Larry, don't talk like a fool, you can't live without money." As he endeavors to find happiness within himself, he goes on to prove her wrong. Maugham confirms as much to Isabel at the end of the film: "His America will be as remote from yours as the Gobi Desert." Before departing for the United States, Larry expresses interest in finding a job at a factory or a garage and then buying a taxi, but also plans to continue looking for answers to his existential questions that Isabel still cannot comprehend. In the film's didactic last line, Maugham informs her, "My dear, Larry has found what we all want and very few of us ever get. I don't think anyone can fail to be better and nobler . . . kinder for knowing him. You see, my dear . . . goodness is, after all, the greatest force in the world. And he's got it."

Isabel thus serves as a foil for Larry, an obstacle he needs to overcome on his quest, and the film establishes her "badness" fairly early in opposition to him. At the end of a night on the town together in Paris, she almost manipulates him into having sex so that if she conceives a child, she will be able to blackmail him into marriage. "One of the few decent things she does is to refuse to go through with her plan," wrote Jack D. Grant in his review for the *Hollywood Reporter*. Grant warned moviegoers, "It is not a pretty role which Gene Tierney plays. Her Isabelle [sic] is an entirely selfish baggage."[108] Press materials show that Fox made no attempt to qualify or contextualize Isabel's actions and motives. "Her beauty could not hide the evil in her heart," read her character blurb in the pressbook's summary of the film,[109] and the production notes describe "the love-mad, covetous Isabel" as "another characterization to put in [Tierney's] memoirs of fascinating and exciting but dangerous women."[110]

Isabel Bradley and Ellen Berent are both, in their own ways, "dangerous women," but *The Razor's Edge* naturalizes a demonization that *Leave Her to Heaven* seems unable to accept without ambiguity. Following the domestic ideology of the postwar era, both women are poised to take up their roles as homemakers for their new husbands (Isabel in the explicit interest of Larry's adjustment from returning veteran to breadwinner). At the same time, they are expected to accommodate men who find their own bourgeois domestic roles restrictive and emasculating. Ironically, Ellen and Isabel are read as dangerous not because they fail to adopt domestic roles, but because they attempt to persuade their male partners to adopt their own. In *The Razor's Edge*, Isabel has no place in Larry's America because of her "badness," a function of her domesticity, which makes her dangerous and incompatible with Larry's values and goals. Larry disavows the feminine domestic to embark on a scholarly globe-trotting adventure that restores his bond to the male soldier who died saving his life. In *Leave Her to Heaven*, Richard retreats to the Maine woods with the intention of escaping to the male-dominated fishing lodge of his youth. The difference is in how this film insists on the possibility that Ellen's dangerousness comes in response to her exclusion from the very homes to which she has been consigned. Dangerousness gets attributed to "badness" to justify and reinforce that exclusion ("leaving her to heaven," as it were). Even in Ellen's diegetic exclusions, though, she remains the film's cynosure to the degree that Richard's story is always dependent on hers. Narratively, visually, and performatively, *Leave Her to Heaven* is all Ellen's show.

While I admit to wishing that *The Razor's Edge* gave Tierney more to do as an actress, the subordination of Isabel to Larry is not so much an issue of the filmmakers' devaluation of Tierney than her position in a cultural crisis of masculinity, which existed alongside and often in relation to the demobilization of women after the war. Outside of individual films and novels, postwar cultural discourse registered what Steven Cohan refers to as "the 'paradox' of hegemonic masculinity."[111] In his book *Masked Men: Masculinity and the Movies in the Fifties*, Cohan illustrates how "the conditions of war forged intense same-sex bonding for straight men."[112] This "buddy relationship" later proved "antagonistic to postwar civilian heterosexuality" when these same men were encouraged to repudiate the masculine behavior valorized in combat.[113]

As white middle-class families in the United States moved from the cities to newly developed suburbs, men assumed the role of the family's moral and psychological leader—husband and father—as it was absorbed in a new domesticity that divided gender roles between male breadwinner and female homemaker.[114] Cohan writes that "the home acquired renewed value after the war as the metonymy of the nation," and in contrast to the war years, the male displaced the female in "representing a coherent national character."[115] During the immediate postwar era, "the enormous growth of the American middle class was perceived as the great accomplishment of postwar life, and the male breadwinner personified that democratic achievement in his domesticity." Paradoxically, cultural critics saw these domestic responsibilities for men as physically, psychologically, and even sexually debilitating, with the breadwinner "pushing too hard to satisfy his wife's ambition and finance her consumerism," not to mention her sexual desires, while also sharing the housework and decision making.[116] At the same time, postwar developments in the field of sexology showed the sex lives of men as more active and varied than previously assumed, contesting monolithic constructions of masculinity. The best-selling book *Sexual Behavior in the Human Male* (1948), coauthored by Indiana University Bloomington researcher Alfred Kinsey, reported such transgressions as masturbation, homosexuality, and promiscuity (both premarital sex and adultery) that raised cultural questions about the definitions of masculinity and lived experiences of men.[117]

Anxiety over the status of domesticated masculinity was a recurring subject in postwar Hollywood cinema, perhaps most explicitly (but certainly not exclusively) in "male melodrama." Whereas the moral and emotional project of melodrama aims to derive pathos from a suffering victim, the romantic-screwball comedy of postwar Hollywood (i.e., the "sex comedy") exploits that suffering for cathartic humor. For one of the earliest examples, we turn to Power and Tierney's next film together, released in December of 1948. Power plays New York City reporter Thomas Jefferson Tyler, a former war correspondent, whose gossip series

"The Life and Loves of Sara Farley" provokes much chagrin from his celebrity subject (Tierney), a millionaire heiress to a grocery store chain. Chaperoned by her aunt (Lucile Watson), Sara travels to a ski resort in Sun Valley, Idaho, to vacation with Count André de Guyon (Reginald Gardiner), who is currently wooing her, and Tom follows them hoping to procure quotes for his next article. Tom poses as the manager of a small-town paper and convinces Sara that his readers believe she has been libeled by the scandal-sheet press. While the two are stuck in an emergency cabin after a minor dogsledding accident, he gives her the opportunity to tell her own story for a rebuttal, and warmed by the fireplace as much as the liquor from Tom's canteen, they realize they are undeniably attracted to each other. Back in New York, where he already has a girlfriend (Arleen Whelan), Tom decides to submit the sympathetic profile story for publication under his real name but not before Sara learns of his deception and plans to get even by discrediting him. She tells the rival papers that she and Tom were married in Idaho, and when his editor (Lloyd Gough) reads about the marriage, he fires Tom. A battle of the sexes ensues as Tom tries to prove to the public that he is no "Cinderella Man."

That Wonderful Urge is nothing if not an example of Hollywood's adherence to the tried and true, both at the level of star casting (pairing Tierney and Power for the third and final time) and popular formulas recyclable within standardized generic models. Neither the film's director nor writer were particularly known for comedy, but they had a template in place. Coming from a background in theater, director Robert B. Sinclair was a captain in the U.S. Air Force who made a training film called *Resisting Enemy Interrogation* (1944) that received an Oscar nomination for Best Documentary (Feature). The screenwriter of *That Wonderful Urge*, Jay Dratler, had worked mainly on crime films such as *Laura*. David Bordwell describes a studio practice called "the switch" or "the switcheroo," which (as director Vincent Sherman explained to him) "involved screenwriters taking stories from movies that have been made before, changing the background and a few details, and presenting them as new." Producer Dore Schary informed Bordwell that the Broadway hit *The Front Page* (1928), for instance, became one of the chief sources of inspiration for writers and directors in the first decade of sound filmmaking, an era of fast, tough, and punchy films usually set in the big city:

screwball comedies, gangster dramas, and backstage musicals. Ben Hecht and Charles MacArthur's Chicago-newspaper comedy led not only to a 1931 film of the same name directed by Lewis Milestone but also to the classic *His Girl Friday* (Howard Hawks, 1940), which changed the gender of one of the main characters and turned a same-sex buddy comedy into a heterosexual romantic comedy about two journalists covering a wrongful execution that is about to occur.[118] The newsman leaving the paper to get married and start a family is now a newswoman played by Rosalind Russell, and the editor desperate to keep his star reporter is her ex-husband played by Cary Grant.

The Front Page, which has been called the "prototype" of the Hollywood newspaper film,[119] influenced the romantic-screwball comedy even before *His Girl Friday*. In her book on the romantic comedy, Tamar Jeffers McDonald writes that the screwball formula of the 1930s follows "a rich woman meeting, being tamed and helped to mature by a poorer or seemingly socially inferior man, such social class commentary being especially appealing at a time when the nation was in an economic depression."[120] Unlike romantic comedy writ large, the screwball comedy "sustains the discord" between the woman and the man, "using the energy of the couple's friction and mutual frustration to drive the narrative forward." Audiences may derive pleasure from their affection for each other, but "this affection is expressed through aggression."[121] The paradigmatic example is *It Happened One Night* (Frank Capra, 1934), a Columbia Pictures screwball comedy and one of the first in the genre, starring Claudette Colbert as a runaway heiress and Clark Gable as an out-of-work reporter hungry for her story. As Matthew C. Ehrlich observes in his book *Journalism in the Movies*, "*It Happened One Night* added new ingredients to *The Front Page* formula: The reporter fell in love with the scoop he was pursuing; the story and love interest became one."[122] This formula continued with screwball comedies such as MGM's *Libeled Lady* (Jack Conway, 1936) and Selznick International Pictures' *Nothing Sacred* (William A. Wellman, 1937).[123]

At Fox, "the switcheroo" was practically a signature element of the studio's brand identity. Mel Gussow's biography of Zanuck points out that his films were distinguished less by subject matter than by formulas, either as remakes of or sequels to the studio's earlier properties. According to Gussow, "Remakes and Sequels were popular throughout

Hollywood, but nowhere were in such abundant evidence as at Fox. A Partial Remake usually took only one ingredient, but a main ingredient, of a successful picture, such as the re-use of a plot device."[124] *That Wonderful Urge* was a complete remake of Fox's Tyrone Power–Loretta Young screwball comedy *Love Is News* (Tay Garnett, 1937), written by Harry Tugend and Jack Yellen from a story by William R. Lipman and Frederick Stephani. Zanuck briefly considered giving *That Wonderful Urge* the title "Love Is Still News."[125] Fox made considerable use of the Lipman and Stephani story, having partially remade *Love Is News* as *Sweet Rosie O'Grady* (Irving Cummings, 1943), a musical-comedy vehicle for Betty Grable and one of the studio's most profitable releases of 1943. Whereas railroad heiress Tony Gateson (Loretta Young) and stage performer Rosie O'Grady (Grable) claim they are engaged to gossip reporters Steve Layton (Power) and Sam Magee (Robert Young), respectively, Sara pretends she and Tom are married in *That Wonderful Urge*. The significance of this "switcheroo" will be discussed shortly.

As a vehicle for Tierney and Power, *That Wonderful Urge* served the purposes of reestablishing studio traditions and rebranding the studio's product after the war. Power and Young had costarred in four other films at Fox: the "woman's film" melodrama *Ladies in Love* (Edward H. Griffith, 1936), the romantic comedies *Café Metropole* (Edward H. Griffith, 1937) and *Second Honeymoon* (Walter Lang, 1937), and the fictionalized biopic *Suez* (Allan Dwan, 1938), which starred Power as nineteenth-century French diplomat Ferdinand de Lesseps (the developer of the Suez Canal) and Young as Empress Eugénie de Montijo.[126] When Zanuck left Warner Bros. for Twentieth Century Pictures, he brought Young with him, and when Twentieth Century merged with Fox Film Corporation in 1935 and Zanuck took over as head of production, Young became one of the studio's major stars. However, as Jeanine Basinger details in her book *The Star Machine*, Young clashed with Zanuck for years and finally refused to renew her contract when it expired in 1939, deciding to move forward as an independent star.[127] Switching Young for Tierney in *That Wonderful Urge*, Zanuck positioned Tierney as the studio's sophisticated brunette of the 1940s and Power's screen partner of the postwar era. Like Grable, Tierney was also a wartime pinup queen, and her star text brought a sexuality to the role absent in the 1937 version. And like her character Sara Farley, Tierney was a celebrity from a well-to-do family and the subject of gossip in the press.

Tierney's romance with a European count and alleged relationship with Tyrone Power make it possible to read the film as a metacommentary on her stardom during the second half of the decade. The release of the film coincided with her reconciliation with Cassini (before they finalized their divorce in 1952), and publicity reaffirmed the strength of her marriage in the face of newspaper gossip that threatened to break it apart. For example, a November 1948 issue of *Silver Screen* (featuring Tierney and Power on the cover) included an article about Tierney's ability to laugh off the stress and embarrassment that goes with being a movie star. The article described how while she was finishing *That Wonderful Urge* in Hollywood, and Cassini was working at his salon in New York, Cassini had been seen dancing with a "lovely blonde" at a nightclub. Supposedly he had already told Tierney that he would be attending an engagement party for a couple of friends, so when he called her to explain that the "blonde" was only the bride-to-be, Tierney reportedly assured him, "I didn't give the silly story a second thought."[128]

Articles also show how the studio-publicity machine sought to absolve itself by blaming gossip journalism for starting the rumors of her affair with Power, setting in motion a new publicity discourse that realigned Tierney with traditional domestic values. A story in a May 1949 issue of *Screenland* responded to the Power–Tierney gossip with the claim, "It was this myth that almost wrecked the one thing that meant more to Gene than anything else—her marriage. She wanted to hold on to her home, her husband and her child." Tierney was said to have been inspired to save her marriage by the "eye-opening statistics on the overwhelming number of divorces in America," realizing "that the American family is an institution which people take too lightly." To save her marriage, according to the article, she had to admit to herself that she still loved her husband and not "care if the Hollywood gossips were snickering up their sleeves."[129] Instead of raising further doubts about her marriage, reteaming Tierney and Power in *That Wonderful Urge* at this time helped the studio demonstrate the marriage's resilience and attribute the breakup to harmful gossip rather than the loss of love from either party. Cassini also designed Tierney's costumes for the film, as he had done for *The Razor's Edge*.

With Power reprising his role from *Love Is News*, *That Wonderful Urge* also gave Fox a vehicle for one of its prewar leading men at a time of postwar uncertainty for the studio system. The film was released the same year as the *Paramount* decree, the U.S. Supreme Court's antitrust ruling that forced the major studios to divorce their operations of production and distribution from exhibition and to divest themselves of their theater chains.[130] Between 1947 and 1949, the studios also suffered an economic decline following the all-time box-office high of 1946, leaving the industry already nostalgic for Hollywood's "golden age."[131] *That Wonderful Urge* was Power's last comedy. Basinger accounts how despite his disappointment with his career options, Fox neither let him go nor reinvented him for a new era, noting, "After the war, they chose to continue exploiting him as if it were still the 1930s."[132]

What helped synthesize this work of reestablishment and rebranding was the film's slightly updated approach to the screwball comedy as an early example of the postwar sex comedy. As McDonald defines it, the sex comedy "pits woman against man in an elemental battle of wits, in which the goal of both is sex. Only the timing and legitimacy of this differs from gender to gender, with women wanting sex after, and men before or without marriage."[133] Under the guidelines of the Hays Code, films could only imply sex through visual or verbal innuendos and suggestive fade-outs at key moments. Because characters could not enact sex on-screen, sex comedies teased the audience with a "will-they-or-won't-they?" story line, hinting at the possibility that sex might take place but delaying the achievement of sex until the end of the film—usually to consummate the couple's marriage to each other.[134] A more titillating title than *Love Is News*, *That Wonderful Urge* signals to audiences that these characters are motivated by "bodily urges rather than emotional impulses" alone.[135] "As with the screwball comedy," McDonald elaborates, "much audience pleasure derives from seeing the couple openly fight and insult each other, underhandedly plot to foil the schemes of the other, and secretly yearn to fall into bed together. The sex comedies suggest the intense animosity between the pair will guarantee a passionate sexual relationship by the film's end."[136]

For the sex comedy to concretize as it did in the 1950s, certain historical conditions had to make greater sexual openness in Hollywood cinema more permissible. McDonald cites 1953 as a pivotal year in this regard. First, Kinsey's *Sexual Behavior in the Human Female* was published, revealing that of the 5,940 unmarried, white, thirty-year-old women in the United States whom Kinsey and his coauthors interviewed, half were not virgins. Kinsey's report challenged the cultural assumption that premarital sex primarily existed in a male domain.[137] Second, the inaugural issue of *Playboy* was published, launching the lifestyle magazine aimed at heterosexual men that included nude centerfolds and served as a consumer guide to the midcentury bachelor apartment. Finally, Otto Preminger released his independent film *The Moon Is Blue* through United Artists without the seal of approval from the Hays Office—and marketed the controversy. Adapted from the 1951 Broadway comedy by F. Hugh Herbert, which Preminger directed on stage, the film was the first feature produced in the studio system to use the word *virgin* since the Hays Code was enforced in 1934. The film's box-office success dealt the first blow to the authority of the code, which waned throughout the decade (it was revised in 1956).[138] While the sex comedy flourished for only the next ten years, McDonald reminds us that it did not disappear. Rather, like the screwball comedy of the 1930s, its elements were gradually integrated into the romantic comedy genre more broadly.[139]

To see *That Wonderful Urge* as a sex comedy, we first need to recognize the differences between and among the three versions of Lipman and Stephani's story. As a Depression-era screwball comedy, *Love Is News* is interested in romance but not necessarily sex. As an escapist wartime musical, *Sweet Rosie O'Grady* is interested in sex but has little sexual tension or chemistry—instead prioritizing musical spectacles to glorify the U.S. showgirl/pinup and show off Grable. This first remake effects the more obvious changes to the original story, reimagining it in a nostalgic Gay Nineties setting, with Grable as an actress on the London stage who calls herself Madeline Marlowe. A *Police Gazette* reporter exposes her as a working-class Irish American from Brooklyn named Rosie O'Grady, a former burlesque queen, creating a scandal in the midst of her engagement to the Duke of Trippingham (Reginald Gardiner, also the count in *That Wonderful Urge*).[140] *Love Is News* gave a substantial role to the paper's exasperated editor (Don Ameche), whose love–hate relationship with the reporter provided a secondary male-buddy story line similar to *The Front Page*, while the count (George Sanders) is a relatively minor character. *Sweet Rosie O'Grady* reduces the role of the editor (Adolphe Menjou, who played the editor in the 1931 film adaptation of *The Front Page*), as the duke gradually becomes the reporter's uneasy friend. Both characters are completely marginalized in *That Wonderful Urge* to allow Power and Tierney to take center stage as the romantic couple. Erasing the ethnic heritage of the Irish American couple from *Sweet Rosie O'Grady*, Fox reused the emergency cabin scenario from *Sun Valley Serenade* (H. Bruce Humberstone, 1941), the studio's hit musical starring Norwegian figure skater Sonja Henie and John Payne, to restore the ethnically unmarked identity of the couple from *Love Is News* and keep any potential sex within the bounds of unproblematic whiteness.[141]

The sex comedy would not yet have been legible to audiences in 1948, but sex is still what distinguishes this film from the previous two versions. Tom and Sara's fireside night together in the emergency cabin establishes their desire for each other early in the film. Uninhibited by the alcohol, Tom and Sara nearly kiss, but the "rescue" team interrupts them. For the duration of the film, they remain keenly aware of this mutual desire (expressing it through mutual antagonism) and the pleasure for them as much as the audience is the anticipation of when that kiss—and maybe more—will finally happen. Even before they meet, what are Tom's articles but thinly veiled attempts to displace his physical attraction for Sara onto a disdain for the upper class? The Farley butler calls it "a kind of left-handed romance, the devastating criticism of a man in love," aptly deducing that "the writer of those articles was trying to avoid showing his affection." Sara wants revenge, as she feels genuinely hurt by Tom's deception, but she also wants Tom. The pretense of marriage allows her to pursue both goals. Selective withholding of narrative information creates ambiguity as to whether they actually did get married in Idaho, and the possibility of marriage hints at the possibility for sex. But when?

On the night of their rescue, after they return to their respective hotel rooms, it is unclear what happens next. Sara lies on her bed with a dreamy, satisfied look on her face, and the next morning Tom awakens in his bed with an apparent hangover to learn that the local courthouse has burned down with all the records. Later in the film, unable to prove that they are not married, Tom colludes with his editor and the paper's seedy lawyer (Porter Hall) to sue Sara for defamation and "great mental anguish" (infuriating the female public that has sided with Sara). The court proceedings reveal that Tom was hospitalized during the war for a head injury that left him with temporary amnesia, and Sara's legal counsel, Attorney Rice (Taylor Holmes), states that while they were married in

Idaho by a justice of the peace, Tom suffered a loss of memory as a result of the dogsledding accident. Attempting to pressure Sara into changing her story, Tom bluffs by admitting to the marriage so he can take over the Farley business. Sara then demands an annulment on the grounds that they haven't "lived together as husband and wife" (i.e., consummated the marriage). The film's funniest exchange essentially clarifies any ambiguity about what is in question:

> **TOM:** Wait a minute, how do you know we haven't?
> **SARA:** After all, I was there. You may have been unconscious,
>   but I wasn't.

For Tom to forestall the annulment, the judge (Gene Lockhart) tells him confidentially, he will need to "remove the grounds." In other words, Sara and Tom need to have sex.

When the judge attempts to reconcile the couple in his chambers, he speaks on behalf of the audience and anticipates the film's inevitable conclusion. "Now everyone in the courtroom, including the jury, is fully aware that you two are eminently suited to each other," he says. Both Sara and Tom are fully aware of this too, but their timing is off. Regretting how he has publicly mischaracterized Sara, Tom understands that she is "a fine, warm human being who's been taught to conceal her true emotions behind an icy wall" and "deeply hurt by all the forces always arrayed against inherited wealth," as he attested in his story before she announces their marriage to the press. Sara realizes that Tom is the first man interested in her for a reason other than her money, as she admits in court before he lays claim to her business. The threat of losing Sara and the guilt over his multiple lies compel Tom to try to win her back in the film's final scene, in her bedroom, where she comes home to find him reading *Sexual Behavior in the Human Male*. After a brief scuffle, they fall to the ground and then sit up next to the bed. Tom confesses his love for Sara, and she responds by reneging the annulment. If this generic romantic comedy resolution rushes to a pat "happy ending," which it does, it is only because it confirms what the characters and the audience already know. What makes the ending more interesting is that it neither confirms nor denies the marriage in Idaho. "That's something you'll never know," Sara tells Tom, although she agrees to "get married all over again" so that he can rest assured their children will be born legally. Their kiss before the fade-out suggests that sex is imminent. The *New York Times* reviewer was not amused, cautioning readers that the "moral tone of the picture leaves much to be desired," especially for a Christmas release when more children are going to the theater. Chief among the objections was the film's reference to the Kinsey report, but the review also scolded Fox for the irreverent treatment of marriage and the court.[142]

Neither the scene in the cabin nor the trial sequence and domestic coda were present in the previous versions of the Lipman and Stephani story, and advertisements for the film promised that the "urge" to which the title referred would eventually lead Power and Tierney to the bedroom. Promotional photos and artwork referred to an earlier scene in the film when Tom waits for Sara to come home from a late night out with the count (fig. 21). Tom lets it slip that he prepared sandwiches and milk for her and was concerned for her safety. Yet if their game is to continue, he must now play on offense, so he also tells her that he wanted to make sure she returned alive in order for him to prove they are not married,

Fig. 21. Tierney shares a bedroom scene with Tyrone Power in *That Wonderful Urge* (Robert B. Sinclair, 1948), which Fox used to promote the film.

encouraging her to call the police to report an intruder and thus verify-
ing he is not her husband. Sara responds by pelting him with perfume
bottles and then pulls out her secret weapon: a long list of women he has
romanced in the past, exposing his double standards for criticizing her
love life in print. The game turns much crueler when Tom takes Sara in
his arms to "surrender" to her husband and plants a stage kiss her on the
lips, assuming that she will publicly deny the marriage if he invokes
the "legal right" for a husband to have sex with his wife. In the context
of the film and its genre, Tom's power play is presented as part of their
game of courtship (presumably Sara is still playing along and not in any
serious danger), but viewed with historical knowledge of the gendered
power imbalances in the postwar U.S. marriage, it reads as an unfair
move in a game that is already rigged.

Named after not one but two former U.S. presidents, Thomas Jefferson Tyler faces a crisis of patriarchal masculinity not unlike Larry Darrell, but he ultimately chooses a domestic life. The film's domestication
of Tom, however, reestablishes his dominance as a postwar husband and
soon-to-be father once the pursuit of romantic love trumps the pursuit
of sex and therefore diffuses the need for sexual sparring. By the end of
the film, sex and marriage are no longer mutually exclusive, suggesting
that through Sara's unlikely help Tom has matured from playboy to adult
heterosexual male within the hegemonic domestic ideology.

Part of this process also involves her holding him accountable to his
own hypocrisy and male ego, and the reporter's comeuppance is harsher
than in either *Love Is News* or *Sweet Rosie O'Grady*. Tom's deposition contends he is "a helpless victim of a diabolical plot" by "an evil, designing
woman" bent on destroying his life, but the proceedings go on to indict
him as the one with the hidden agenda. It was Tom who "lured" Sara to
the cabin, as Attorney Rice puts it, where he could be "alone with her
in the seclusion of a cabin in the woods." While Tom insists his motives
were strictly in the interest of his interview, his article betrays a more
"personal interest" in Sara, whom he describes as a woman of "charm," a
"young and desirable" woman who would "naturally attract the attention
of most men." Rice reminds him of his accusation: "You maintain that
while you were collecting material for your articles, the defendant was
so overcome by your manly charms, your magnetic personality and duty
that without any encouragement from you, she dreamed up a fraudulent

marriage to you and threw her considerable fortune at your feet." The discourse that Tom had once controlled—newspaper gossip—turns on him with humiliating headlines such as "Tyler Flops as Witness" and "Defense Blasts Tom-Tom." Sara may never be able to level the playing field, but the film gives her participation greater stakes. Hardly the "evil, designing woman" Tierney played opposite Power in *The Razor's Edge*, Sarah is nevertheless dangerous in that only she knows what really happened in Idaho, and she understandably wields this knowledge against Tom as a weapon (however comically).

Juxtaposed with Tierney's public image as the wife of Oleg Cassini, the domestic nurturer familiar to audiences in the 1940s, all three films in this chapter can be understood as complementary representations of women's demobilization after World War II. As women committed to marriage, readjustment, and homemaking, respectively, her characters in *That Wonderful Urge*, *The Razor's Edge*, and *Leave Her to Heaven* not only act in accordance with the hegemonic domestic ideology of the time but also expose the restrictions, contradictions, and competitions endemic to a patriarchal-capitalist domestic sphere. By overinvesting in these roles, her characters (if only temporarily) unsettle the postwar reorganization of the U.S. home front that such roles were constructed to support, ironically making the "real" Tierney an impossible, perhaps undesirable ideal to achieve.

On March 13, 1949, Lipman and Stephani's story for *Love Is News* was recycled once more, this time on radio in an adaptation of *That Wonderful Urge* for an episode of *Lux Radio Theatre*. Starring Tierney as Sara and switching Power for Don Ameche, the broadcast returned the story to its origin with the actor who played the editor at the paper in *Love Is News*. This adaptation also reunited Tierney with her costar from *Heaven Can Wait* (Ernst Lubitsch, 1943), the film that introduced her image as a mother, the subject of the next chapter.

3

The Front Lines of
Life and Death

Motherhood and Mortality

Almost every major Hollywood genre or production trend in the 1940s included at least one film starring Tierney by the end of the decade: the romantic comedy with *Rings on Her Fingers* (Rouben Mamoulian, 1942) and *That Wonderful Urge* (Robert B. Sinclair, 1948); the war film with *Thunder Birds* (William A. Wellman, 1942), *China Girl* (Henry Hathaway, 1942), and *A Bell for Adano* (Henry King, 1945); film noir with *Laura* (Otto Preminger, 1944); and both the "woman's film" and "male melodrama," respectively, with *Leave Her to Heaven* (John M. Stahl, 1945) and *The Razor's Edge* (Edmund Goulding, 1946).[1] What we have not yet examined are fantasy and Gothic horror—the former including *Heaven Can Wait* (Ernst Lubitsch, 1943) and *The Ghost and Mrs. Muir* (Joseph L. Mankiewicz, 1947) while the latter being the genre in which historical audiences would have identified *Dragonwyck* (Joseph L. Mankiewicz, 1946). This chapter analyzes all three films, arguing that as they make the spectral "real" according to the narrative and thematic conventions of their genres, they both confront and manage the fear of death. Each film posits a different representation of motherhood, with Tierney playing maternal figures, to show how it is possible to live with and through the presence of death, even one's own.

Looking for constructions of the maternal in fantasy and horror might seem odd given how the majority of writing on motherhood in Classical Hollywood cinema has been devoted to "woman's film" melodrama. Classic maternal melodramas such as *Stella Dallas* (King Vidor, 1937), *Mildred Pierce* (Michael Curtiz, 1945), and *Imitation of Life* (John M. Stahl, 1934; Douglas Sirk, 1959) have inspired works of scholarship that, in turn, have become classics of feminist film theory.[2] But as Lucy Fischer advises in her book *Cinematernity*, it behooves us to consider how maternity functions in other genres to gain a more expansive understanding of the relationship between gender and genre, or "how narrative and cultural forms imply specific sexual politics."[3] Indeed, genres themselves are not merely catalogers but generative systems that perform the "'maternal' task of endless propagation and proliferation."[4] The politics of motherhood during and immediately after World War II will be our particular focus with respect to the genres of fantasy and horror, and also how a single star was used in relation to popular genres to embody different types of mothers. That Tierney should develop a maternal star image at this time is not terribly surprising. Hollywood was addressing an audience that saw an upsurge in the national birth rate, and Tierney herself gave birth to her first child in 1943. What motherhood meant in the context of her image, however, is a more difficult question to answer.

Boom Years: The U.S. Maternal Ideal
and Gene Tierney as Star Mother

We have seen how during the war years in the United States, the home front was a gendered space of women's labor in a public workforce, but what needs to be emphasized is the degree to which working *mothers* participated in the war effort. Andrea S. Walsh describes how in certain respects "the relentless wartime search for happiness" and "'now or never' ethic" accelerated family processes and supported traditionalism through heterosexual marriage and monogamy.[5] In other ways, though, the absence of men on the home front and new job opportunities for women created "a de facto temporary matriarchy" in which a woman could be employed, independent, and a parent at the same time.[6] Most women in the United States favored contraception for married couples, and family planning was accepted in the mainstream. Abortion remained illegal except in rare therapeutic cases and was less accepted than contraception, though still common. According to surveys conducted in the late 1930s and early 1940s, more than 80 percent of white urban women used contraception and nearly 25 percent of affluent women had illegal abortions (with over 75 percent in the latter category reporting few long-term negative emotional effects). Yet between 1940 and 1943, the national birth rate rose from 17.9 percent to 22 percent, including both legitimate and illegitimate births. From these statistics, Walsh surmises that outside of the very young or conservative, U.S. women in the early 1940s wanted their pregnancies.[7]

At the same time, the experience of a sexually segregated home front could be a source of duress for women separated from their G.I. husbands or boyfriends. Walsh explains that as "the loneliness, anxiety, and uncertainty of waiting were psychically interwoven with new freedoms," women found comfort in companionship with other women (through social activities such as moviegoing and card-playing) as well as parenthood (if they were not isolated and could rely on support from grandparents).[8] Despite the greater power women held on the home front in wartime, the work performed by men and women did not receive equal cultural value. As absent men were idolized for heroically serving in combat, the increased responsibilities for service wives put additional strains on their time and energy that they were simply expected to endure. Temporary single mothers who also worked outside the home were less available for their children and feared contributing to juvenile delinquency, encouraging their older children to help out with child-rearing duties and household chores, particularly older sons eager to succeed their fathers as the "man of the house."[9]

Being a mother and workingwoman also came with new social regulations on "acceptable" models of femininity. Dana Polan finds that wartime discourse in the United States transformed earlier models—representing woman "as nonutility, as beauty-for-beauty's sake, as the display of seductive charms"—into one based in scarcity and sublimated desire that ultimately served a nurturing role.[10] Women (particularly older women) were taught to practice self-denial in order to establish unity and optimism on the home front, ensure efficiency in running the family, and enable pragmatic solutions to wartime problems. If their war work was understood as an influence on male preserves of the war effort (e.g., casting bullets fired by men in combat), it was also represented as a complement to or even the fullest realization of their domestic labor (e.g., learning to keep a cleaner house from training in the WACs).[11] Moreover, gaining access to a public labor force traditionally occupied by men meant that women would be better able to empathize and identify *with* men, learning to become more understanding wives in the process.[12] While it was important for them to maintain their love for men away from home, their love should not interfere with the war effort. Excessive desire and sexual manipulation were seen as qualities the "enemy" possessed.[13] Polan interprets these discursive strategies not as means of promoting "the triumph *over* scarcity" but rather to demonstrate "the triumph *of* scarcity." "Here," he writes, "the shortages of war will be represented as a positive good, a force that will help Americans cast off a modern decadence and rediscover their fundamental resourcefulness, a basic 'know how.'"[14]

Like many of her female fans, Tierney became a mother during World War II and joined a group of Hollywood stars as models of motherhood for the U.S. "baby boom," active and productive, nurturing and conventionally feminine, practical and self-sacrificing. The fan magazine *Movies* published an article titled "The High Cost of Star Babies" in December of 1943 that cited Joan Bennett, Alice Faye, Betty Grable, Brenda Joyce, Brenda Marshall, Rosalind Russell, Lana Turner, and Cobina Wright Jr., in addition to Tierney, as new or expectant mothers. Of all the studios, Fox was "dealt one of the heaviest blows in its stellar talent" as an increasing number of stars reportedly took leaves to have children.[15] The article detailed the need for studios to change production schedules when losing a major star or brace themselves for box-office losses and to revise scripts to accommodate new replacements, but as a publicity piece, it also reinscribed the ordinariness of these star mothers. Revealing this project of demystification and remythification quite clearly, it stated, "Human history shows that each war creates an up-swing in the birth record. This war is no exception. America's birth-rate increased twenty-five percent over what it was in pre-war days. And movie stars are human beings first, glamour notwithstanding."[16] Tierney had just finished shooting *Heaven Can Wait*, and with Cassini waiting for her and their new baby at Fort Riley, readers were told that this army wife would be unable to engage in Fox's promotional plans for the film.[17]

Where Tierney differs from her contemporaries are the circumstances surrounding the birth of her first daughter, Daria, in October of 1943. Born deaf and partially blind with a severe intellectual disability, Daria spent most of her life in care facilities. Working in film after film in the early 1950s, Tierney attempted to provide the annuity for her care.[18]

Daria's disabilities were caused by a case of rubella, or "German measles," which Tierney contracted while entertaining troops at the Hollywood Canteen during her pregnancy. A female marine carrying the virus had escaped quarantine to see her perform, and only after meeting the fan a year later did Tierney realize she was the source of the infection.[19] This information stayed hidden from the public until the late 1950s when the press began covering Tierney's psychiatric treatments (see chapter 4), and the story later inspired Agatha Christie's Miss Marple mystery novel *The Mirror Crack'd from Side to Side* (1962).[20] On the subject of Daria in her autobiography, Tierney posited motherhood as its own distinct wartime labor: "I have long stopped blaming the lady marine, myself, God, or Hitler for what happened to us. But Daria was, of course, a war baby, born in 1943. I suppose it has always been true that, in wartime, the most innocent suffer, too. Daria was my war effort."[21] While the particularities of this labor were not yet apparent to the public in the mid-1940s, Fox was able to represent Tierney's motherhood by either idealizing it or accentuating her homemaking in lieu of normative child-rearing duties.

Studio-controlled publicity gave every indication that Daria was both a physically and mentally abled child living under Tierney's domestic care. In May 1944, the press reported that Daria was "born two months prematurely," calling her an "incubator baby," and that doctors would not allow a nurse to bring her to Hollywood until then for her "camera debut."[22] Fan-magazine articles would eventually assure readers of her health and parents' contentment, such as an August 1946 piece in *Modern Screen* titled "Leave Heaven to Her," referring to Tierney as a wife, mother, and dog owner. The article proclaimed that "Daria is [. . .] a beautiful child. Her bone structure is exquisite, her coloring lovely." Humorous and heartwarming anecdotes supported the rhetorical question, "With such an adorable moppet at home, is it any wonder the Cassinis prefer nurseries to nightclubs?"[23] One story described the two-and-a-half-year-old child mischievously hiding her parents' car keys in the coffee pot.[24] Another scenario had Daria running up to Tierney's friend Cobina Wright Jr. (a fellow Fox star), mistaking her for "Mama," but instead of hugging the woman, she recognized her in time to slow down and meekly say, "Oh, hello."[25] The article ended with Tierney tiptoeing into Daria's nursery to hang glow-in-the-dark pictures she brought home from New York and surprised to find that Daria was not asleep. When Tierney asked why she was still awake, according to the article, Daria replied, "To see," and nodded at the new pictures.[26]

Whatever struggles Tierney faced were characterized as the sort of "civilian problems" a middle-class army wife experiences during her husband's absence, balancing motherhood and work outside the home.[27] The press referred only to a nurse whom Tierney entrusted with Daria's day care. For example, in an August 1945 article titled "Gene Tierney Has Her Troubles Too!," *Screenland* covered Tierney's return to acting after her stay in Fort Riley. Tierney reportedly moved Daria's furniture piece by piece into her Beverly Hills home when movers failed to arrive, and to prevent Daria from catching pneumonia, she then had to find a heater for the nursery. The article alleged that Tierney borrowed several heaters from the Fox props department, demonstrating wartime resourcefulness and making Hollywood compatible with the home.[28]

From 1946 to 1948, Tierney's estrangement from Cassini required further efforts to align Tierney with a family image. In 1947, the market for her audience expanded to include young girls with the publication of *Gene Tierney and the Invisible Wedding Gift* by Kathryn Heisenfelt, one of the Whitman Authorized Editions, an illustrated series of young adult novels featuring stars such as Shirley Temple, Judy Garland, Roy Rogers, and Gene Autry as protagonists in mystery or adventure stories. The same year, Whitman also added Tierney in its paper-doll line, not to be confused with Mel Odom's popular "Gene doll" introduced in 1995 for adult collectors (a 15.5-inch fashion doll named Gene Marshall inspired by female stars of the Hollywood studio era and resembling Tierney in particular).

Connecting Tierney's persona to specifically postwar U.S. values, publicity evoked motherhood through a conservative discourse on homemaking. Fox issued a press release in 1947 announcing that she sold her Beverly Hills mansion and all its furnishings. After completing *The Ghost and Mrs. Muir*, she would be moving into a bungalow near the studio with Daria and her nurse, making New York City their permanent home between films.[29] Another press release read: "The cottage has a living room, two small bedrooms, a dining room, kitchen, and bath. Gene has used unpainted furniture[,] space-saving, built-in cabinets and desks, and a lot of 'finds' unearthed in second-hand stores and junk shops. GI's and brides can take a tip from her ingenious planning for this inexpensive home, the total cost of which is in the same class as their own budgets."[30] Also living in this Hollywood bungalow would be Tierney's younger sister, Patricia, acting as her personal secretary and helping her run the new home. Fans would have recalled their close companionship while Cassini served in the U.S. Army Cavalry. Gene had attracted publicity as the responsible yet compassionate "big sister" to Pat, then sixteen years old. *Modern Screen* informed readers how the Tierney sisters served as confidantes and chaperones for each other, shared the same clothes, and wore the same shoe and glove size but that Gene advised Pat to stay in school before she were to consider becoming an actress herself.[31]

Even following Tierney's reconciliation with Cassini, the bungalow remained part of her maternal image. An October 1950 issue of *Photoplay* ran an article featuring the Tierney-Cassini residence in its Star in Your Home series, which offered "Hollywood ideas to decorate your home."[32] Fox art director Lyle Wheeler, an Oscar nominee for *Laura* and *Leave Her to Heaven*, was the credited author of the piece. Purporting that Tierney "has reduced movie-star living to its simplest form" and that she was done with her "big glamour house phase," Wheeler accounted her ordinary domestic leisure activities such as hosting buffet-style dinners and small parties with Cassini (including games of charades, ever the performer) and playing canasta with her movie-star friends. Although Tierney employed a "combination cook and housekeeper," Wheeler promised readers that she could manage all of the housework herself were she not working at the studios.[33] To support this thesis, the majority of the article focused on her interior design and decoration of the home, spotlighting her traditional and cost-effective furnishings and providing ample illustrations. Among the rooms described were the living room, Tierney and Cassini's bedroom, a room for Tierney's second daughter, Christina (two years old at the time), and a guest room. Daria's room is inexplicably absent from this tour of the house. The only mention of Daria is in a reference to a large painting of mother and daughter hanging over the mantel of the living-room fireplace—like Laura Hunt, an absent presence.[34]

Of course, Tierney's maternal star image also derived from her films between 1943 and 1947. By the early 1950s, when Fox began loaning her out to other studios, one can still see the maternal Tierney in a film such as *Close to My Heart* (William Keighley, 1951), a "woman's film" melodrama from Warner Bros. about a suburban housewife unable to bear children. Discouraged by the thought of adding her name to the adoption agency's two-year waiting list, she desperately hopes to adopt a baby that has been abandoned at the local police station, but her journalist husband (Ray Milland, on loan from Paramount) is wary of accepting a foundling whose parentage he cannot verify. Taken together, her maternal roles on-screen in the 1940s constitute a heterogeneous representation of motherhood wherein a given film may celebrate certain ideals over others. The roles of mother and wife overlap in *Heaven Can Wait*, which views motherhood as an eternally redemptive force in the lives of wayward men; Tierney's character both assumes a maternal position in her relationship with her immature husband and raises their son who takes after his father. *Dragonwyck* looks to motherhood as a precious family resource that must be protected by a semipatriarchal male to safeguard the family's productive future. Offering a more negotiated maternal position, *The Ghost and Mrs. Muir* endorses the possibility for women to be good mothers and at the same time inhabit an identity for themselves independent from motherhood. All three of these films deploy maternal figures to inspire optimism when faced with death, metaphorically conveyed through the spectral, and displace contemporary anxieties about loss onto the turn-of-the-century past.

The Redemptive Maternal: *Heaven Can Wait*

At first glance, the comedy *Heaven Can Wait* would appear to be another entry in the cycle of escapist films popular from the Great Depression through World War II—and especially on-brand for Fox—that romanticized small-town middle-class family life in the Gay Nineties. Sean Griffin remarks that period films set in the turn-of-the-century United States were so prevalent at the studio during the early 1940s that it was nicknamed "Nineteenth Century Fox."[35] In other ways, though, the film was an unorthodox choice for a wartime production. Director Ernst Lubitsch wrote, "I encountered partly great resistance before I made this picture, because it had no message and made no point whatsoever. The hero was a man only interested in good living, with no aim of accomplishing anything, or doing anything noble."[36] Lubitsch's first Technicolor film and his first film at Fox after developing the famed "Lubitsch Touch" at

Paramount, *Heaven Can Wait* tells the life story of Henry Van Cleve (Don Ameche), a handsome lothario from an affluent New York City family, who lives from 1872 to 1942 and seems neither aware of nor affected by the historical events leading up to (and including) the U.S. intervention in World War II. Despite the resistance Lubitsch described, *Heaven Can Wait* was his most commercially successful film of the sound era and earned Academy Award nominations for Best Picture, Best Directing, and Best Cinematography (Color).[37] Not since *The Love Parade* (1929) had Lubitsch received a Best Director nomination.

The film's darkly comic wit makes it especially distinctive, a credit both to Lubitsch and his frequent screenwriter Samson Raphaelson, adapting Leslie Bush-Fekete's 1934 play *Birthday*.[38] In the wake of his death on the day after his seventieth birthday, Henry narrates his story to Satan himself (played by Laird Cregar and identified only as "His Excellency"), defending his "case" for admission to Hell in the red art deco waiting room. And who is the devil, really, but a surrogate for an audience implicated in taking sinful pleasure from hearing Henry tell this tale? Lubitsch scholar William Paul notes how the film's flashback structure transforms the linear narrative of Henry's life "into a form of historical inquiry, helping to create a cinema of memory that proliferated in this period."[39] Henry's birthdays and the successive deaths of his relatives not only mark the passage of time but also serve as a constant reminder of his eventual death. By limiting the film's scope to Henry's myopic point of view, Lubitsch and Raphaelson invert the genres of the biographical film and the historical-period drama in their portrayal of a "hero" who apparently matters little to the course of the history through which he lived. In fact, the only line of dialogue that might be interpreted as a social comment is His Excellency's droll greeting to Henry in the opening scene: "I hope you'll forgive me, but we're so busy down here. Really, sometimes it looks as if the whole world is coming to Hell." Not guilty of any crime, Henry has come to Hell for a life that has been, in his words, "one continuous misdemeanor." As Paul points out, "Lubitsch strips everyday events of the pretentions biopics artificially place on them in order to make events of little dramatic consequence dramatically significant in themselves." Adding to the humor of this clever twist on the formula is the casting of Ameche, who had been a regular in Fox's bio-pics at the time.[40]

Neither a conventionally nostalgic family comedy nor a historical-period drama, *Heaven Can Wait* is better understood within contemporary production trends as a fantasy. Thomas Doherty details how Hollywood films of the 1940s approached death in conciliatory ways, often by incorporating fantasy into the quotidian. As long as Hollywood cinema has been dedicated to action and emotion, death has served the drama of films as a theme or subject and raised the stakes for violence on-screen—of which death is often a result. In the 1940s, however, Hollywood's wartime audience was all too familiar with death in their everyday lives. Whether in a comic or melodramatic register, fantasy films engaged in "recovery" work for the departed, invoking the possibility of an afterlife and the presence of ghosts, spirits, and angels for "a transparent allegorical reach and cultural purpose."[41] Doherty explains that this "more down-to-earth and consciously therapeutic variant [of the fantasy genre] used the ethereal to assuage the grief of families and friends left with only memories and gold stars in the windows."[42] Once characters learn to let go of the past, they can begin to build a better future. Sentimental films such as *The Human Comedy* (Clarence Brown, 1943) and *Tomorrow Is Forever* (Irving Pichel, 1946)—family melodramas set in wartime on the U.S. home front—certainly took on similar projects without elements of fantasy, but fantasy allowed filmmakers to deal with the effects of loss more gently and indirectly, situating the problems of a wartime audience within transhistorical concerns about change and mortality.[43] While *Heaven Can Wait* turns to the past to see the humor in a "great man" theory of history, a fantasy such as *The Ghost and Mrs. Muir* uses the past to contrast traditional constructions of family against its modern female protagonist.

Even the most ordinary lives matter greatly, fantasy films asserted, but death is nothing to fear. Films such as *Here Comes Mr. Jordan* (Alexander Hall, 1941), *A Guy Named Joe* (Victor Fleming, 1943), *The Canterville Ghost* (Jules Dassin, 1944), *Between Two Worlds* (Edward A. Blatt, 1944), *It's a Wonderful Life* (Frank Capra, 1946), *The Bishop's Wife* (Henry Koster, 1947), *Down to Earth* (Alexander Hall, 1947), and *Portrait of Jennie* (William Dieterle, 1948) are among a few examples of how fantasy represented death as an inevitable part of life. So linked were these films that some of their titles became interchangeable. *Heaven Can Wait* was actually the title of Harry Segall's 1938 play that inspired *Here Comes Mr. Jordan*, which directors Warren Beatty and Buck Henry remade in

1978 under Segall's original title. When directors Chris and Paul Weitz remade the film again in 2001, it was called *Down to Earth*, borrowing the title of *Mr. Jordan*'s 1947 musical sequel starring Rita Hayworth.

There is also more to these films than the assurance of a life after death. Fantasy in the 1940s relied on the spectral to affirm the physical, showing how individual human self-knowledge and agency are capable of resolving conflicts. Drawing from literary theorist Tzvetan Todorov, Polan observes that this particular kind of fantasy was usually set in the realm of the "marvelous," or "that realm in which human and physical laws are suspended." Yet he insists that what is important about the marvelous in these films is that it "leads the human subject [. . .] to a new certainty, to a new faith in the psychological self. The marvelous becomes an aid that mediates the sacred and the desacralized—an aid by which humans can fulfill human ends and tasks."[44] By accepting that the marvelous is in fact "real" and resides in human beings (however unbeknownst to them), the marvelous serves as a vehicle for characters to realize their human potential, vanishing once they satisfy their goals in the narrative.[45] For example, Henry's worth in *Heaven Can Wait* is not assigned by divine (or demonic) forces but demonstrated through his own autobiographical narration. Henry's memory allows him to rediscover his love for his patient, faithful wife Martha (Tierney), whom he outlived after a happy twenty-five-year marriage, and he is redeemed by the love she evidently maintained for him.

The film not only puts Henry's life and death on a continuum, but it also equates the significance of his life with his marriage to Martha. After all, their October 25 wedding anniversary coincides with his birthday. Although Henry resigns himself to damnation, he laments, "There are several people up there [in Heaven] I would love to see. Particularly one. A very dear one." Upon finishing his story, His Excellency dismisses him, encouraging him to defend his case for admission to Heaven instead, where he believes Martha will be there to "plead" for him. Henry might be able to register in "a small room vacant in the annex, not exactly on the sunny side, not so very comfortable." If one of the messages in *It's a Wonderful Life* is that "no man is a failure who has friends," *Heaven Can Wait*, for all its irony and cynicism, at least proposes the idea that no man is a failure who had the love of a good wife—not even someone as disreputable as Henry.

Martha's goodness manifests in her steadfastly maternal role, both as a maternal figure for Henry and the mother of their son, Jack. The film's spiritual idealization of Martha as mother requires that she deny herself the extramarital romances in which Henry indulges, emerging as his "better" half by displaying virtue and forgiving him of his adolescent transgressions. According to Lubitsch biographer Scott Eyman, linking Tierney to blue and lavender colors was the exception to an unusually restrained palette for a 1940s Technicolor production at Fox,[46] and I would add that it paints Martha as cool, modest, and tasteful. When she dies before Henry, the film practically canonizes her as a saint, but that intervention of the marvelous ultimately desacralizes her image as Henry comes to understand that what qualified her for sainthood was her self-sacrifice as a wife and mother while she was alive. This socially "acceptable" model of femininity for the U.S. home front would later define the feminine ideal of the homemaker after World War II.

Using the objective correlative of a fictional self-help book for newlywed women, *How to Make Your Husband Happy* by "Dr. Blossom Franklin," the film defines her relationship with Henry in terms of her eagerness to please and Henry's failure to see what is in plain sight until it is too late. Henry first meets Martha when he follows her into a Brentano's store on her way to buy the book, not knowing she is engaged to his cousin Albert (Allyn Joslyn), a successful lawyer and the pride of the Van Cleve family. Displayed in the store window, the book causes Martha some embarrassment with its cover illustration of a woman peering out from behind a curtain, giving the reader a wink and a smile. Henry poses as a clerk, and when Martha asks if there are any women working in the store, he assures her that the management entrusts him with customers' "more delicate situations," going as far as to call him "the bookworm's little mother." Swayed by his feigned concern that losing a customer may cost him his job, she reluctantly asks him to fetch the book. Sexuality is socially acceptable for her as a bride-to-be, especially if it makes her husband happy, but it would be in "excess" if taken outside the marriage—a social double standard that the film reflects, although does not exactly condemn. Just before Henry's death, as he tries to convince Jack to hire a younger woman to read to him, he pulls Dr. Franklin's book from a shelf in his library and, recognizing the cover, stops midsentence. The book reminds Henry of his late wife, but more important, he fully realizes how for twenty-five years of marriage, she made his happiness her priority. Feeling more sympathy for his father's loneliness as Henry sadly returns the book to the shelf, Jack reconsiders the old man's request. "Father," he tells him, "her last thought was that you should be happy, and I promised her I'd see to it."

The film offsets some of its sexism by refraining from characterizing Martha as either a completely passive victim of Henry's dalliances with other women or a dupe who believes his prevaricating excuses. Ten years after their marriage, she finally (albeit temporarily) leaves him. Heading for her parents' home in Kansas, she sends a telegram to inform him that she will soon make plans for Jack but asks Henry not to follow her, offering no explanation. Henry's grandfather (Charles Coburn) insists that Henry try to save the marriage (in effect, saving his soul). "If a woman like Martha runs away from her husband, there must be a reason," he bellows, threatening to wait for Henry at the gates of Heaven to hit him on the head with a baseball bat if he cannot earn Martha's forgiveness (sending him to Hell, where we came in). When Henry arrives at her home, he accuses *her* of doubting his sincerity and agrees to a divorce, but Martha calls his bluff. "Oh, Henry," she responds, "I know your every move. I know your outraged indignation. I know the poor, weeping little boy. I know the misunderstood, strong, silent man. The wounded lion who's too proud to explain what happened in the jungle last night." Martha even sees through Henry's attempt at an apology with an expensive Cartier bracelet. Earlier, while developing a wallet photograph she took with Jack, she checked the size of Henry's wallet only to find the receipt from Cartier—dated months ago. Never having received the bracelet, she correctly assumes it was a gift intended for another woman. Virtuous, but not purely innocent, Martha is capable of deception herself. It is when Henry overhears her lying to her mother on a department store phone that he first takes an interest in her (she tells her mother that she is delayed at the hairdresser, though is actually on her way to Brentano's, so the film quickly establishes her intentions as good).

Martha's motivations for staying with Henry over ten years are also made explicit. After Albert coincidentally meets her on the train to Kansas, he escorts her to her parents' home and presumes that marrying

Henry was a "mistake" she has "paid for." "Now, Albert," she objects, "I don't want anybody to get the impression that I've been the victim of ten years of misery. Nothing of the kind. On the contrary, I can say there were moments in my marriage which few women have been lucky enough to have experienced." Fearing that she would die an "old maid" (in Kansas!), Martha also saw marriage as her only to opportunity to escape her bickering parents, the Strables (Marjorie Main and Eugene Pallette), who accumulated their wealth from her father's meatpacking plant and its popular advertising character, "Mabel, the Cow."

The conservative, sycophantic Albert was her first suitor on whom her parents could agree and, while he may have been a more stable husband, Martha is genuinely attracted to Henry for his charm and romantic passion, qualities that Albert does not possess in the slightest. At a party hosted by Henry's parents (Spring Byington and Louis Calhern) to celebrate Albert's engagement, Martha is presented to the Van Cleves and their guests, who welcome her with gawks. Tracking into a medium shot of Tierney, the camera also introduces the film's female star, but rather than solely showing her off as a beautiful attraction for the audience's own gawking, the shot draws attention to Martha's uncomfortable smile as she surveys Albert's world. Henry and Martha recognize each other from their Brentano's encounter (triggering that flashback) and then find themselves together again, this time in the family library, where Albert sends Martha for sneezing during an aria performed by one of his clients. Never would Albert have expected Martha to leave with Henry to get married, literally swept of her feet in the foyer. Toward the end of the film, as the couple sits in the same library on their twenty-fifth anniversary, they reflect on Henry walking up to Martha to kiss her. Henry remembers her as "a frightened little girl," but Martha corrects him and to his surprise confesses that she was not frightened at all, adding, "Do you know what was in my mind? I thought, 'What's the matter with him? Can't he walk faster?'" Twenty-five years later, she considers herself "the happiest woman in the world."

Imbricated in her continued romantic desire for Henry is also a maternal understanding and care for him that the film illustrates by doubling Henry with Jack. As Henry and Martha grow older together, Henry may still see her as "the innocent little girl from Kansas," but the film shows how Henry is actually her "obstinate little boy." This childishness is what endears him to Martha and causes her to take him back after he follows her to Kansas. Henry tells her how their beloved Jack somehow reconciled with his girlfriend after making her jealous by buying ice cream for another girl. With generous affection, Martha deduces that Jack told his girlfriend another one of his "little stories." Martha knows these stories are obvious fibs, but she cannot help but accept them because "he wants you to believe them so bad that you wish you could." Although this "like father, like son/boys will be boys" rationalization excuses Henry's actions for Martha and perhaps also for Lubitsch and Raphaelson, the film's humor is never at Martha's expense. Rather, Henry becomes the object of some ridicule as her "little Casanova." Attempting at the age of fifty to pursue a chorus girl named Peggy Nash (Helene Reynolds), he sends her a note with roses and visits her dressing room. Peggy patronizes him until his shocking and humiliating discovery that Jack is her current beau, and Henry agrees to pay $25,000 for her silence. The blackmail scheme recalls the flashback at the beginning of the film, when, as a child, Henry's first crush cons him out of his pet beetles in exchange for a walk with her in the park.

Nowhere is the comparison between Henry and Jack more apparent than when Jack tells his parents about his newest girlfriend. Playing an adult Jack, Tod Andrews (credited as Michael Ames) bears a close resemblance to Ameche, which allows the film to articulate this symbolic comparison between father and son at the level of the visual as much as the narrative (fig. 22). Henry has just privately broken the news to Martha that Jack is dating a "showgirl," and he proposes buying her off to stay away from Jack, but, as usual, Martha is two steps ahead. She knows about Peggy and surmises that Henry has already paid her. To preserve the happiness of the family, Martha allows Jack to sow his wild oats, just as she pretends to be ignorant of Henry's affairs or at least his flirtations (how far Henry has gone during their marriage remains ambiguous). Questioning Jack about his romantic life, Henry looks to Martha for support, but her sarcastic refrain of "I don't know, and don't ask me" underscores what she does know: how men like Henry and Jack form crushes easily, how they grow tired of women quickly, and the problems that arise when they decide "to get rid" of these women. Following this pattern, it turns out that Jack has broken up with Peggy, and while Henry is relieved by this news, he is less enthusiastic to know that Jack has

Fig. 22. Martha Van Cleve (Tierney) observes how her grown son, Jack (Michael Ames, *right*), takes after his father, Henry (Don Ameche, *middle*), in *Heaven Can Wait* (Ernst Lubitsch, 1943).

moved on to another showgirl. Henry worries that Jack has grown up to be like him but may not be as lucky to marry a woman like Martha. "I have no illusions about myself," Henry admits to her. "Martha, if I hadn't met you, I'd hate to think where I'd be right now." Of course, the audience knows where Henry is as he tells his story in the narrative frame, and it will be the cumulative memory of her that ultimately grants him deliverance.

The childishness that Martha fondly sees in Henry does not obscure his actual age to her, and realizing that their time together is limited, she begins keeping secrets from him to ensure his happiness. Middle age is a source of chagrin for Henry, but Martha accepts it matter of factly (reminding him to wear his reading glasses to prevent headaches) and even optimistically (knowing that once he gained a "little tummy," their marriage was more or less secure), to the point that when she becomes terminally ill, she assures Henry it is "nothing at all." Henry has mistaken her phone calls and afternoons out as signs of an affair, acknowledging,

"You're still very attractive, and you know it." While Martha enjoys seeing him jealous for the first time, her secrecy has selfless intentions; she
wants to spare him any distress.

Remembering their twenty-fifth anniversary, Henry thinks of waltz-
ing with Martha in the foyer of their home, where she exits the film. The
poignancy of the scene lies in the discrepancy between what Henry does
not know in this flashback—that he and Martha are sharing their last
dance and spending their last anniversary together—and what he does
know in the narrative frame, creating dramatic irony for the audience
through Ameche's voice-over. "There were only a few more months left
for Martha," Henry says, "and she made them the happiest of our lives
together." Telling "little stories," the sort that Martha cannot resist, has
always been Henry's way of weaseling out of trouble. The difference with
this story is that he succeeds not because of what he tries to disguise but
for what he reveals in spite of himself. Martha gives value to his other-
wise uneventful life, and through his renewed appreciation of that value,
she also (in a maternal fashion) yields his spiritual rebirth.

Maternal Plentitude: *Dragonwyck*

Birth and reproductive capability are among the chief preoccupations in
Dragonwyck, a film about the anxiety of patriarchal family lineage during
the Anti-Rent War of the 1840s, when tenant farmers in upstate New York
rebelled against the "patroons," the male landowners who ran a manorial
system established by their Dutch colonial ancestors in the seventeenth
century. In the role that introduced him to audiences as the Gothic villain
he would famously personify throughout horror films of the 1950s and
1960s, Vincent Price plays Nicholas Van Ryn, the patroon of the fictional
Dragonwyck manor in the Hudson Valley.[47] After the birth of his daughter, Katrine (Connie Marshall), his wife, Johanna (Vivienne Osborne),
learns she is unable to bear more children, making him the last of the
Van Ryn patroons. Tierney plays the ingenue as Miranda Wells, his distant cousin from a farm outside Greenwich, Connecticut (the star's home
state), whom he invites to Dragonwyck for an extended stay in exchange
for her service as a companion to eight-year-old Katrine.

The servants believe that the Van Ryn bloodline is cursed and that
the spirit of Nicholas's great-grandmother Azilde haunts the "Red Room"

of Dragonwyck, where her portrait hangs over her treasured harpsichord. Driven mad by Nicholas's great-grandfather, who rejected her after she gave birth to his son (fulfilling his sole desire for her), Azilde committed suicide in this room when she was Miranda's age. Dragonwyck's housekeeper, Magda (Spring Byington), informs Miranda that whenever tragedy is about to strike the Van Ryns, Azilde returns to sing and play the harpsichord, which her husband forbade, but that since Miranda is not a blood relative, she will be unable to hear the ghostly music. However, the central mystery of Dragonwyck turns out not to be whether the manor is haunted by Azilde's spirit (it is) but whether Nicholas is a murderer and whether Miranda will be his next victim. Following Johanna's sudden death, Nicholas marries Miranda despite the reservations of her Christian fundamentalist parents (Walter Huston and Anne Revere). Miranda longs to see the world beyond her family farm and is captivated by Nicholas's aristocratic glamour, while he, the film eventually confirms, poisoned Johanna with the intention of marrying Miranda—expecting her to bear him a son. In this respect, *Dragonwyck* works in the opposite way of the postclassical horror trend Fischer identifies in films such as *Rosemary's Baby* (Roman Polanski, 1968).[48] Rather than focusing on the trauma of a monstrous parturition, it plays on the fear of infertility, of *not* giving birth at all.

Based on Anya Seton's best-selling novel of the same name, published one hundred years after the Anti-Rent War in 1944, the film capitalized on the renewed popularity of the "Female Gothic," or works in the Gothic literary mode written by women authors—Clara Reeve, Ann Radcliffe, Mary Shelley, Charlotte and Emily Brontë, and Daphne du Maurier, among others—that were addressed to and read by women.[49] The 1938 publication of Du Maurier's novel *Rebecca* and 1940 film adaptation directed by Alfred Hitchcock not only revived interest in Charlotte Brontë's Victorian Gothic novel *Jane Eyre* (1847), which *Rebecca*'s producer David O. Selznick recognized as an intertext, but also energized a wave of Gothic film melodramas in the 1940s.[50] In addition to Fox's 1944 adaptation of *Jane Eyre* (Robert Stevenson), examples from other studios included *Suspicion* (Alfred Hitchcock, 1941), *Experiment Perilous* (Jacques Tourneur, 1944), *Gaslight* (George Cukor, 1944), *My Name Is Julia Ross* (Joseph H. Lewis, 1945), *Undercurrent* (Vincente Minnelli, 1946), *Secret beyond the Door* (Fritz Lang, 1947), and *The Two Mrs. Carrolls* (Peter

Godfrey, 1947). Seton's novel was first serialized during 1943 in *Ladies' Home Journal*, with Tierney on the cover of the issue containing the first installment. Although Tierney's appearance on the cover was likely coincidental (Fox acquired the rights to the novel in 1944 and the film went into production in 1945), the studio nevertheless used the cover in the trailer to market the film as an adaptation of Seton's novel, a vehicle for Tierney, and a "woman's film."

The trailer quoted the magazine's explicit comparison between the novels *Rebecca* and *Dragonwyck*, grouping the latter in the recent adaptations of Gothic literature in the Du Maurier tradition. Miranda's work as a governess and references to a "Red Room" also evince the continued intertextual function of *Jane Eyre* in the genre.[51] Film scholars such as Diane Waldman and Mary Ann Doane have since termed these films "Gothic romance films" and "paranoid woman's films," respectively,[52] but at the time they were received as horror films that made claims to "quality" or "prestige" through their associations with femininity.[53] Indicating Fox's investment in *Dragonwyck* as such a film, it was "presented" by Darryl F. Zanuck and, at $1.9 million, cost more than the average black-and-white production.[54] Horror was unusual for the film's writer-director Joseph L. Mankiewicz, making his directorial debut after establishing a career as a writer and producer, but he would later be known as one of the most sophisticated filmmakers of women's melodrama in Hollywood (with *A Letter to Three Wives* [1949] and *All about Eve* [1950], he made Oscar history by winning awards in two consecutive years both for writing and directing).[55] The film earned a domestic profit of $2.57 million, just ahead of *Heaven Can Wait*, scoring yet another box-office hit for Tierney in the middle of the decade.[56] Price and Tierney both reprised their roles for a *Lux Radio Theatre* adaptation that aired during the Halloween season on October 7, 1946.

While the Gothic novel originated in the eighteenth century, the revival of Gothic narratives in the 1940s retained many of the same conventions. Doane cites a range of examples that can be found in *Dragonwyck*: "the large and forbidding house, mansion, or castle; a secret, often related to a family history, which the heroine must work to disclose; storms incarnating psychical torment; portraits; and locked rooms."[57] If we understand the film genre in Doane's specific terms as "paranoid woman's films," or variations on the Bluebeard tale, the distinguishing element of female paranoia should not be taken for granted. As she explains this terminology, "[T]he paranoia [is] evinced in the formulaic repetition of a scenario in which the wife invariably fears that her husband is planning to kill her—the institution of marriage is haunted by murder. Frequently, the violence is rationalized as the effect of an overly hasty marriage; the husband is unknown or only incompletely known by the woman."[58] Miranda's suspicions build gradually, shifting from nervous curiosity about Azilde's curse on the Van Ryns to her detection of the possible threat posed by Nicholas himself. Upon her arrival at Dragonwyck, she forms a maternal bond with Katrine, who confides in Miranda that she does not love her parents and wonders whether Nicholas loves her, his daughter, either. On the stormy night of Johanna's murder, Miranda comforts Katrine when the girl awakens and claims to hear lullaby-like music from the "Red Room," which frightens her as the singing and harpsichord playing grow louder (fig. 23). Moments later, Miranda discovers that Johanna has died.

Fig. 23. Miranda Wells (Tierney) comforts Katrine Van Ryn (Connie Marshall) on a dark and stormy night in *Dragonwyck* (Joseph L. Mankiewicz, 1946).

The circumstances surrounding Johanna's death are strange enough, but Miranda does not yet suspect Nicholas of murder. Dr. Jeff Turner (Glenn Langan), the tenant farmers' young physician, is unable to determine the cause of her death. Having diagnosed her with a cold that evening, he regretfully assumes she was more ill than he realized (in actuality, Nicholas asked Dr. Turner to call on Johanna and invited him to spend the night at Dragonwyck in order to blame her death on his lack of medical experience). As Miranda attempts to console Nicholas, she is surprised to learn that he and Johanna merely tolerated each other and that they dropped the facade of a happy marriage once they knew that Johanna could not have children after Katrine. Nicholas also tells Miranda he has fallen in love with her, appealing to her religious faith by averring that destiny has brought her into his life.

After they are married, Nicholas is overjoyed when Miranda announces she is pregnant, but their happiness together comes to an abrupt end when their son is born with a malformed heart and dies immediately following his baptism. Nicholas secludes himself in the tower room of Dragonwyck, as he did during his marriage to Johanna, where he becomes a drug addict. One night Miranda decides to investigate and finds him in a disheveled, intoxicated state. The film overtly shows Nicholas's cruelty in his condescension to her that displaces his bitterness over the loss of their child. Insulting her "ordinary standards" of living and incredulous of her ability to understand him, Nicholas expects her to react with fear or shock. Instead, she calmly rejects his overwrought self-pity and victim-playing to indict him for "just plain running away" from problems he cannot control. She reminds him that "his" son was also their son. Neither passing moral judgment nor offering to save Nicholas, as he anticipates, Miranda wants only to help and even share in his grief, pleading, "Let me be part of you. Let me love you, and love me too." There is no ambiguity over Nicholas's capability for misogynistic violence in his next confrontation with Miranda when he slowly and quietly enters her bedroom, startling her as she begins to read the Bible her father gave her as a gift. The film implies Nicholas's desire to rape if not murder his wife by alluding to his feeling of entitlement to her body (when she asks with tired exasperation why he has come to her room, he replies, "Inasmuch as this is my house, must I explain my presence in it?"). Approaching Miranda, he remarks on her "beauty," "strength," and "grace" while at the same time undermining her for what he smugly describes as the "earthiness" of her "peasant stock" and her "unexpected look of quality," and finally he threatens, "It would be a pity if we were not to have another . . . if you were barren."

That *Dragonwyck* should so closely follow particular conventions of the Gothic is a testament to its transatlantic endurance for centuries as a popular genre, but it also points to the entrenchment of women's horror within the Hollywood genre system by the middle of the 1940s. Waldman identifies various cultural factors that created an especially receptive environment for the "Gothic romance" to flourish on-screen, as these films "place an unusual emphasis on the affirmation of feminine perception, interpretation, and lived experience" at a time when U.S. women underwent a process "of role redefinition, frustration, and confusion."[59] When the country entered the war, the home was no longer the center of the husband's life, leaving women dissatisfied without their traditional occupations as housewives. The war provided opportunities for higher-paying jobs in a public labor force at a time when greater sexual openness and knowledge about birth control made it culturally possible for women to have lives outside of the home. What followed, however, was the rechanneling of women back into the home after the war, the reunion with their husbands after long separations, and the rise of divorce in response to hasty prewar marriages.[60] Waldman claims that this transition for women "gave the 'marrying a stranger' motif of the Gothics a specific historical resonance."[61] Wartime and postwar Gothics of the 1940s affirmed the female protagonist's experience by proving her suspicions about her husband to be true. The husband's murderousness is not presented as a surprise twist but as consistent with his attempts to confine the woman exclusively to the domestic sphere (as we see in *Dragonwyck*) and, in certain cases, manipulate her visual and aural access to knowledge (as we see in the husband's attempt to drive his wife insane in *Gaslight*).[62]

This narrative pattern of revealing patriarchy as tyrannical does not necessarily mean that women's horror of the 1940s formed a counterhegemonic narrative in Hollywood cinema. Another aspect of these films involved the intervention of a young male savior figure who validates the woman's suspicion, rescues her from the husband-villain, and supplants him to give the film narrative closure.[63] While the first husband usually represents a nineteenth-century condition or period (e.g., the patroon system in the New York Hudson Valley), the prospective second husband signals a historical change to which the first husband cannot adapt, introducing the possibility of the semipatriarchal family ideal of the 1940s. The sexual division of labor of the semipatriarchal bourgeois family remained organized according to the male-breadwinner and female-homemaker dynamic that existed before the war, but it encouraged a more egalitarian relationship between husband and wife.[64] *Dragonwyck* contrasts Nicholas with Dr. Turner, the male savior of the film, to position the latter as a democratic alternative to the man Miranda has married: Dr. Turner is an ally to the tenant farmers, standing up for one (Harry Morgan, credited as Henry Morgan) whom Nicholas evicts for refusing to pay rent; he shows sympathy for Johanna, whose insatiable appetite for food, he infers, sought nourishment and satisfaction to compensate for an emotionally empty marriage; and he is a caring physician, whereas Nicholas scolds Miranda for hiring a clubfooted maid (Jessica Tandy) because he finds "deformed bodies" depressing, a projection of his fear that he will not have a healthy son able to continue his legacy (Nicholas later resents the maid simply for living when his son died prematurely).

Dr. Turner's attraction to Miranda is also made known at key moments in the film and, in contradistinction to Nicholas, he seeks a companionate relationship with her. First meeting her at the annual Dragonwyck kermis (the outdoor Dutch festival in which the tenant farmers pay rent and tribute to Nicholas), he is struck by her beauty and asks for the "honor" of seeing her again soon. Katrine expresses her admiration for Dr. Turner, wishing he could be her doctor, and tells Miranda that he and her father share a mutual dislike of one another. The next time Dr. Turner sees Miranda is when they sit together at Dragonwyck by the fireplace after he treats Johanna's cold. Knowing the tensions between him and Nicholas, Miranda resists his attempts at friendly conversation, but the scene of hearth and home is nevertheless uncharacteristic of the gloomy, cavernous manor house. Following Johanna's death, as Miranda temporarily leaves to return to Connecticut, he catches up to her carriage and asks if she will permit him to visit her at her family farm—if the next week wouldn't be too soon. Miranda invites him to see her whenever he is "passing through," but he presses the issue, stating that over time he wants to be able to show how he feels about her.

On the other hand, Nicholas is drawn to Miranda exclusively for her biological potential to give birth to his son. By the time Miranda goes into labor, the farmers have already been granted their constitutional rights to own their land, a sign that the dissolution of the patroon system is imminent. Nicholas summons Dr. Turner to Dragonwyck, discrediting the physician from New York City whom he first hired to perform the delivery. Surprised by the urgency of Nicholas's request, Dr. Turner asks whether he has reason to think Miranda is in danger, but Nicholas can only respond, "Nothing must happen to my son," and demands that Dr. Turner "take every precaution." The previous physician is only too willing to let Dr. Turner relieve him, calling Nicholas a "maniac" who seems capable of murder if a problem were to occur in the delivery (he claims that when he tried to resign from the case, Nicholas locked him in his guest room and seems to be "mesmerizing" him). Sitting at Miranda's bedside, Dr. Turner gently awakens her:

> **MIRANDA:** I don't know whether to believe this or not.
> **DR. TURNER:** You can believe it.
> **MIRANDA:** Are you going to take care of me now?
> **DR. TURNER:** Yes, I'm going to take care of you now.
> **MIRANDA:** That's good. It's . . . it'll be all right now. I'm not afraid anymore. Jeff . . .
> **DR. TURNER:** Don't be afraid.

After the delivery, Nicholas neither believes Dr. Turner's warning about the baby's heart defect nor appears affected by his consolation that Miranda has "come through beautifully" and will be able to have other children in the future. As both her protector/savior and the "good" patriarch who will eventually take Nicholas's place, Dr. Turner guarantees that Miranda will be able to assume her maternal role within a new, socially preferrable family system that ensures her prosperity.

It is also Dr. Turner who exposes Nicholas's murder of Johanna. Nicholas poisoned her cake with his "favorite oleander," which he had displayed in her bedroom under the pretense of trying to cheer her up during her illness. After noticing the plant on the night of her death, Dr. Turner begins research on botany and learns that oleander contains lethal toxins, but he does not confront Nicholas with this evidence until Miranda's maid describes his abuse and implores Dr. Turner to take Miranda away from Dragonwyck, commenting on the "ugly-looking" plant he sent to her bedroom (ostensibly a gesture of amends after the argument in the tower). The view of the oleander between Nicholas and Miranda in the following scene—the confrontation in Miranda's room—performs the double duty of confirming Dr. Turner's suspicions and those of the audience, setting the stage for Miranda's climactic realization. Decrying a god "who giveth life and also takes it away," Nicholas demands that Miranda answer for her god who took his son's life, reasoning, "No one gives life, [and] takes it without purpose." He tells her that it was by his will, not God's, that Miranda came to Dragonwyck: "What you are is the reflection of what I wanted you to be. You live the life that I gave you." Miranda replies that she can think only of Johanna but does not know why, intuiting Nicholas's designs through an emotional identification with his first wife rather than the deductive logic Dr. Turner has employed.

The last-minute rescue of Miranda recuperates the wife and mother within a semipatriarchal family first by vindicating the spirit of Azilde, the original victim-mother in Dragonwyck's more traditionally patriarchal, dynastic system. When Nicholas is interrupted by a strange sound and dismisses it as only "the wind through the trees," Miranda insists that he is hearing Azilde's music, the same music Katrine heard the night of Johanna's death. "I never believed it really," she says, "but now I do," referring both to the superstitions about the Van Ryn curse and her suspicions about Nicholas. Just as Miranda recognizes herself in the legacy of female trauma at Dragonwyck that the Van Ryn men have perpetuated over history, she also understands Azilde as the avenging force through which that legacy is felt and remembered. The film evokes Azilde's spectral presence entirely through the score composed by Alfred Newman, the head of Fox's music department. Compelled to follow the music to the "Red Room," Nicholas looks terrified to see the harpsichord bench empty and Azilde's painted visage staring at him from her portrait. In a fit of distress as the music builds in intensity, he covers his ears and shuts his eyes, but the music stops only to announce the arrival of Dr. Turner, who (paraphrasing Miranda) was "just passing by." Dr. Turner replaces Azilde as the dispenser of justice in Dragonwyck. After accusing Nicholas of Johanna's murder and cold clocking him in self-defense, he leaves with Miranda. When they return with the mayor and a group of farmers to arrest Nicholas, they find him at the kermis site in the midst of a psychotic episode—hallucinating and raving about his son inheriting Dragonwyck—and he is shot dead before he is able to fire his gun at the crowd.

For all of the film's overtures to the spectral, it concludes with the victory of "a new certainty," not unlike fantasy films of the 1940s, achieved through human methods of detection—masculine logic and feminine intuition—that converge to impose a semipatriarchal order on a family system deemed dysfunctional. About to embark for Connecticut, Miranda admits to Dr. Turner that she never truly had a home other than her family farm. She reflects on her mother's caution to her, that "you can't marry a dream," before she moved to Dragonwyck to become Nicholas's wife. This adolescent romance, as she now comprehends it, has been nothing more than a detour on her way to appreciating the middle-class family values to which she has awoken, exchanging passion for safety: "Some dreams are very real, I guess. So real that they get confused with reality. And then when you wake up and look around, you find yourself saying, 'What am I doing here? How did I get here? What has this to do with what I am and what I want?' Then I guess you make up your mind you've had a nightmare, and you go crawlin' to your ma and pa." Reminding Dr. Turner that "Greenwich isn't so far away" and that he may be "passing through sometime," she now clearly knows what she wants as an adult woman, and he asks again whether the next week would be too soon to visit. Miranda's renunciation of the dream to enter into a courtship with Dr. Turner means that she is ready to accept motherhood correctly, not as mistress of the manor but as a homemaker, where, the film promises, "reality" will be its own reward.

The Resisting Maternal: *The Ghost and Mrs. Muir*

If *Dragonwyck* is about a woman learning to disavow her dreams to become a proper wife and mother, *The Ghost and Mrs. Muir* is about a mother who unapologetically surrenders to her dreams to satisfy her desires on her own terms. For this reason, I propose we think of this romantic fantasy as an example of what E. Ann Kaplan calls "the 'resisting' maternal woman's film." Whereas traditional films in the genre "comply passively with the dominant patriarchal mother-discourse,"

Kaplan contends that a cycle of U.S. films between 1930 and 1960 opened a space for the genre to "question or expose this discourse," including melodramas such as *Stella Dallas* and both versions of *Imitation of Life*. Unlike a "complicit" maternal woman's film, *The Ghost and Mrs. Muir* resists the nineteenth-century paradigm of the self-sacrificing mother (the "angel") versus the evil "phallic" mother (the "witch") to construct the maternal ideal. The narrative does not assume that the mother is "positioned by unconscious, mythic processes beyond her control" but rather "sees her positioned historically by social institutions (theoretically open to change)."[65] Lucy Muir (Tierney), the film's protagonist mother, moves with her daughter, Anna (Natalie Wood), and devoted housekeeper, Martha (Edna Best), to the English seaside village of Whitecliff after the death of her husband, Edwin, where she seeks to live unbound to the social expectations for a widowed mother in the early twentieth century (fig. 24).

Fig. 24. In *The Ghost and Mrs. Muir* (Joseph L. Mankiewicz, 1947), Tierney plays the widowed mother Lucy Muir, who raises her daughter, Anna (Natalie Wood), in the English seaside village of Whitecliff at the turn of the twentieth century.

The first line in the film states Lucy's intentions to move out of her London home, away from her mother-in-law, Eva (Victoria Horne), and grandmother-in-law Angelica (Isobel Elsom), who value her only as a reminder of Edwin. "And now my mind is made up," Lucy announces, more than a year after Edwin's death. Eva and Angelica accuse her of acting inappropriately for a bereaved woman, showing ingratitude to them and disrespect to her late husband, but Lucy asserts herself in what will be the first of a series of rebuttals to characters who impose unfair demands on her: "You mustn't think I'm not grateful. You've both been so very kind to me, but I'm not really a member of the family, except for marrying your son, and now he's gone. I have my own life to live, and you have yours, and they simply won't mix. I've never had a life of my own. It's been Edwin's life and yours and Eva's. Never my own." Eavesdropping from the kitchen, Martha and Anna are excited to join Lucy on what Martha calls a "bloomin' revolution."

As deeply as Lucy cares for Anna, she also refuses to be defined by motherhood alone. After moving into their new home, the supposedly haunted but very affordable Gull Cottage, Lucy helps Martha with the chores and confesses that she feels "useless," reflecting, "Here I am nearly halfway through life and what have I done?" Martha challenges Lucy's regret that she has "nothing to show" for the past years by reminding her of Anna, to which Lucy replies, "I can't take any credit for her. She just . . . happened!" The film will focus less on Lucy's work raising Anna, who is largely absent from the story, and more on her romantic and creative relationship with the ghost of Daniel Gregg (Rex Harrison), the blustery sea captain who used to live in Gull Cottage and died in his sleep after accidentally kicking on the gas that powers the heater in his bedroom.

Working together, they write a book called *Blood and Swash* based on Captain Gregg's seafaring adventures and Lucy publishes it under her name. Lucy's "unvarnished" biography of a sailor grabs the attention of a sexist editor, who praises it as "a man's book," admitting that he would have rather taken up sailing than "turning out indigestible reading matter for a bilious public" in order to support his mother and sisters. The editor is surprised by the coarse language of "such a nice-looking woman" and amazed she should know about a sailor's life, let alone a man such as Captain Gregg, initially assuming her writing is no different from the "twenty million discontented females in the British Isles" he imagines currently at work on a novel ("I've got to publish this bilge in order to stay in business," he shouts at their meeting, "but I don't have to read it!"). *Blood and Swash* proves enormously successful, and the royalties allow her to pay the rent on Gull Cottage. More significantly for Lucy, the experience of writing with Captain Gregg gives her the feeling of happiness and personal accomplishment for which she has searched.

The Ghost and Mrs. Muir was adapted from the novel of the same name by Josephine Leslie, who published under the pseudonym R. A. Dick out of concern that a female author's name would deter book sales,[66] and Fox acquired the rights to the novel the year it was published in 1945.[67] With multiple film authors involved in the adaptation (screenwriter Philip Dunne, director Joseph L. Mankiewicz, producer Fred Kohlmar, and Zanuck heading the studio's chain of command), German film critic Frieda Grafe makes the persuasive case that the production defies a straightforwardly auteurist assessment. As Mankiewicz believed that a film should be directed by its writer, he viewed the project as an "apprenticeship" under Zanuck to demonstrate his ability to direct a film with a script and actors assigned to him.[68] Meanwhile, Zanuck was interested in exploiting the popularity of ghost stories in the 1940s but wanted the film to establish a supernatural environment through literate means of dialogue and acting rather than visual effects.[69]

Conceived with a projected female audience, *The Ghost and Mrs. Muir* relies on the iconography of the Gothic melodrama at the same time as it subverts the genre's formula by eschewing the usually macabre atmosphere and infusing it with humor.[70] In Grafe's reading, "The old house [. . .] becomes [Lucy's] refuge from the prison of conventions. She has the feeling it wants to be rescued by her. Its ghost becomes her confidant and her accomplice in freeing herself from any fetters of marriage."[71] Despite the best efforts of her fastidious real estate agent, Mr. Coombe (Robert Coote), to dissuade her from renting Gull Cottage, Lucy finds the idea of a haunted house "perfectly fascinating." Lucy is hardly insulted when he calls her the most obstinate young woman he has ever met, retorting, "Thank you, Mr. Coombe. I've always wanted to be considered obstinate." Although director of photography Charles Lang received an Oscar nomination for Best Cinematography (Black-and-White) and some reviewers appreciated the whimsical take on the ghost story,[72] the film performed only moderately well at the box office.[73] Mrs. Muir and Captain Gregg later reappeared in public consciousness when Fox adapted the film for a sitcom starring Hope Lange and Edward Mulhare, which aired on NBC from 1968 to 1969 and ABC from 1969 to 1970, relocating the story to New England and updating the time period to the present (Lange won Emmys for both seasons).

The humor of the film was instrumental to its marketing as a supernatural-themed and sexually titillating romantic comedy starring Tierney and "Sexy Rexy," as Harrison was known at the time, but Fox's promotional strategy was also a mischaracterization of the actual film the studio released. Alison L. McKee, in her book *The Woman's Film of the 1940s*, discusses how the film's period setting, elegiac sense of lost time, and aching score by Bernard Herrmann are incongruous with advertising material that illustrates Tierney wearing a hairstyle and clothing consistent with 1940s fashions, as well as a tagline that reads, "The flesh . . . so weak! The spirit . . . so willing! Gene Tierney with taunt in her smile, Rex Harrison with that haunt in his kiss, and George Sanders without the ghost of a chance."[74] Halfway through the film, Sanders enters the story as the suave yet predatory author Miles Fairley (Lucy's editor also publishes his books), who becomes a rival of sorts for the captain. This active/male, passive/female dynamic in the advertisements casts Tierney as a body to behold and possess: the seductive though weak-willed object of competing male desires in a romantic triangle.

To render the novel's subjective qualities in more classically cinematic terms at the visual level, the filmmakers transformed Captain Gregg from a character who may exist only in Lucy's imagination or subconscious mind into a "real" ghost she can see, partly adapting to the conventions of the romantic "woman's film" of the studio era. The film comes close to acknowledging this issue in a self-reflexive way when Captain Gregg compares himself to the protocinematic illusion of a magic lantern slide, a literal projection. Yet what the film's marketing distorted was "both a mournful ineffability and a complex rendering of subjectivity and gender" that McKee sees as typical of the "ghost films" released during and after World War II.[75] Through its cinematography, editing, and score, she argues, the film links Lucy and Captain Gregg's subjectivities in sequences that "construct a diffused, sexually undifferentiated point of view that is often as much about space as bodies, and that both the camera and Herrmann's score articulate across the divide of gender difference."[76] Even while Captain Gregg appears to dictate his life story to Lucy as she writes *Blood and Swash*, she is not his stenographer, typist, or "ghostwriter" but a collaborator who shares in equal authorship over the book.[77] Lucy's editor is therefore more correct than he realizes when he asks whether she has been "empowered by the captain to act for him" in submitting his authorized biography for publication. The film's system of point of view and identification achieves what McKee calls "a kind of spectatorial androgyny." For example, Lucy adopts the captain's salty expressions in her everyday life ("blast!") and, in other moments, characters seem to hear the captain's outbursts through her. Captain Gregg, by contrast, is relegated to a stereotypically feminine position of "waiting and watching," sometimes as an invisible onlooker, always as a spiritual muse, without the ability to participate in the action himself.[78]

As the opening scene of the film illustrates, Lucy's moxie is not brought on by imitating Captain Gregg; to the contrary, the captain reflects and emboldens attitudes that she demonstrates prior to their relationship in the thrust-and-parry dialogue of Dunne's script. Lucy first defends herself against Eva's intimations that she is neglecting her maternal obligations to Anna by moving away from the Muir family in London:

> EVA: Lucy, have you considered Anna?
> LUCY: Yes, Eva, I have.
> EVA: And you're willing to take responsibility for what might become of her?
> LUCY: She's *my* daughter, Eva.
> EVA: And what do you mean by that?
> LUCY: Only what I said.
> EVA: You're insinuating that I interfere with Anna. Don't deny it, Lucy. Don't deny it, I say!
> LUCY: I'm not denying it, Eva.

When reviewing homes available for rent in Whitecliff, she contests Mr. Coombe's dismissal of Gull Cottage as a suitable option for her:

> LUCY: But if I'm going to live in the house, I should be the judge.

> MR. COOMBE: You'll only waste your time.
> LUCY: But it's *my* time.

Finally, when she meets Captain Gregg during her first night in the cottage, Lucy does not react in fear. He materialized earlier that afternoon while she napped in his bedroom, opening the window and observing her sleep, but Lucy awakened with the sensation of having had "a curious dream." Seeing him now for the first time, she rebukes him for trying to scare her away and then for doubting her competence:

> LUCY: I thought I dreamed it. Did you open the window to frighten me?
> CAPTAIN GREGG: I opened the window because I didn't want another accident with the blasted gas. Women are such fools.
> LUCY: You, of all people, should not have brought that up.
> CAPTAIN GREGG: I wouldn't call that remark in the best of taste.
> LUCY: Well, I'm sure it was very kind of you, but I am quite capable of taking care of myself.

What Eva interprets as selfishness and Mr. Coombe calls "obstinance," Captain Gregg admires as strength and self-possession, eventually nicknaming her "Lucia" because "women named Lucy are always being imposed upon." Touched by her commitment to Gull Cottage, he allows her to stay on a trial basis under the condition that she move his portrait to the primary bedroom, where he agrees to remain. He soon helps her expel her in-laws, who insist she return home to London when Edwin's gold mining shares stop paying dividends, and then rids her of a potential suitor in Mr. Coombe, who believes that a woman living in such an isolated location needs protection by the "right man."

In addition to revising the conventions of the Gothic melodrama, the film also reverses the "dream" narrative of *Laura*, with Tierney in the role of the haunted dreamer who falls in love with a character presumed dead. Captain Gregg's portrait and former dwelling may conjure a space of romantic fantasy similar to that in *Laura*, but *The Ghost and Mrs. Muir* rights the gendered imbalance of power between Laura and Mark by merging Lucy and the captain's subjectivities. To whatever degree Lucy is "awake" when she sees and hears Captain Gregg, the film never entirely discounts how she "dreams" him into being. The film is less concerned with delineating dreams from reality than with showing how they comingle as Lucy attempts to navigate her new life as a single mother and writer, charting a course for herself at the beginning of the twentieth century. Prior to beginning their collaboration on *Blood and Swash*, Captain Gregg assures her, "I'm here because you believe I'm here. And keep on believing and I'll always be real to you." Therefore, he is not so much an object of obsession for Lucy that she wishes to control but a projection of her desires, personifying them in a more socially acceptable voice and body. Lucy relates to his spirit of adventure, yearning to live beyond what the conventions of Victorian femininity have allowed her as an "Angel in the House," while he is sympathetic to her as a fellow outsider, feeling misunderstood and taken for granted when he was a seaman.

Although Captain Gregg admits his attraction to Lucy, their relationship completely depends on emotional intimacy since it can never be consummated physically, a condition made explicit by their sleeping together, as it were, in the primary bedroom of Gull Cottage. Correctly surmising that her marriage to Edwin was a loveless one, Captain Gregg shows an understanding that no other character affords her. Lucy recounts how Edwin was an architect working on an addition to her father's library and she accepted his marriage proposal after he kissed her in the family orchard. Then only seventeen years old, she expected the "happily ever after" ending of the novel she had just finished "in which the heroine was kissed in the rose garden" but grew disappointed to realize that Edwin was content to live without passions or achievements ("I'm afraid he wasn't even a very good architect," she muses). Captain Gregg, however, has engaged in a variety of aesthetic pursuits during his lifetime: he designed Gull Cottage, which he hoped to convert into a home for retired seamen; he tended its garden, where he planted his cherished "monkey puzzle tree"; and he read Romantic poetry, at one point quoting "Ode to a Nightingale," Keats's meditation on death and transcendence. What is more, when Lucy worries about the uncertainty of her future after completing *Blood and Swash*, he loves her enough to encourage her to see other men. He materializes while she sleeps to tell her that she has been "dreaming," that she wrote the book alone and imagined him from his portrait, the seaside cottage, and the maritime belongings he left behind.

This disavowal of the dream does not give *The Ghost and Mrs. Muir* the resolution found at the end of *Dragonwyck* but instead leaves its maternal protagonist adrift in the melancholy of "reality." Miles Fairley, the other man in the film, is paradoxically never a realistic alternative to Captain Gregg despite being "real"—Lucy's only justification to Martha for why she might marry him. When they first meet at their mutual publisher, Miles's impression of Lucy is no less sexist than the other men in the film whose assumptions Lucy disabuses; he gathers she must be the author of a cookbook, a biography of Romantic poet Lord Byron, or a "book of social graces." In certain respects, he is correct when he guesses she has written "a book of dreams," but his glib tone speaks to his phallocentric and logocentric disdain for such an endeavor. Quipping that he does not share the "weakness for feminine literature" that he figures their editor has developed, he tells her that he is "surprised to find a lady author infinitely more exciting than her heroine could possibly be."

Miles's contempt for his own genre—children's literature—obviously identifies him as the villain of the film. Despite how Lucy rationalizes his "forward" behavior as a symptom of the twentieth century ("we must rid ourselves of the old fetishes and taboos," she declares to Martha), he does not entirely fool her. Lucy describes him to Martha as "conceited and erratic, even childish," but she also cannot deny her loneliness, her desire for "companionship and laughter and . . . all the things a woman needs." When she turns up at his London home to surprise him, she discovers that he is already married with children of his own, confirming that Miles wants only to satisfy his sexual desire for an affair. Mrs. Fairley (Anna Lee) responds to Lucy's embarrassed apology for her "mistake" by empathetically apologizing to her, acknowledging that "it isn't the first time something like this has happened," and Lucy returns to Gull Cottage alone. Convinced that her relationship with Captain Gregg has been a series of dreams, she nevertheless hopes to see him rematerialize in their bedroom, but she will not see him again until she dies years later.

The third act of the film depicts the end of Lucy's life in Whitecliff as Anna (now grown and played by Vanessa Brown) comes home from college with her fiancé, a sublieutenant in the British Royal Navy. Reintroducing Anna neither reinscribes a traditional family unit, with a young, semipatriarchal couple of the 1940s ousting the matriarchy of Gull Cottage, nor does it force Lucy into a traditional maternal role, investing in the "reality" of her daughter's life to secure her happiness at the expense of her own. Rather, Anna's arrival affirms Lucy's fantasy when they both realize they shared the same dreams during their first year at Gull Cottage. Anna attributes her lifelong "weakness for sailormen" to the "dream game" she used to play as a child, talking to the ghost of Captain Gregg with whom she was "hopelessly in love" but who stopped visiting her as she grew older. Lucy is shocked by this bittersweet revelation, inferring that she must have relayed her own dreams about the captain to Anna at an impressionable age. Even as Anna entertains the possibility that Captain Gregg was real, Lucy reiterates that they both "made him up." The film's narrative verifies neither Lucy's nor Anna's versions, but the truth of one is less important than what transpires between the two women in their reunion: the strengthening of a mother–daughter bond through their recognition of their *mutual* desires that Captain Gregg has represented for them both. "She'll have her own way," Martha remarks about Anna, "same as her mother." Martha too seems to have shared Lucy's dream, teasing Anna that her fiancé is "only a lieutenant" when she herself would prefer a captain.

In keeping with the conventions of the 1940s Hollywood fantasy film, *The Ghost and Mrs. Muir* approaches Lucy's death not as final but as an extension of her existence on earth. This ending also reconnects her with her inner life, redeeming the role of fantasy in shaping her experience of reality. Lucy declines Anna's request to move in with her, wishing to remain in her own home until she dies ("You can be much more alone with other people than you are by yourself," she explains, "even if it's people you love"). She maintains that she was not meant for conventional happiness but has taken solace in Anna, Martha, and Gull Cottage, adding that she still has her memories, "even if it was a dream." However ambivalent Lucy may sound in her conclusion, the film upholds this sentiment as she sits in the same chair where she first dreamed of the captain and drifts off to sleep for the last time. Captain Gregg awakens her as the younger "Lucia," and she leaves her aged body behind to walk with him arm in arm through the doors of Gull Cottage. Enveloped by the Whitecliff fog, the couple disappear into the night, and Lucy enters a misty dream from which she will happily never return.

The resisting maternal image of *The Ghost and Mrs. Muir* does not supersede the more romanticized images of mothers in *Dragonwyck* (as vulnerable and dependent on men) and *Heaven Can Wait* (as a guardian angel for men) but exists alongside these representations in the same way that Tierney's publicity reflected contradictory expectations for working mothers in the mid-1940s. Tierney was a woman who parlayed her skills into a successful career and supposedly enjoyed work outside the home at the same time that she remained committed to homemaking, a pursuit that became even more encouraged after the war. Publicity would have fans believe that these traditional feminine roles of wife and mother provided her with true happiness and also sustained the well-being of her family. So naturalized was this construction of the white middle-class family that the story of Daria would threaten its presumed invincibility rather than reinforce the qualities of maternal love and labor that the culture actively promoted. By the 1950s, the events of Tierney's private life proved impossible to conceal, and a new narrative would need to be written. Psychologically unwell, she would be affixed to a public identity based on the struggle to attain the very family-domestic ideal she was thought to possess.

4

Into the Whirlpool

Psychological Disorder and Rehabilitation

The first indications of Tierney's mental illness presented themselves well before the public learned about her psychiatric treatments in the late 1950s. At the age of twenty, she was diagnosed with "a chronic nervous stomach" that gave her attacks of debilitating pain, which she later documented in her autobiography.[1] Participating in wartime bond tours, she also experienced "seizures of stage fright" that overcame her when "having to make an unscripted talk to ordinary people." The way she described it, "As long as I was playing someone else, I was fine. When I had to be myself, my problems began."[2] She became fully aware of her illness, though, when she fell into a depression on location in Argentina shooting *Way of a Gaucho* (Jacques Tourneur, 1952).[3]

Following her divorce from Cassini later that year, she felt that "keeping busy" would cure her.[4] Tierney received custody over her second daughter, Christina (Cassini had visitation rights), but shared joint custody of her first daughter, Daria.[5] Over the next three years, Tierney starred in six more films: for MGM, she played one of the Mayflower Pilgrims in *Plymouth Adventure* (Clarence Brown, 1952) and a Russian ballerina in the Cold War romance *Never Let Me Go* (Delmer Daves, 1953); for the British production company Two Cities Films, she played a woman whose schoolteacher husband is suspected of murdering an infatuated female student in *Personal Affair* (Anthony Pelissier, 1953); and for Fox, she played a respected Broadway actress in the posh whodunit *Black Widow* (Nunnally Johnson, 1954), an ancient Egyptian princess in the historical epic *The Egyptian* (Michael Curtiz, 1954), and a U.S. missionary nurse embroiled in the Chinese civil war in *The Left Hand of God* (Edward Dmytryk, 1955).[6] After spending more than a decade under contract at the studio, Fox still had not learned how to "type" her and was content to cast the star in nearly every popular genre or production trend at the time. "I tried to work harder and harder," she confessed in her autobiography, "thinking that would cure everything. All it did was make things worse."[7] Fox planned to cast her in another film, but she wrote that when she left Hollywood for New York City, where her mother kept an apartment, the studio assumed her departure was a "walk out" and suspended her for "being prima-donna-ish."[8]

In 1954, while rehearsing for an episode of the CBS anthology drama *General Electric Theater*—an adaptation of Henrik Ibsen's *A Doll's House* in which she would play Nora—she suffered what the press later called a "nervous breakdown" and withdrew from the series. It was announced that she had a viral infection.[9] Articles came out with the information that she moved back to her remodeled childhood home in Connecticut to be with her family.[10] Columnist Cobina Wright reported that she then took "a long rest" and spent a year "regaining her health after an illness," "several unhappy personal experiences," and "a long series of pictures" that left her "simply exhausted."[11] Tierney actually underwent an estimated total of thirty-two electroconvulsive treatment (ECT) sessions at Harkness Pavilion in New York City and the Institute of Living in Hartford, Connecticut.[12]

By the end of 1957, she had attempted suicide on the ledge of her mother's Manhattan apartment facing the Sutton Place neighborhood and right across from the building where Marilyn Monroe lived with her husband, Arthur Miller. When a neighbor reported the incident to the police, Tierney and her mother covered it up by claiming that they had decided to wash the windows; shortly thereafter, her mother checked her into the Menninger Clinic, then located in Topeka, Kansas.[13] At Menninger, she was subjected to a form of hydrotherapy known as a "cold pack," which involved binding the patient from the neck down in wet ice-cold blankets for a period of thirty minutes.[14] Upon her discharge, talk of future projects gave renewed attention to her career, which had been on hold since *The Left Hand of God*. Fox slated her to star in the comedy *Holiday for Lovers* (Henry Levin, 1959) as the wife of a psychologist (Clifton Webb),[15] and CBS gave her the opportunity to reprise her role in the teleplay of *A Doll's House*.[16] Both parts were recast, however, when she was admitted to Menninger again in 1959 and reemerged in the Topeka neighborhood of Westboro as a part-time salesgirl at Talmage's Ladies

Apparel Shop.[17] Working short, irregular hours, the thirty-eight-year-old star brought an upsurge in business to the chic local clothier.[18]

Beginning in 1958, Tierney's treatment received widespread press coverage in publications ranging from the general-circulation magazine *Life* to the fan magazine *Modern Screen* to the women's confession magazine *True Confessions*. Articles framed her as a "troubled beauty"[19] and attributed her years of depression to her "hopeless" situation as a wife and mother,[20] who "struggled to be a normal woman" only to be "Hollywood's unluckiest star."[21] Not only had she been ill for the past six or seven years, the press confirmed, but she had suffered a series of "emotional blows" beginning with the birth of a disabled child.[22] Almost ten years after Daria's birth, Tierney and Cassini had divorced. And in 1954, the year she withdrew from *General Electric Theater*, her fiancé, Ali Salman Aga Khan ("Aly Khan"), reportedly called off their wedding. The wealthy Muslim prince was a celebrity in his own right and had been previously married to Rita Hayworth. *True Confessions* referred to these events in Tierney's life as "one failure after another."[23]

Just as the previous three chapters challenged the assumption that Tierney was significant only as an aesthetic object of beauty, this chapter argues that to understand her as a pitiable victim of personal tragedy only reframes her as an equally passive star. The constructed subjectivity evident in the press coverage of her treatment shows a star struggling to negotiate (however unsuccessfully) a double bind between a stereotypical role as wife/mother and a professional who could recover from her illness simply by working through it. Compounded by the 1978 publication of her autobiography *Self-Portrait*, a best seller that revived interest in her films from the 1940s, the discursive signs of her labor established a new set of interpretive strategies to read her work that continues to circulate. To that end, in the second half of this chapter, I will turn to *Whirlpool* (Otto Preminger, 1950), a film in which Tierney played a character suffering from a psychological disorder.

Gene Tierney Reframed: Publicity and Press Commentary

Tierney's public image at the end of the 1950s provides an example of how a star is recuperated within particular ideological determinants (according to discourses on female labor and mental health) and at a particular historical moment (during the last years of the Classical Hollywood era, when studio-controlled publicity began to give way to star gossip). The press wrote a comeback narrative for her that identified her mental illness as a female illness and *work* as the source of psychological rehabilitation. By aligning her image with professional acting (as opposed to the "natural" charisma of stardom), this narrative redefined social roles for women in the postwar era in terms alternative to the domestic sphere and yet also reinscribed a traditional construction of femininity by attributing Tierney's illness to marital and maternal trauma, precipitating the need to get back to work. What we find is a reconciliation of work, on the one hand, and marriage and motherhood, on the other, masking a social expectation for women to "work through" illness to prove their professional capabilities.[24] This process stabilized Tierney's star image at a moment of potential disturbance.

Members of Hollywood appear to have known that Tierney was to some degree unwell, but it is unclear whether her illness was an open secret exactly. Jules Dassin, the director of the London-based film noir *Night and the City* (1950), said that Zanuck called him to request he create a larger role for the minor character of Mary Bristol, the girlfriend of Richard Widmark's hustler-cum-boxing promoter. Quoting Dassin, "Zanuck called me, and said, you owe me one. I want you to cast Gene Tierney . . . she's just had a bad time, a very unhappy love affair and she's rather suicidal and she needs us to help."[25] Dassin seems to be referring to her separation from Cassini between 1946 and 1948, prior to their temporary reconciliation that resulted in the birth of Christina. Tierney's own stories about the films that followed show how her illness took its toll during productions. Describing herself as "snappish and rude" on the *Way of a Gaucho* shoot, she insisted that she was not liked: "I was impatient with the hairdresser, critical of the director, annoyed by the chatter of the crew."[26] Accompanied by her mother, Christina, and a nurse while filming *Never Let Me Go* in England, she "was still subject to abrupt personality changes." For example, when her costar Clark Gable joined them for lunch in the hotel dining room and the band began to play the theme from *Laura* (Otto Preminger, 1944), she was convinced the band was making fun of her.[27] While filming *Personal Affair*, she struggled to remember her lines, and on the set of *Black Widow* she experienced face blindness with people she had known for years.[28] By the time she was acting in *The Left Hand of God*, her costar Humphrey Bogart recognized the signs of mental illness from his sister.[29] He warned the studio bosses about Tierney's condition and helped her through the production with "patience and understanding" (at the time, he was going through his own health problems with esophageal cancer).[30]

Earlier publicity and press commentary characterized Tierney in ways that might be taken as coded, unconscious, or inadvertent references to her mental and emotional distress. Published three months before her departure in 1954, an article in *Movieland* about "Gene's destiny" reads almost as preemptive damage control on the part of Fox.[31] Author Fredda Dudley Balling quoted the following "outcry" from Tierney: "Why CAN'T I be anonymous? Why can't I do the simple things other people do without attracting attention?"[32] Ostensibly referring to Tierney's futile attempt to bargain-hunt in Rome "as merely another American tourist," Balling added, "The things she most wants sometimes seem to be the things she can't have." Most of the story considered her possible marriage to Aly Khan following her divorce from Cassini. After Tierney initially turned down the playboy prince for dates, one of her friends reportedly told her, "I think you're crazy not to give a date or two to such a terrific guy!" Balling replied, "Who wants to be considered crazy?"[33] Finally, in the article's most protective move, it promised readers that "whether they marry or not there is one thing certain: Gene will emerge in company with light laughter. She has no time, or use, for tears."[34] The article created continuity with another interview Balling published six years earlier in *Silver Screen* titled "Laugh or Go Mad." Here, Tierney revealed her secret to withstanding her stresses as "one of the most popular human beings in Hollywood, not only in her own circle of friends, but with studio employees and with the press." As a "constantly in demand" star, she told the magazine, "I laugh and preserve my balance." She spoke of "certain times when only laughter could have kept a person from grabbing the nearest pair of trophy horns and gorging someone to death, or hurling himself from the Alps."[35] On the cover, she appeared with Tyrone Power in a promotional image for their comedy *That Wonderful Urge* (Robert B. Sinclair, 1948), looking only madly in love.

Other articles had addressed rumors about her tempestuous marriage to Cassini. One of the most curious examples was a column published in the *Hollywood Reporter* as early as 1945, purportedly written by Tierney herself, that denied the existence of a "mad room" in their home. As she explained to readers, "I'm just an ordinary gal who gets angry once in a while. My mads take on a peculiar, but far from violent flavor." She elaborated with the following: "When I get a mad-on, I don't throw things; I don't cry; I don't shout, much—though any of those symptoms would probably be the fastest way out of a mad-jag. I do talk a blue streak about whatever has annoyed me, until I have exhausted myself. Then I generally laugh helplessly and I am over it. But I don't need or have a special room to explode in!"[36] While separated from Cassini, her marriage came under even closer scrutiny. Cassini's brother was credited as the author of a *Modern Screen* article that attributed the couple's separation to their different careers, incompatible schedules, and mutual pressures as public figures, which led to "heated arguments."[37] Another article in *Modern Screen* titled "Miss Tierney Regrets" described her as "depressed" both during and after her separation but added that she remains focused on "her career and her daughter and her home" and therefore regrettably declines marriage proposals.[38]

The separation between Tierney and Cassini broke in 1946 with stories of a "spat" and rumored "rift."[39] Louella Parsons predicted that "divorce will probably be only a matter of days now," reminding readers of Tierney's trip to New York City for an extended period after she and Cassini "quarreled violently."[40] Accusing Cassini of "cruelty" that inflicted "grievous mental suffering," Tierney filed suit for divorce in 1947.[41] Cassini had a "violent temper," she said, citing an incident in which he threw a hot spoon at her (although missed contact). The abuses with which she charged him were not only physical. At a party they hosted at their house, according to the *Los Angeles Examiner*, Cassini spent the evening dancing with ten women whom he knew Tierney disliked and whom he demanded she invite.[42] In her words, "Oleg loved to give parties but never helped with them. He always came as a guest. [. . .] He expected me to be a gay wife and a hard-working actress at the same time. I told him I just couldn't do it."[43] The divorce was not finalized, and in a 1948 column published after their reconciliation, Hedda Hopper described "a wistful sort of sadness" in the star, who "seemed lonely." With rumors that Fox found her "difficult to handle," that she "developed a loathing for Hollywood and the acting profession," and that she had a "secret romance in

New York," Hopper gave Tierney a chance to explain that she traveled to New York during the separation to see her family in the Northeast, including her daughter. Tierney told Hopper that Daria stays with her sister and her children, as her disabilities were then unknown to the public.[44]

Some of these rumors may have been stoked by her temporary suspension at Fox. Although Tierney had been reportedly "designated as the First Lady of the studio" by 1947, Fox put her on suspension for turning down the "woman's film" melodrama *The Walls of Jericho* (John M. Stahl, 1948). The film would have starred her alongside Cornel Wilde, Linda Darnell, and Kirk Douglas in the role that went to Anne Baxter.[45] After *Anna and the King of Siam* (John Cromwell, 1946), *Forever Amber* (Otto Preminger, 1947), and *Chicken Every Sunday* (George Seaton, 1949), it was the fourth film she refused.[46] When John Ford was preparing to shoot *Mogambo* (1953) in Africa, she also declined the role that went to Grace Kelly, not wanting to separate from Christina for six months or travel abroad with a small child.[47] Nevertheless, she maintained a reputation as an agreeable star while under contract.[48] Well into the 1940s, publicity championed her as a star with a "kind heart and devotion to duty."[49] As she later reflected in *Self-Portrait*, "Perhaps I should have been less anxious to avoid a fight, and refused more scripts than I did. But I was not cut out to be a rebel. Those instincts that made me vulnerable in private served me well in my work. The studio bosses liked the fact that I was not difficult. The public perceived me, I think, as a nice person and held me blameless."[50] In addition, she pointed out how a doctor informed her that a "more tranquil life" would have kept her "weakness," as he referred to it, in abeyance.[51]

It is difficult to determine how much of the press coverage and interviews with Tierney after 1958 represented Tierney speaking for herself, how much represented gossip journalism, and how much represented the studio's public relations campaign to defuse a potential scandal over its well-liked star. A combination of the three was likely at work. What I find more compelling is how that ambiguity only amplifies the contradictions in Tierney's stardom and the construction of her subjectivity as a woman negotiating the contradictions in her social and psychic life during the 1950s.

Associated Press journalist Cynthia Lowry wrote three articles in November of 1958—published a day apart from one another—that show the somewhat strange incongruities this discourse held in tension. Quick to absolve the studio of any responsibility, Lowry's story in the *New York Daily Magazine* declared, "Her mental breakdown [. . .] cannot be scored as another black mark against the film city and its frantic mores." The quotes attributed to Tierney suggest a kind of internalization of the attitudes toward her illness as a "weakness," concealing the systemic power in studio and star relationships that encouraged stars to comply with exploitative labor practices. "Perhaps the most important lesson I had to learn was to admit and accept defeat," she said. "I had to learn to say, 'I can't solve that: I give up.'"[52] Lowry's second article, published in the *New York Post*, focused exclusively on the circumstances of Daria's birth and Tierney's love life, but here Tierney's own words problematize the implication that she was simply a victim of unhappy events. In refusing to blame Cassini as the cause of her depression, she also resisted being an object of romantic pity: "'I was already very ill mentally when I met him,' the actress says. '[The divorce] may have speeded things up a little, but it didn't bring it on. I was due for a collapse.'"[53] The third and most nuanced of the articles, published in the *Newark Evening News*, suggested that Tierney was not a defeated star who "had to learn" to know when to "give up" but a woman who gained "maturity" by realizing the importance of reclaiming her agency. Tierney explained that "maturity means not doing anything I feel I'm not up to. It means eliminating from my life people who affect me unpleasantly; it means to have no truck at all with those who upset me emotionally, who make me angry or frustrated, or boil me up. I must not allow myself to get into situations where I feel trapped." At the end of the article, Lowry addressed Tierney's new commitment to spreading awareness about mental illness and raising funds to help the majority of the population unable to afford it.[54]

Most articles presented Tierney's illness less as an *illness* than a gendered condition of individual problems, relying on vague, indirect language. A September 1958 issue of *Life* featured a story titled "Welcome for a Troubled Beauty" with her announcement, "I am back in town and available for work."[55] Tierney embraced director George Cukor at Paramount in one photograph captioned, "It's great to see you back. You are looking marvelous." In another, she received a kiss on the cheek from Samuel J. Briskin, chief of studio operations at Columbia; this caption read, "'You haven't changed a bit,' he said. 'Let's find something for you.'"[56]

Additional photographs depicted Tierney sitting in a camera operator's chair at Fox to observe a rehearsal for *The Sound and the Fury* (Martin Ritt, 1959) and visiting with the film's star, Joanne Woodward.[57] The article concluded, however, with the story of "the birth of an abnormal baby"—Tierney's contraction of rubella, Daria's disabilities, the revelation about the infected fan—and called this experience "Gene Tierney's first wound."[58] Good publicity for Tierney's Hollywood homecoming also made her mental illness legible by eliding the contradictory demands of women's work in the public sphere and motherhood in the private sphere, tacitly defining women's psychology primarily within the realm of the maternal and reinforcing the social pressures on women's public and private roles. Similar articles ran throughout the year with headlines such as "Gene Tierney Back at Job," "Reborn Star," "Gene Eager for Film Work," and "Gene Tierney Gets a Second Chance," with little discussion of how to improve women's mental health care and destigmatize mental illness.[59]

On the surface, there may be something "positive" about this story of a woman apparently overcoming an illness and returning to work, but this particular comeback narrative fails to imagine a possibility in which Tierney could live a happy life as a woman raising a disabled daughter. According to the social expectations of motherhood, having an "abnormal baby" would make Tierney an "abnormal mother," so Tierney can be affirmed only for returning to work in a role other than a maternal one. It would be wrong to assume that the condition of Daria's birth was itself a trauma that created Tierney's psychological disorder (what the comeback narrative suggests). As she later acknowledged in *Self-Portrait*, "[T]he main cause of my difficulties stemmed from the tragedy of my daughter's unsound birth and my inability to face my feelings." The last part of this statement is key: Tierney's mental illness made it impossible for her to "face [her] feelings" adequately about Daria's situation and it was *this* emotional impasse that caused her to suffer. Tierney dedicated an entire chapter to Daria in *Self-Portrait* wherein she describes the guilt she experienced after making the difficult decision to place Daria in a care facility. In addition to feeling anxiety over the "social taboo" of childhood-intellectual disabilities, Tierney also resented that she had been "cheated" out of a daughter and that Daria had been deprived of privileges afforded to other children.[60] The insistence upon Tierney's return to work therefore misses the point. "My kind of mental illness is a stress disease. The problem is in the blood, in the chemical balance," she asserted.[61]

Domestic concerns of mother–daughter relationships were also coterminous with ideas about heteronormative romance in Tierney's star biography at the end of the 1950s. A December 1958 article in *Modern Screen* titled "Gene Tierney Comes Home" took a three-pronged approach, highlighting "a hopeless baby," "a hopeless marriage," and "a hopeless love" as its (now familiar) principle concerns (fig. 25).[62] Aly, her "hopeless love," had been romantically linked to Tierney in 1953, and rumors of their impending engagement provided grist for the Hollywood gossip mill.[63] Refusing to blame him for her illness, Tierney later told the *New York Journal-American* that they never realistically planned to marry and called him a close friend who knew she was "in no [mental] state for an international social life."[64] Yet the end of their royal affair was acknowledged as the final blow that broke the fragile Tierney, as if to narrativize her experience in the form of a fairy tale. A story in the *Los Angeles Examiner*, for example, included a photograph of the couple with the caption, "Breakup of their romance left Gene Tierney despondent.

Fig. 25. "Gene Tierney Comes Home," *Modern Screen* (December 1958). Courtesy of Media History Digital Library.

Now the actress, ill, is confined and the dashing Aly Khan is long gone."[65] Other stories elaborated on the breakup, such as a *Los Angeles Times* item that commented how Aly's father, Sultan Mahomed Shah, Aga Khan III, threatened to disinherit his son if he and Tierney were to wed.[66]

Even after Aly's death in 1960, *Photoplay* turned to his breakup with Tierney once again. A feature article rehearsed the series of events in her life that were thought to have led her to seek treatment, culminating in "the words, 'I cannot marry you.'" The story recounted a night in which Tierney allegedly sat alone in a nightclub, deliberately removed long white gloves from her hands one finger at a time, and then put them back on with equal care. Dazed from Aly's rejection, the story went, Tierney performed this ritual over and over again.[67] While this article claimed that Tierney first looked at her former lover's death as a bad omen, having been recently discharged from Menninger for the second time, it also reassured readers that she has discovered new love in Texas oil tycoon Howard Lee and a newfound sense of solace.[68] The couple had married in July of 1960 following Lee's divorce from Hedy Lamarr.

Despite the feminine-domestic ideal promoted in the maternal and romantic images of U.S. mass culture after World War II, Adrienne L. McLean and other film and cultural historians have shown that women did, in fact, work outside the home in the postwar era. Following the influx of women in the workforce during the war, women remained working at a gradual increase after the war even if they traded their "war jobs" for service or clerical positions.[69] However, as McLean elucidates in *Being Rita Hayworth*, star-making was based on "basic tenets of middle-class respectability," and for studios to market stars as ordinary, promotion and publicity demanded "that all stars *want* to be married and *should* be married because they are always so ordinary."[70] Female stars therefore modeled the problems of the middle-class wives and mothers who were still held to the standards of hegemonic domestic ideology in their pursuit of a career. For instance, Hayworth was forced to raise her children as a single mother after her divorce from actor and singer Dick Haymes. The press viewed her career as both an interference with her responsibilities as a mother and her only means with which to work as her family's provider. In other words, McLean argues, Hayworth was "urged to stay home and to stop working *at the same time* that her career is named as being all that she has left with which to support herself and her children."[71] With Tierney, we see repeated assertions of her status as a professional actor, and in certain respects that discourse probably reflected Tierney's desires to keep her illness private and "go back to work" (i.e., to prove her professional capability after an illness in order to be taken seriously). Being a dutiful employee of the studio was expected and had been rewarded, and she owed Fox one last film to fulfill her contract obligations. "My illness was a curable one," she wrote in *Self-Portrait*, "not cancer or something worse. I was responsible for it, not anyone else."[72] At the same time, though, the press could not recognize an identity independent from Daria, Cassini, and Aly.

The coverage of Tierney's treatment also coincided with a larger U.S. cultural interest in psychoanalytic therapy that gained ground in the press and peaked in the late 1950s, including discussions of psychoanalytic theories and practices, as well as magazine features on "pop psychology" aimed at middle-class housewives. In her book *Couching Resistance*, Janet Walker explains that psychiatry expanded after World War II from servicemen to both male and female civilians. Walker claims that the "feminine adjustment" in postwar psychiatry, or the "process of fitting a woman into a rigid gender stereotype," emphasized women's roles as wives and mothers, which "often amounted to a prescription of exclusive domesticity" authorized by the institution of "objective" medical science and promoted through mass culture to justify the social oppression of women.[73]

Although women's psychological problems dominated popular discourse on psychiatry, men equaled if not outnumbered women as psychiatric patients.[74] Veterans helped legitimize psychiatry for the public as "more deserving patients emerging from wartime experience" rather than the insane and the disenfranchised, but Walker points out that women's stories were more prominent for two reasons: (1) the postwar bias against men's expressions of vulnerability or admission of illness and, more significant, (2) the way in which psychiatry reinforced society's assumption that "the problem of woman" is the only problem that cannot be disavowed.[75] Thus, while not discounting the actual mental illness of women or what she phrases the "very real adverse psychological effects of women's inequality," Walker makes clear that "certain psychiatric discursive practices themselves were motivated by and even contributed to the attribution of illness to women."[76]

A series of *New York Journal-American* interviews with Tierney published in November 1958 shows how the influence of this psychiatric discourse set certain terms for interpreting Tierney's rehabilitation. Journalist Phyllis Battelle described her as Menninger's "most beautiful patient, but possibly one of their most emotionally repressed," as well as "a romanticist and a dreamer—and ever an optimist." Battelle reported that doctors instructed Tierney to cry in order to confront memories from her past, beginning with her estrangement from her father, Howard Tierney Sr., that followed the breach-of-contract suit he brought against her at the start of her career.[77] Until she turned twenty-one, her contract with Fox was to be not in her name but rather in that of Belle Tier Corporation, the holding company her father had set up for her (and had named after her mother, Belle Tierney) to administer her finances. Gene allocated a quarter of her total earnings to Belle Tier, as did her parents, brother, and sister, which allowed her immediate family to share the company's profits evenly. Each member of the family codirected the company, but her father served as president. Unbeknownst to the rest of the family, he also held complete control of the company stock, as he retained 51 percent of the stock in his own name. After eloping with Cassini at the age of twenty, Tierney, as a married woman, was eligible to manage her own career, so Fox drew up a new contract. Tierney's father still felt that Belle Tier was her rightful agent, but the suit was supposedly thrown out of court.[78] Immediately after her parents divorced in 1942, her father married a woman with whom he was having an affair, and Gene saw him for one of the last times in his life.[79]

Tierney grew up in an Episcopalian home of New England Republicans, and the public was already aware of her family drama that began as early as 1941 when her marriage to Cassini met with the staunch disapproval of her parents. Her mother told reporters that she was "just a misguided child [. . .] carried away by this suave man of the world."[80] As Fox's 1943 biography summarized the events, Howard "instigated a smear campaign in the press, slandered Cassini both mentally and morally, accused him of being a fortune-hunter and even attempted to get the marriage annulled."[81] During Tierney's courtship with Cassini, Howard wrote to her threatening to declare her mentally unstable if they were to marry.[82] Adela Rogers St. Johns published an article in the *Los Angeles Examiner* about these "love troubles," predicting that "her experience—maybe heartbreak—passion—her first battle with the world" could turn her into "a great actress, a woman of real courage and deep emotion."[83] When Belle Tier went bankrupt in 1941, Louella Parsons wrote how "an unhappy Gene Tierney" was unable to save her parents' home from foreclosure (not yet established in her career under her new contract, she herself was "broke" and owed taxes on her past salary).[84] It was Gene's turn to sue Howard, claiming he embezzled the money she made under her old contract. A quarter of her total earnings went to Belle Tier, but Howard supposedly set aside the other 75 percent for her in a trust fund. She received no returns on what she put in the company, and what he saved for her had vanished. The court ruled in favor of Howard, who appeared in court with financial records that accounted for how "every cent of this money had been spent on her in one way or another."[85] According to Gene's version, he had stolen from her to save his sinking business right before his divorce from her mother.[86]

In Battelle's configuration of Gene's relationship with Cassini, he became a substitute for her father, but her divorce from Cassini was therefore made doubly traumatic as it registered with the loss of her father that she already felt. Battelle went as far as to refer to Cassini as "her first therapist" in that "he was someone to talk to and confide in" for Tierney at a young age.[87] The comparison of Cassini to therapist locates this story not only in postwar ideologies of marriage but also in representations of psychiatry itself, which imagined women in need of and dependent on protection from patriarchal authority figures. We have seen how the studio discursively functioned as benevolent patriarchal family structure for Tierney, and here both Cassini and the institution of psychiatry fulfill similar roles.

The last of Battelle's interviews told readers that Fox kept her on salary during her three years of treatment. Despite the two to three years the doctors anticipated for a recovery at Menninger, "she was out—and pronounced cured—in eight months." Tierney insisted she did not want "to capitalize on [her illness]" but believed her experience would make her "a better actress." Prior to her treatment, she said she thought women who cried easily were "terribly weak," but now, she remarked, "I weep like crazy. Like a weak woman should. I'm normal." As she prepared for her comeback, Battelle quoted her saying that her "main problem" was "to take off weight."[88]

Not until 1960 did she make her return to the screen (after her release from Menninger the second time). Starring on an episode of *General Electric Theater*, it was also a return to the same series she had left six years earlier, albeit a different episode.[89] The last time audiences would have seen her on television was in 1957, immediately before her first stay in Menninger, when she appeared on the CBS panel show *What's My Line?* as a mystery guest. Fox then signed her to play Constance MacKenzie in *Return to Peyton Place* (José Ferrer, 1961) but replaced her with Eleanor Parker when she had a miscarriage.[90] Tierney's first film credit since *The Left Hand of God* came with *Advise & Consent* (Otto Preminger, 1962), a political drama helmed by the director of *Laura*, who cast her as a Washington society hostess. Here was the film that "br[ought] Gene Tierney back from retirement," or so the marketing proclaimed, directed by "the man who helped to launch her as a star."[91] The following year, she played the aristocratic mother-in-law of a newlywed ne'er-do-well in *Toys in the Attic* (George Roy Hill, 1963), an adaptation of Lillian Hellman's Southern Gothic play set among a dysfunctional New Orleans family. Heralding "a triumphal return to the screen as a portrayer of strong dramatic roles," promotion for the film credited her performance in *Advise & Consent* as the basis for her casting.[92]

Neither *Advise & Consent* nor *Toys in the Attic* led to Tierney's portended comeback, and as they were both independent productions, she was still beholden to her contract with Fox for one last feature. The runaway production *The Pleasure Seekers* (Jean Negulesco, 1964) was to be her final film released theatrically. A hip musical set in Madrid, the film follows a trio of young women from the United States looking for love and excitement on their tour abroad. Tierney, billed as a "guest star," had evidently passed the torch to a new generation of sex symbols: Ann-Margret, Carol Lynley, and Pamela Tiffin. At the age of forty-four, she more or less began her retirement in Houston, where she lived with Lee for the rest of her life, although she did show up in small parts on three television programs: ABC's *The F.B.I.*, guest starring in a 1969 episode as a witness to a murder who is unknowingly targeted by the Cosa Nostra; *Daughter of the Mind* (Walter Grauman, 1969), an "ABC Movie of the Week" produced by Twentieth Century–Fox, playing the wife of a cybernetics professor (Ray Milland) who believes that his recently deceased daughter is communicating from beyond the grave; and the hit miniseries *Scruples* (Alan J. Levi, 1980), a primetime CBS soap opera adapted from Judith Krantz's bestselling 1978 novel, with Tierney in the role of a Manhattan fashion-magazine editor. She continued taking medication and was still, in her words, "subject to periods of odd behavior."[93]

Tierney's personal struggles in the 1950s mark a shift in the cultural perception of stars' lives and work that came to dominate the following decade. Although Tierney was not the first or even the most famous case of a star who received public attention for suffering from mental illness, the conditions of this public revelation were distinct from those of her peers. After concerning public behavior, bipolar star Frances Farmer was committed to the Western State Hospital in Washington State from 1945 to 1950. Farmer's so-called autobiography *Will There Really Be a Morning?* was published posthumously in 1972 and is thought to have been ghostwritten and fictionalized by her friend Jean Ratcliffe. Two biographies followed, William Arnold's book *Shadowland* (1978) and the Jessica Lange film *Frances* (Graeme Clifford, 1982), contributing to further myths and misinformation about the details regarding her life and treatment.[94] The other major difference between Tierney and Farmer is that the latter was a comparatively minor star. Both women actually costarred with Tyrone Power in *Son of Fury* (John Cromwell, 1942), with Farmer as the "bad" woman Power doesn't get in the end. They shared no scenes together and rarely crossed paths with each other during filming, but in *Self-Portrait* Tierney lamented that "no one seemed to realize, or care, that [Farmer] was seriously ill." What Tierney later learned about her costar "frightened" her: "A very gifted actress had been crying out for help, and no one was listening."[95]

Another earlier (and better-known) example is Judy Garland. In 1950, the press reported that she had attempted suicide when she cut her throat with a shard of broken glass. Then addicted to pills and alcohol, she had already experienced a nervous breakdown in 1947, stayed in psychiatric hospitals, and been suspended by MGM three times after the studio replaced her in *The Barkleys of Broadway* (Charles Walters, 1949), *Annie Get Your Gun* (George Sidney, 1950), and *Royal Wedding* (Stanley Donen, 1951). Unlike Tierney, whom Fox found cooperative, Garland failed to arrive on time (if at all) when filming *Royal Wedding* and *Annie Get Your Gun*. On the latter film, she fought with director Busby Berkeley, whom the studio subsequently fired from the project.[96] In her book *Scandals of Classic Hollywood*, Anne Helen Petersen points out how MGM described the cut on Garland's throat as "superficial" and her actions as "hysterical," characterizing her as a star suffering from exhaustion. However, publicity was "sympathetic, generous, and boldly recuperative," viewing her as an overworked former child star who still remained "a girl."[97] The discourse on Garland had always suggested that "she lacked the motherly care and compassion Freud posited as essential to normal development," and in the aftermath of her breakdown, her star discourse "textually maintained her juvenile status."[98] By contrast, the discourse on Tierney framed her as an adult woman in the postwar era (a wife, mother, and worker). This comeback narrative not only shows how the Hollywood star machine responded to the mental illness of one of its biggest stars but also how that response sought to resolve contradictions between women's domestic and nondomestic roles, creating a double bind for its seemingly rehabilitated star. Garland's Hollywood comeback with *A Star Is Born* (George Cukor, 1954) ensured her status as an icon of "resilience,"[99] whereas Tierney's comeback was short lived, relegated to supporting roles, and in the shadow of her earlier films.

Playacting and Sleepwalking: *Whirlpool*

One of the reasons stars continue to matter past the synchronic moment of their stardom is because their films continue to circulate. This afterlife allows for repeat viewings in later contexts and introduces older stars to different audiences (often through television broadcasts, home video platforms, and, more recently, streaming services such as the Criterion Channel and Watch TCM). When new information is uncovered about stars' lives and careers, new meanings become available to their films. Indeed, a process of recycling and canonization granted a new lease on studio-era filmmaking as early as the mid-1950s when the major studios started selling or leasing their back catalogs of pre-1948 titles to television syndicators.[100] Television remained an important ancillary market for the film industry, and a new generation gained an appreciation for the history of Hollywood through film cults, college film societies, and the formalization of academic film studies in the 1970s. Directors such as Otto Preminger had been of great interest to postwar French film critics and were the subjects of serious cultural attention in the United Kingdom and United States following the Anglophone take-up of *la politique des auteurs*. Apropos of Preminger's *Laura*, critic turned filmmaker Paul Schrader introduced U.S. audiences to the term *film noir* in his program notes accompanying the first Los Angeles Film Exposition series in 1971, which he published the following year in the cinephile magazine *Film Comment*.

The publication of *Self-Portrait* in 1978 coincided with this wider rediscovery of Hollywood's studio-era cinema that had been gathering momentum over the previous twenty years. In reconstructing Tierney's image from an autobiographical perspective, the book's articulation of her discursive agency cannot be overstated. Of course, one may never know where the star ends and the "real" Gene Tierney begins, but by laying claim to the telling of her own story, she vies for the public control of her identity and gives readers the impression that a "real" woman still exists to take back. *Self-Portrait* reminded readers of how Tierney often found her self-worth in the validations of others, which made accepting her illness and pursuing treatment more challenging than the press had fully acknowledged. When a psychiatrist "offered no suggestion" after an appointment, she wondered whether it was that he did not believe in the severity of her condition or that as an actress she had "deceived" him.[101] At the Institute of Living, a doctor shamed her for wearing French beach sandals, which he referred to as "bedroom slippers," effectively severing her last connection to the world of fashion and a personal style in which she had long identified.[102] In addition to fearing and even dreading the ECTs, which caused nausea and memory loss, she also experienced terrible guilt, feeling responsible for bringing her illness upon herself and her family.[103]

Yet she also shared stories of resistance during her institutionalization, such as her escape while taking a "walk around the grounds." Tierney recounted how a distracted nurse and an open gate created an opportunity to flee to a nearby store and call her brother just before the nurse and a group of attendants caught up to her. As she put it, "I had gone through my life saying yes, being nice, doing as others pleased. Now, when I no longer had full control of my mind, I was subconsciously indulging a desire to resist and say no."[104] After awakening from one of her ECTs, she struck a nurse for allowing it and was punished with solitary confinement in a "box" that had no toilet, running water, or windows.[105] Tierney regretted the violent impulse, recalling that it frightened her more than the nurse. "I considered it a weakness to show temper," she conceded, "and I always tried to control mine, probably at a cost to myself."[106]

How might we then read one of Tierney's films in the discursive contexts of psychological disorder and rehabilitation that publicity, press commentary, and autobiographical writing have created since the 1950s? If we take *Whirlpool* as an example, we can draw on what Rebecca Bell-Metereau and Colleen Glenn call "the erotics of suffering" for a more deeply emotional appreciation of her performance as a kleptomaniac framed for murder, whose psychiatrist husband disbelieves her innocence. Not to be confused with "sadomasochistic identification," the erotics of suffering have less to do with "feelings of disempowerment" or "a position of victimhood" than an empathetic relationship the audience forms with the star.[107] "On some level, we see ourselves in the stars," Bell-Metereau and Glenn claim, "and just as we triumph with them, we also suffer with them."[108]

Although Tierney's suffering first received public attention with the *General Electric Theater* incident, four years *after* the release of *Whirlpool*, she was already experiencing various forms of private suffering at the time, and audiences would have recognized her as a star who was to some degree troubled. The following, however, is not an exercise in decoding what was known about Tierney to speculate how the film would have been received at the time of its release, nor does it presume that the film was made as an allegory for Tierney's real life. Rather, it looks at how cinematic elements of character and performance intersect with extracinematic discourse on Tierney's mental health (including her own autobiographical narrative) in the construction of her subjectivity as a star who suffered in silence. Historians of stardom such as McLean and Danae Clark have argued that film texts reveal "the social relations of labor and subjectivity" in a star image,[109] and the previously inaccessible meanings in *Whirlpool* give that subjectivity diachronic significance. If the star system appears to reconcile "the dominant contractions in social life," as Richard Dyer theorizes,[110] the suffering of performer and character further collapses the boundaries between star and person, continuing to bridge the divide between the public and the private for the star's audiences. The image of Tierney's body on-screen mediates her suffering but in this context is never a site of abjection. On the contrary, she models a kind of suffering in which "it is possible to triumph over, transcend, successfully live out contradictions" that one suffers to negotiate.[111]

Latent in *Whirlpool* is an invisible, stigmatized form of suffering on both psychological and gendered levels. As Bell-Metereau and Glenn remind us, stars may attempt to mask their private suffering, such as Columbia Pictures' cosmetic transformation of the Hispanic Margarita Cansino into the more Anglo-American Rita Hayworth or the closeting of gay actor Rock Hudson until the "forced public revelation" that he was HIV positive. Both of these cases shift an understanding of their screen roles from acting to the performance of identity.[112] "The spectacle of an actor's suffering, both onscreen and in private, gives audiences a sense of the actor's authenticity," the authors write, "and yet in order for the performance to accomplish its psychological goal of arousing and then displacing anxiety, it must come across as something hidden from view, beneath the obvious surface and artificiality of acting."[113] Either by design or by accident, the mirroring of a star's on-screen and private suffering threatens to disrupt a star's image. Yet it can also allow for retroactive readings of their films, creating new sources of pleasure and identification in audiences eager to see the "real," ordinary actor through the manufactured, extraordinary star image. The suffering of stars has as much power to end careers as to determine an iconicity beyond an industry- or audience-bound meaning at a particular moment in time.

When *Whirlpool* was first released in January 1950, Fox marketed it as "another *Laura*,"[114] the film that made Tierney a major star. *Whirlpool* was a reunion project of sorts at the studio: a film noir starring Tierney and directed by Preminger with a score composed by David Raksin. According to the trailer, "Not since the unforgettable *Laura* . . . has the screen stormed to such heights of suspense!"[115] The film is part of Preminger's "Fox quintet" as producer-director, which includes *Laura, Fallen Angel* (1945), *Daisy Kenyon* (1947), and *Where the Sidewalk Ends* (1950).[116] Of the five films, Tierney starred in three, but she was also chosen to play Manhattan career woman Daisy Kenyon before the role went to Joan Crawford, who costarred with two of Tierney's previous screen partners, Dana Andrews and Henry Fonda.[117] *Whirlpool* was her first film after a two-year acting hiatus during which time she gave birth to her second daughter, Christina. Recall that Daria was born in 1943, a year before the release of *Laura*. The pressbook called *Whirlpool* Tierney's "best film since then," giving her "what she has described as her best part," and referred to her children as the "good luck signs on the road of her career."[118]

In addition to its place in Preminger's Fox quintet following *Laura*, *Whirlpool* should also be historically understood in the context of its release as a follow-up to Fox's *The Snake Pit* (Anatole Litvak, 1948).[119] One of the first films to depict the treatment of mental illness in a psychiatric hospital, *The Snake Pit* starred Olivia de Havilland in an Oscar-nominated performance as a schizophrenic woman put through hypnotherapy and electric shock treatment, but Tierney was one of the actresses originally considered for the role.[120] Both *The Snake Pit* and *Whirlpool* were entries in a cycle of films produced across multiple studios—*Cat People* (Jacques Tourneur, 1942), *Now, Voyager* (Irving Rapper, 1942), *Spellbound* (Alfred Hitchcock, 1945), *The Locket* (John Brahm, 1946), *Shock* (Alfred L. Werker, 1946), *Nightmare Alley* (Edmund Goulding, 1947), *Possessed* (Curtis Bernhardt, 1947), *Caught* (Max Ophüls, 1949)—that reflected Hollywood's fascination with psychology and Freudian psychoanalysis in the 1940s.[121]

That most of these films came out after World War II is not incidental. Philippa Gates writes, "Only once the war was over, it would seem, did Hollywood begin to interrogate the myths it had constructed during wartime. Now that unity was no longer the theme of the day, filmmakers began to explore America's home-front discord."[122] Women in mystery-suspense films occupied a more contained position by the 1950s, as the heroic female detectives of the previous two decades had more or less disappeared. Female investigative work might be occasionally taken up by homemakers controlled by their patriarchal husbands, such as Barbara Stanwyck's domesticated newspaper columnist in *Crime of Passion* (Gerd Oswald, 1957), or women who saw their very sanity questioned, as in *Witness to Murder* (Roy Rowland, 1954), another Stanwyck vehicle.[123] With Hollywood films increasingly turning inward to investigate the origins and effects of trauma, repression, and psychosis in ordinary white Americans, discord was manifest at both social and psychological levels and in conscious and unconscious ways. Fittingly, the source of *Whirlpool* was the novel *Methinks a Lady* (1945) by the leftist author, screenwriter, and social critic Guy Endore (born Samuel Goldstein), who received an Oscar nomination for writing *The Story of G.I. Joe* (William A. Wellman, 1945) but who remains better remembered for his novel *The Werewolf of Paris* (1933) and his scripts for the MGM horror films *Mark of the Vampire* (Tod Browning, 1935), *Mad Love* (Karl Freund, 1935), and *The Devil-Doll* (Tod Browning, 1936).

The emphasis on psychology in *Whirlpool* is therefore not necessarily motivated by what Fox may or may not have known about Tierney but rather is consistent with larger Hollywood production trends. Mary Ann Doane calls the 1940s "the decade of the most intense incorporation of psychoanalysis within the Hollywood system," tracing these films back to the larger popularization of psychoanalysis of the late 1930s and 1940s that resulted from the influx of refugee analysts and psychiatrists

from Europe. The psychiatric establishment balked at cinematic representations of the profession—reductive or altogether incorrect representations that made no distinction between psychoanalysis and
psychology. Responding to such criticisms, Hollywood made appeals to
authority by employing experts to serve as consultants on films including *The Dark Mirror* (Robert Siodmak, 1946) and *Sleep, My Love* (Douglas
Sirk, 1948).[124] For example, Fox recruited hypnotist Fred Schneider as a
technical adviser on *Whirlpool* and advertised his contribution to the film
in the pressbook as a way to promote its credibility.

Despite the popularity of *Laura* and films about psychoanalysis,
reviews of *Whirlpool* were mixed at best. Bosley Crowther of the *New
York Times* reserved praise only for José Ferrer's performance as the villain,
writing that "haughty Gene Tierney plays the lady who is slightly off the
track and Charles Bickford and Richard Conte are the detective and husband, respectively. All together, along with several others, they labor to
cast a spell. But their efforts are bleakly artificial."[125] Lambasting the con-
voluted plot, Richard L. Coe of the *Washington Post* opined, "I'm afraid it
all seems absurd while Gene Tierney, Jose Ferrer and Richard Conte stalk
through their stark, elegant paces."[126] Mae Tinee, the pseudonymous critic
of the *Chicago Tribune*, quipped, "This film nearly put me to sleep, and it
wasn't hypnosis but sheer boredom that did it."[127] In a characteristically
generous review for the *Los Angeles Times*, Philip K. Scheuer approved of
the "smooth storytelling," however "outrageously contrived." Compared
to *Laura*, he wrote, "I can't state with assurance that *Whirlpool* is the better
of the two; but then time and sentiment always give a half-remembered
pleasure an advantage, sometimes unfairly."[128]

The comparisons Fox invited between *Laura* and *Whirlpool* are not
without merit, but Tierney's physical appearance actually calls attention to how much she has changed in the years separating the two
films and the striking contrast between her two characters. Playing
an upper-middle-class housewife in *Whirlpool*, she wears her hair in an
almost matronly perm, shorter with tighter curls than the long, curled
bob that rounded her face in 1944. Faint lines around her eyes and mouth
show signs of age, and her slightly sunken cheeks and heavier eyelids give
her face a harder look than the youthful Manhattan advertising executive (figs. 26 and 27). For *Laura*, Bonnie Cashin dressed her in costumes
that suggested women's white-collar professional work during wartime,

Figs. 26 and 27. Tierney as Laura Hunt (*top*) in *Laura* (Otto Preminger, 1944) and as Ann Sutton (*bottom*) in *Whirlpool* (Otto Preminger, 1950), from New York City advertising executive to Los Angeles housewife.

inspiring real "ready-to-wear" fashions, but to play Ann Sutton in *Whirl-pool*, Cassini created a wardrobe that typified a very different woman, although still quite stylish (audiences would have expected no less from Tierney). Fox even singled out Cassini's costumes in the pressbook.

Ann and her husband, Bill (Richard Conte), live in the Westwood neighborhood of Los Angeles where Bill practices psychoanalysis from their home. Unbeknownst to Bill, Ann suffers from kleptomania, and an astrologer named David Korvo (José Ferrer) learns of her secret when she is caught shoplifting a pin from a local department store. However, Korvo gains her trust by persuading the store manager to give up the shoplifting report from the store file on the grounds that Ann is not a thief but a "sick woman," therefore leaving no record of an incident that might tarnish Ann's reputation or that of her prominent husband. When she later reveals to Korvo that she is also an insomniac, and that pills only cause her to "jump inside," he offers to put her under hypnosis, convincing her that seeking help from her husband would lead him to discover her kleptomania and that another doctor would likely expose it to him.

The incredible hypnosis scene provides the film's first explicit link to *Laura*. Preminger biographer Chris Fujiwara quite rightly describes *Whirlpool* as the director's "critique of the male need for perfection in the woman," explaining that the film "expands from the conflict between self-will and external will, making this conflict an instance of the battle between a woman's self-definition and a definition imposed by men."[129] Fujiwara associates Korvo with the role of a director, "exploiting the weakness of women for his gain," as well as to the institution of Hollywood itself, "promising escape [. . .], designing traps for the unsatisfied desires of women."[130] A Svengali-like figure with society connections, a dandy's personal style, and a taste for acerbic bon mots, David Korvo is also another Waldo Lydecker (the villain in *Laura*). Ann's hypnosis takes place in a private room at a party for Korvo, held in the home of one of his society acquaintances, where in the background viewers can see the same Asian statue from Waldo's collection that appears in the first post-credits shot of *Laura*[131] (later, Korvo's collection of "exotic" masks hanging in his apartment shows his own Orientalist decor).

Associating Korvo with Waldo was intended. After reading the script by Andrew Solt, Zanuck felt that the film could possess "much of the quality and strangeness of *Laura*," noting, "[W]e must make David an interesting and intriguing character, just as interesting as Clifton Webb was in *Laura*."[132] Preminger hired Ben Hecht to rewrite the script. One of the most prolific screenwriters of the Hollywood studio era and a former journalist, author, and playwright, Hecht was a proponent of the Freudianism en vogue at midcentury.[133] Zanuck suggested revisions to the ending that we might read as (perhaps unconscious) references to Waldo's fate at the end of *Laura*: the staircase in which Korvo hides and his prerecorded speech that plays over his death.[134] The image of the record shards on the turntable in *Whirlpool* graphically matches with the shattered clock face at the end of *Laura* (both obliterated by gunshots after implicating Korvo and Waldo as murderer and attempted murderer, respectively).

In other respects, Korvo serves a distinct function in *Whirlpool* that may be less obvious when viewed as simply a recycling of *Laura*. The host of the party (Constance Collier, Tierney's acting coach) brags to her guests that Korvo "reads souls, guides human destinies with the aid of the stars and makes fortunes for other people at a nominal fee," and she encourages them to attend one of his lectures on hypnotism. At the risk of being mistaken for a mere "fortune-teller" or a "hypnotist," Korvo clarifies, "I use a number of sciences in my experiments with the human family." In this way, he might be understood as a double for Bill Sutton. Both men are "competitors vying for control of Ann's loyalty and for her very psyche," observes Janet Walker. "And, if Korvo and Sutton are flip sides of the same coin," she continues, "then Sutton's analytic technique, by implication, is as suspect as Korvo's overtly authoritarian brainwashing tactics."[135] This reading shows how *Whirlpool* discursively resists patriarchal social formations of both doctor/patient and husband/ wife linked in the figure of the psychiatrist husband.

The way Korvo sees it, Ann is already a "patient" of his. "The fact that I know of your kleptomania," he reasons, "the fact that I know your mind is sick and threatening to get out of hand gives me a medical position in your life, doesn't it?" As she sits down in a chair, he crouches in front of her and leans in to begin a kind of incantation, "You're relaxed with me. You don't have to exhaust yourself trying to seem normal: the serene and devoted wife who doesn't dare upset her busy husband. Your soul can undress in front of me. That means that your cure is already beginning." In a close-up shot that lasts just over thirty seconds, Korvo's shadow stretches across Ann's face, and she slowly closes her eyes, then lets her head drop (fig. 28). Once she has completely fallen asleep, she robotically follows a series of arbitrary commands. She opens her eyes, walks to the window to draw the curtains, walks to the door to close it, and walks back to the chair to resume sitting with her eyes shut, but refuses to hold Korvo's hand when he extends it to her (under hypnosis, she still cannot perform an action against her will). Before he awakens her with no memory of the hypnosis session, he instructs her to sleep for nine hours beginning at eleven o'clock. One of the party guests, Theresa Randolph (Barbara O'Neil), warns her about Korvo's history of preying on women for their money, but the next morning Ann rises feeling completely refreshed and agrees to continue seeing him for hypnosis therapy.

At their first appointment in Korvo's apartment hotel, Ann insists they meet in the bar rather than his room. Korvo defensively accuses her of being afraid of her "unwifely impulses," but Ann calls him "smug" and "stupid," suspecting that he seduces vulnerable women into love affairs by making them feel "close and dependent" on him. In spite of her doubts about his integrity and her disinterest in whatever romantic relationship

Fig. 28. David Korvo (José Ferrer) puts Ann under hypnosis.

he may solicit, she also believes that he understands her emotionally in a way that Bill cannot. "I know you, Ann, better than you know yourself," Korvo tells her. "You're unhappy. You're miserable. You've locked yourself away in a characterization: the serene and devoted wife. That playacting is destroying you." He promises to "release" her "from a torture chamber called Mrs. William Sutton." The film appears to confirm Korvo's impression of Bill as the source of Ann's "neurosis," an equally controlling male presence in her life but one who projects an identity through benevolent sexism rather than manipulating her actions through hypnosis.

Earlier in the film after Ann is caught shoplifting, she returns home from the department store in a state of agitation and instructs her maid, Miss Hall, to interrupt one of Bill's sessions. At first, Ann plans to confess the shoplifting to him, but changing her mind at the last minute, she instead happily greets him in their bedroom and suggests they attend a Heifetz concert that evening. By unclipping the pen from the outside breast pocket of his jacket and placing it on the inside pocket, she "playacts" her role of "the serene and devoted wife." Ann sees the pen as a reminder of the pin she nearly shoplifted earlier that day, triggering the feelings of guilt and shame she wants to repress. Assuming it was Miss Hall who misinterpreted Ann, Bill glibly remarks, "Hall must be losing her grip on reality. I guess she's so used to my poor patients that everything sounds like hysteria to her."

The playacting continues as Ann dutifully removes a handkerchief from a chest of drawers and stuffs it in Bill's breast pocket where the pen hung. Bill meanwhile says he would rather skip the concert and "do some writing," then retrieves the pen from his inside pocket. Afraid he has detected her secret, she breaks eye contact and looks down at the pen, but he fidgets with it and redirects his thoughts back to his work. The bits of business with the pen and the handkerchief allow Tierney to communicate Ann's nervousness with an excessive use of "expressive objects," a term James Naremore defines in his book *Acting in the Cinema* as theatrical objects that become "signifiers of feeling" when under a performer's control.[136] As Ann struggles "to conceal or repress [her] sincere feelings," Tierney "exhibit[s] dissonance within the characterization" through a moment of performance-within-a-performance, or "expressive incoherence" in Naremore's language.[137] Bill's practice of recording his sessions with his patients—"wiretapping the subconscious," as Korvo puts it—ironizes his inability to "hear" his own wife, and in this respect

Korvo is entirely correct when he later tells Bill, "If you can rid yourself of your husbandly egomania, maybe we can both help save Ann."

Throughout this scene, Bill remains oblivious to Ann's performance codes and her suffering more generally. His main concern lies with one of his patients, a young World War II veteran unable to talk, whose suffering is more legible to him. Preoccupied with an upcoming convention when Ann returns home from Korvo's party later in the film, Bill shows her similar patronizing attention (seeing her identity as entirely dependent on his own). "You know," he says, "the greatest kick I get when we go to a party together is when people stare at you and say, 'Who is that lovely girl?' 'Why that's Dr. Sutton's wife. She's very devoted to him.' My head swells up like a balloon." Lying down on her bed behind him, Ann passes out from the sleeping instructions Korvo gave her under her first hypnosis. Apparently unconcerned, all Bill can say in response is, "Well, my sleeping beauty. Take off your robe and slippers" (the mise-en-scène puns on the phrase "bad bedside manner," implying Bill is no better a lover than he is a doctor). Ann's sleepwalking under Korvo's direction is similar to her "playacting" for Bill as "the serene and devoted wife," and Tierney's expressive incoherence makes the connection between these two modes of performance explicit during this scene.

Not only is Korvo Ann's "director," but he is also an actor himself, pretending to want to help her when actually trying to get to socialite Theresa Randolph, his ex-lover and former client currently in Bill's psychiatric care. Under Korvo's hypnosis one night, Ann steals phonograph recordings of Theresa's sessions with Bill, which exposes Korvo as a con artist, while Korvo murders Theresa and frames Ann for the crime. Korvo designs it so that the police suspect Ann was carrying on an affair with him and murdered Theresa out of jealousy. And in the film's most preposterous twist, he establishes an alibi by undergoing a gallbladder operation the week of the murder, only to hypnotize *himself*, sneak out of his hospital room, and strangle Theresa with Ann's scarf (leaving behind Ann's pin as evidence). If Ann is driven from Bill to Korvo, Theresa serves as a double for Ann, driven from Korvo to Bill. The portrait of Theresa hanging above her fireplace mantel, which looks down at her corpse propped on her sofa, evokes the portrait of Tierney's almost-murdered socialite in *Laura*, which hung over Dana Andrews asleep in her chair (figs. 29 and 30).[138]

Figs. 29 and 30. Laura (*top*) and Ann (*bottom*) enter crime scenes that mirror each other.

Laura and Ann are women who have both been framed. The men in Laura's life compete to possess her body, tell her story, and determine her future based on their ideation of the perfect woman (represented by Laura's framed portrait), while Bill and Korvo, respectively, induce Ann's performance of "serene and devoted wife" and obedient patient (leading to her framing in a murder). Between *Laura* and *Whirlpool*, Tierney's performance engages in a critical dialogue about female image-making and female role-playing, but whereas Laura's fashion and professional work give her a sense of agency in the public, Ann hardly ever steps out from behind a mask of placidity she wears for the approval of others. When Ann steals the phonograph recordings, she is not simply seized by Korvo's control but is passed from Bill to Korvo. Sitting at her bedroom desk while Bill is away at his convention, she begins writing him a letter: "My DARLING, Just a few words to tell you how deeply and how desperately I love you." The interruption of clock chimes puts her in a trance; she dons her coat and gloves, descends the staircase to unlock Bill's walk-in safe, lifts the records and drives to Theresa's house, and finally hides them in Theresa's closet before finding her corpse under the portrait. With the arrival of the police, Ann is again interrupted and passed from Korvo to Lt. James Colton (Charles Bickford, the ex-cop from *Fallen Angel*).

Preminger composes shots of Tierney in primarily in one of two ways. First, as Fujiwara points out, he "establishes an attitude toward Ann that could be described as relaxed but persistent in its continual medium-shot surveillance of her movements," suggesting "that we are watching Ann watch herself."[139] The scenes we have just examined—the business with the pen and the handkerchief, Ann's somnambulant hypnosis session, and her theft of Bill's records—are all examples (figs. 31, 32, and 33). As Fujiwara interprets Preminger's decision, "The space around her, in the frame, figures the mental space of her own unconscious self-observation."[140] A second, equally important way Preminger films Tierney is by crowding her with other actors in the frame. The long shots of men interrogating Ann at the department store and the police station extend the film's critique of patriarchal marriage and psychiatry to what Walker calls the "controlling presence of medical, corporate, or legal collective gaze at the woman."[141] Here, we observe men observing Ann from

Figs. 31, 32, and 33. Ann "playacts" for Bill (Richard Conte) and later sleep-walks for Korvo.

Figs. 34, 35, and 36. Director Otto Preminger crowds Tierney with other actors in the frame.

a meta-level of surveillance (figs. 34, 35, and 36). "I couldn't have done it," she cries at the police station, "I couldn't . . . unless . . . unless I'm crazy? Unless I'm crazy?" The blurring between Ann's waking and sleeping life seems to register when she breaks down in front of Colton and weeps, pleading, "I don't know what happened. I can't remember anything. I'm dreaming all this!"

During the second half of the film, as a subject of legal investigation, Ann gets written into a narrative over which she has no control. Tierney visibly holds back tears when Bill visits Ann at the police station. "Please, don't cry," he says prescriptively, to which Ann replies, "I won't." Bill's request to Ann and his "thanks" in return are not unlike Korvo's hypnosis instructions in how he tries to manage her outward behavior and emotional inner life from a clinical distance. When Bill questions her about her relationship with Korvo, she finally breaks character, responding, "You won't believe me. No matter what I tell you. You don't want to hear the truth. You won't let me tell it. You think I'm lying!" The scene almost reprises Mark's interrogation of Laura about the murder of Diane Redfern when Laura responds, "What difference does it make what I say? You've made up your mind I'm guilty." This time, however, Tierney's performance is more desperate, almost to the point of exhaustion. Ann knows she was not having an affair but convinces herself she is "crazy," and her inconsolable sobbing communicates the helpless feeling of not being heard or believed.

Later in the film, Bill's lawyer informs her that they have decided to plead "not guilty by reason of insanity" and will attempt to prove that her relationship with Korvo "unbalanced" her and drove her to cover up for a murder he committed. "He had nothing to do with me," Ann interrupts defiantly. "He didn't unbalance me or drive me to anything. Bill did." She goes on to accuse Bill of running away from the truth as long as they have been married. "You made me playact," she tells him, borrowing Korvo's theatrical term. "I had to pretend I was healthy and happy when I was sick and miserable. Headaches. I couldn't sleep. Afraid to tell you. Afraid to lose your wonderful love. Locked away in the characterization of a serene and devoted wife." Preminger literalizes Ann's imprisoning characterization with the prison bars in the mise-en-scène, visually equating the patriarchal structures of power represented by Bill, Korvo, and Colton (see fig. 36). The second half of the film looks at Ann as a fully "institutionalized" woman at the levels of marriage, psychiatry, and the law.

We have seen how Tierney was expected to pretend she was "healthy and happy" when she was "sick and miserable," "playacting" both as an actress who performed different roles and as a woman "locked away in the characterization" of a star image. Tierney worked to conceal an identity that threatened to disrupt this image, not only immediately after leaving the industry in 1954 but also in the years leading up to it. As she stated in the last paragraph of *Self-Portrait*, "I traveled in a world that once was—Hollywood of the war and immediate postwar years. And I existed in a world that never is—the prison of the mind."[142] The "prison of the mind" to which she refers is a potential way we might understand Ann's suffering as a kleptomaniac who feels compelled to steal. From this vantage point, *Whirlpool* is less about "disordered" femininity than the factors that contribute women's psychological disorders and feelings of shame and guilt that come with them. Ann suffers in part because she is afraid Bill will discover her kleptomania and stop loving her. One of the reasons I find *Whirlpool* such a powerful film is due to the knowledge that Tierney was struggling with her own private disorder at the time of its making and continued to experience the very real anxiety of maintaining her "characterization" for the studio and public into the 1950s. The press coverage following her first release from Menninger shows her in the middle of different patriarchal authority figures (the studio, her psychiatrists, her ex-lovers) that publicists and journalists cited in their narrative of disorder and rehabilitation, encouraging a new kind of "playacting" as Tierney (prematurely) announced herself cured and ready for work.

Like Ann, Tierney experienced different and sometimes conflicting expectations from these authority figures over who she was supposed to be. Fox had promoted her as a "very contradictory type,"[143] from an Orientalist "exotic" to a white pinup queen, from an "all-American" workingwoman to "war bride" and mother. At home, Cassini had wanted her "to be a gay wife and a hard-working actress at the same time."[144] When she confided in her mother that she needed to see a psychiatrist, Tierney said that her mother replied, "Don't be silly, all you need are some new clothes," and took her on a shopping trip to Paris. Tierney admitted that when she would "get nervous and withdraw," Aly Khan would "cover up" for her and continue assuring her mother that "all she needs to do is live on a farm."[145]

In order to reclaim her agency, Ann turns to stealing. She explains to Colton and her lawyer that her kleptomania began with her father, who refused to allow her to spend money (tying up "thousands and thousands of dollars" in a trust fund even after he died). The kleptomania returned with her domestication as Bill's wife ("he treated me like my father did," she says). Julie Grossman contends that at a time when women were encouraged to return to the home after working in a wartime public labor force, Ann is able to rebel not only from her "trophy wife" status married to Bill but also from the financial restrictions her father imposed on her since childhood.[146] When viewed in this feminist-historical context, Grossman claims that Ann's kleptomania can be read as "her need for validation" and "a violent critique of patriarchy" in pursuit of economic independence.[147] In this way, *Whirlpool* shifts "the standard focus of postwar trauma on men to the gender chaos the postwar period introduced for women."[148]

Yet the film is also open to a sympathetic reading of Ann's actions in the context of the Tierney's biography. Recall that part of her treatment involved confronting her relationship with her father, Howard, who presided over the holding company to which she allocated a quarter of her total earnings. Tierney explained the following in *Self-Portrait*: "Until I was married, I lived on an allowance and never saw my paychecks. I couldn't buy a dress or order steaks for the household without running the bills through the company. Once, when my mother was in the East, I walked into a store and charged an alligator handbag for $85, an extravagant and frivolous thing to do. My parents hit the ceiling. But I still own that purse today, which proves that quality lasts."[149]

According to Fox's publicity biography, Howard sued her when she married Cassini and signed a new contract with Fox, and she later charged Howard with stealing the money in the trust fund where he saved the other 75 percent of her earnings. Fox had downplayed these events in the press at the beginning of Tierney's career, suggesting this reading strategy may not have been widely available in 1950, but they reentered public discourse with the press coverage of her treatment and the publication of her autobiography.

The reconciliation between Ann and Bill at the end of the film is perhaps too pat, restoring Ann to her socially acceptable position as the "serene and devoted wife" under the proper care of psychiatrist husband, Bill (a surrogate for her father, much in the way Cassini was identified as a surrogate father and psychiatrist for Tierney). When Ann returns to Theresa's home with Bill and Colton to search for the hidden records, Bill is finally able to recognize her as a psychologically disturbed woman and confidently promises to "cure" her, offering a positive alternative to Korvo, the "bad" doctor. "When you married me," he deduces, "I insisted that you start with me as a poor doctor's wife, that you don't spend your own money. That brought back the neurosis. My acting like your father made you steal again." Meanwhile, Korvo has snuck out of the hospital again (another self-hypnosis!) and intrudes on the reconstituted couple. After hearing the incriminating record and watching Korvo bleed to death from his unhealed surgical wounds, Colton hands Ann back over to Bill's "custody" (Colton's word) and clinches the happy ending.

There is more emotional complexity to this ending, however, that problematizes what might appear to be Ann's total assimilation into the domestic order. While she is quick to redeclare her love for Bill, it is only after Bill admits to having "injured" her "by being blind" to her needs as his wife. Therefore, as Grossman argues, "this ameliorative ending doesn't elide the movie's use of personality disorder to underscore the gender prisons in which women are locked up."[150] Ann vows never to lie to him, but Bill assures her, "You don't have to. I love you as you are." What redeems Bill is the trust he now shows toward Ann. It is her mutual trust in Bill that unblocks her memory of what happened the night of the murder, not Bill's psychiatric deduction (he only provides information that she and the audience already know).

The trailer for *Whirlpool* characterized Ann as a stereotypical femme fatale much in the same way the trailer for *Laura* painted the portrait of a "beautiful," "exotic," and "dangerous" woman. According to the trailer, Ann is not a mentally ill housewife suffering from her conflicting desires to please her husband and maintain a subjectivity for herself but instead an opaque object of mystery who turns bad under the influence of a bad man. In the reading the trailer suggests, Ann needs to be psychologically corrected to fulfill her role as Bill's wife, requiring the protection and detective work of good men (psychiatrist and police lieutenant). The credits introduce the principle characters as follows: "Gene Tierney[,] who gives her heart to *one* man . . . and loses her soul to another . . .";

"Richard Conte[,] groping for the secrets of his wife's hidden past . . .";
"Jose Ferrer[,] who introduces the most *sinister character* ever to come
to the screen"; "Charles Bickford[,] the detective who holds *a girl's life* in
the balance." Ann's problem thus becomes her transgression from the
domestic norm that rocks the foundations of patriarchal knowledge and
authority (as the tagline asks, "Do you believe a woman can commit a
sin . . . when she is hypnotized?"). Writing in *Film Comment* in 1974, critic
Michell S. Cohen compared *Whirlpool* to an earlier kleptomania-themed
film, RKO's *The Locket*, as examples of what he saw as a major theme
in postwar film noir: "the hidden, dangerous nature of woman beneath
her beguiling façade." Ann is then another "beautiful neurotic" with a
"schizophrenic dichotomy." In film noir, Cohen supposed, "*all* women
were to be mistrusted," a symptomatic reading that interpreted noir as
a reflection of sexual insecurities experienced by returning servicemen
after years apart from women. This reading allows characters in noir
only to fall along a neat (and usually gendered) binary of either victim or
villain.[151] Based on the trailer for *Whirlpool*, Fox likely encouraged such
a reading of the film.

Both the trailer for *Laura* and for *Whirlpool* speak to the hegemonic
anxieties about women's social roles during and after World War II (pur-
chasing power as wartime workers and their readjustment as postwar
wives, respectively). But as I have tried to show in this book, plot does
not trump other ways that films produce meaning, nor can it account
for the range of meanings in a given film, and interpreting films purely
as symptoms of dominant ideology occludes alternative readings that a
star image makes possible. We have seen how Tierney's costumes in
Laura materially ground the film in emerging ways of fashioning oneself
as a white-collar workingwoman at a time when women's public identities were intensely "policed." The extratextual discourse on her mental
health and emotional labor in the 1950s strengthens an identification
with Ann (as opposed to Bill) in *Whirlpool*. Tierney's biographical legend
helps us understand Ann not as deviant, a victim, or an enigma but as a
woman living with and facing her pain amid a chorus of voices claiming
authority over women's experiences. Further, Tierney was one of many
women who negotiated between having an illness and feeling expected
to return to work and who tried to satisfy contradictory roles of wife,
mother, and working professional in the postwar era. In the context of

her biography, then, *Whirlpool* is not "about" Tierney's experiences so much as postwar female trauma located in the gender prescriptions for the feminine-domestic ideal after World War II (and the social oppressions they support). Tierney's personal story continues to remain part of her star image, but as it gets rediscovered and refracted through her films, what that story means for us is still being written.

Conclusion

The Reproducible Gene Tierney

After Gene Tierney, the pinup queen; Gene Tierney, the war worker; Gene Tierney, the wife and mother; and Gene Tierney, the tragic beauty, we are left with "the girl in the portrait" from *Laura* (Otto Preminger, 1944). The size of Tierney's roles reduced considerably following *Whirlpool* (Otto Preminger, 1950), even when she appeared on-screen later the same year in *Night and the City* (Jules Dassin) and *Where the Sidewalk Ends* (Otto Preminger). The few films that did star Tierney in a leading role—*The Mating Season* (Mitchell Leisen, 1951), *Close to My Heart* (William Keighley, 1951), and *Personal Affair* (Anthony Pelissier, 1953)—were not made at Fox and are no longer well known outside of niche cinephile circles. We can speculate as to the reasons for her fading in the star system (her personal life in the 1950s and the film roles available to women at her age are both probably contributing factors),[1] but no hypothesis about her career trajectory fully accounts for why *Laura* remains her signature film when many of her films were quite popular in the 1940s. As *Leonard Maltin's Movie Encyclopedia* asks, "Can anyone remember this dark-haired, radiantly beautiful 1940s star without hearing the haunting strains of David Raksin's theme for *Laura* (1944), her most famous film?"[2]

Fans may be tempted to make claims to *Laura*'s "timelessness" as a Hollywood classic, and although I would not dispute its greatness, I want to suggest that its afterlife has more to do with the appropriations of its famous prop—the painted portrait—than any "quality" the film intrinsically possesses. An enlarged glamour photograph by Frank Powolny, the portrait both indexes Tierney's physical presence as an actress and empties it of an aura to guarantee her stardom, enabling the reproduction and citation of her image over time. The portrait does more than identify Tierney with the role; it is a total image of female stardom that makes her synonymous with the character. But whereas Laura Hunt proved that she was, in actuality, alive, usurping the portrait of a woman presumed dead, the *Laura* portrait has since been called upon as a kind of "living" object to defy the so-called death of Classical Hollywood cinema and the mortality of its stars. Therefore, in its subsequent uses, the portrait is usually not a visual metaphor for male fantasy projections, the way it originally functioned in *Laura*. More often, it is used uncritically as a nostalgic object to signify the traditions of female star glamour and film noir that retroactively inform popular ideas about the history and cultural value of Hollywood cinema. Seeing the portrait helps audiences remember Tierney for *Laura*, but without the context of the original film, audiences risk misremembering the character as the passive woman in the black evening gown.

From its opening credits played over the portrait, *Laura* helped circulate elements of Tierney's "picture personality." Not only did it reproduce a name and promotional photograph (levels of discourse that corresponded to biographical knowledge of the star gained from fan magazines), but it also identified the star with a particular role (the role that made her a star) announced in the credits. Moreover, the film mediated her star image in two overlapping ways: first through promotional photography and, second, through mise-en-scène (the portrait, after all, is a prop and part of the profilmic space to be recorded by the camera). Recall Walter Benjamin's thesis on painting in the age of photography stating that "technology of reproduction detaches the reproduced object from the sphere of tradition." He explains, "By replicating the work many times over, it substitutes a mass existence for a unique existence."[3] This loss of an artwork's "aura"—its ontological authority that may be experienced in an unmediated presence—applies both to Preminger's recorded image of the portrait and Powolny's recorded image of Tierney. Apropos of Benjamin, James Naremore points out that "mechanical reproduction deprives performance of authority and 'aura,' even as it greatly enhances the possibility for stardom."[4] Whether for a film or a photograph, shooting any star allows for the reproducibility of the star's image, and, of course, Tierney is no exception here. By incorporating Tierney's photograph into the mise-en-scène, though, *Laura* doubles the reproduction of her image and makes it doubly reproducible. Technologies of reproduction retain a cult of remembrance of the absent subject while endowing the subject with an "exhibition value" that ensures wider conditions of possibility for public display.[5] It is no surprise that when Dell published a paperback edition of Vera Caspary's original novel in 1961, the cover image was designed to look like the *Laura* portrait from the film adaptation.

The screen version of *Laura* thus represents the first stage in a series of reproductions that identify Tierney with the film, the character, and, most important, the portrait. Prior to the film, the portrait was first conceived in the pages of Caspary's novel, and portraits also featured prominently in film noir and Gothic melodramas during the 1940s and 1950s. As Steven Jacobs and Lisa Colpaert detail in their book *The Dark Galleries*, characters "identify paintings with the persons they represent—a psychological process that is not that different from the role actual artworks have played throughout history."[6] Such portraits are usually paintings of women, which Jacobs and Colpaert argue correspond to "the origins of portrait painting in the Renaissance when male portraits had first and foremost a representational function whereas female portraits were often presented as allegories of Beauty." In this way, Jacobs and Colpaert contend, the portraits "channel an unfulfilled desire for an unreachable woman" that seeks to turn the female subject into an image, a process of subjugation duplicated by the painting and reinforced by the film[7] (I would add even as it is possible to see that process laid bare in films such as *Laura*). The audience, in turn, feels the same affective weight of the portrait experienced within the diegesis. Cinematic devices of narrative continuity—music and sound effects, camera movement and framing, lighting, and shot composition—render the painted subject as significant a character as any embodied by an actor in the mise-en-scène.[8] According to Jacobs and Colpaert, *Laura* is the most famous example of this cinematic use of a portrait,[9] but the *Laura* portrait is unique in that it was not an actual painting. The Fox Special Effects Department employed techniques of painting to create the *Laura* portrait from Powolny's photograph of Tierney just as portrait painting has imitated techniques of photography since the nineteenth century,[10] a case of remediation par excellence.[11]

When writing about Tierney, film critics risk reproducing the process of subjugation that Jacobs and Colpaert describe, making her an especially challenging star to evaluate at the level of performance. Steven Rybin's close reading of *Laura* in his book *Gestures of Love* shrewdly acknowledges how "[t]he analyst of performance courts complicity with the desire of these male characters to reduce Tierney and her characters to stillness," freezing frames on DVDs and Blu-rays to study and appreciate still images of the star, whereby Tierney is inevitably "captured."[12] At the same time, a moment-by-moment analysis of performance also reveals how "she projects a stillness and coldness when the narrative calls upon her to play a character under the control of another."[13] If one accepts that "Tierney's own ways of positioning herself are in fact presented as ways of being posed and positioned by others," her films remain open to questioning "how much agency Tierney and her characters have in shaping gesture, movement, and expression."[14] Yet to whatever degree one understands her films as self-reflexive, it seems impossible to discuss her performances without referring to stillness (therefore always in relation to the conventions of portraiture) and perhaps makes the *Laura* portrait an inescapable intertext both in Tierney's star image and her acting style.

The *Laura* portrait also exists as a mobile image, and I would argue that we need to look beyond *Laura* and even Tierney herself to see how it has retroactively given the star iconic status. We have seen how recycling and remaking older properties was a common practice at Fox, but we have not looked at how the studio continued using the *Laura* portrait into the 1950s. The first instance occurred in *On the Riviera* (Walter Lang, 1951), a musical comedy starring Danny Kaye in a dual role: Henri Duran, a French aviator-cum-industrialist on the verge of bankruptcy, and Jack Martin, a struggling impressionist from the United States who performs at a nightclub on the French Riviera. When Henri's business partners learn that he will be absent from a major social event held at his home, leaving him vulnerable to a buyout from a competitor who will be in attendance, they hire Jack to impersonate Henri. Jack's impersonation leads to further complications when he inspires jealousy in his girlfriend, Colette (Corinne Calvet), and starts wooing Henri's neglected wife, Lili (Tierney). The film essentially served as a vehicle for Fox's next cohort of female sex symbols (e.g., Calvet) and male musical comedians (e.g., Kaye).

At the same time, it also asserted continuity with the past by repeating tried-and-tested formulas and paying tribute to stars of the 1930s and 1940s (sometimes through gentle parody). Fox made *On the Riviera* previously with *That Night in Rio* (Irving Cummings, 1941), starring Don Ameche in the Kaye role, Alice Faye in the Tierney role, and Carmen Miranda in the Calvet role, and earlier still with *Folies Bergère de Paris*

(Roy Del Ruth, 1935), starring Maurice Chevalier in the Kaye/Ameche role, Merle Oberon in the Tierney/Faye role, and Ann Sothern in the Calvet/Miranda role. Kaye imitates both Chevalier and Miranda at different points in the film, while the studio promoted Tierney in press materials as one of its resident fashion mavens (a model for Cassini's latest designs and the subject of merchandising tie-ins at women's shops and department stores). Tierney appeared on-screen in one of her most celebrated costumes: a red off-the-shoulder jersey gown with purple sash, which Fox showcased in the film's promotion. Marilyn Monroe, one of the studio's rising stars at the time, wore the same dress to the premiere of her comedy *Monkey Business* (Howard Hawks, 1952) and made it famous in a photo shoot of her own. The *Laura* portrait in the background at the Duran home aligns Tierney with Fox's tradition of great beauties, affording audiences the opportunity to see the portrait in color for the first time (fig. 37). Framing Tierney, literally, through a *Laura* intertext, the film participates in the construction of the studio's legacy by exhibiting one of the glamorous star images it created, to be admired in a fraught period of political, economic, and technological change for the U.S. film industry.[15]

Fig. 37. The *Laura* portrait in *On the Riviera* (Walter Lang, 1951).

A subtler appropriation of the portrait occurred two years later in *Woman's World* (Jean Negulesco, 1954), a Fox film that did not star Tierney. Something of a heritage production for the studio, it derived from what Fox historian Aubrey Solomon calls "the sturdiest of warhorses" in Zanuck's story repertoire.[16] The reusable story line of "three attractive young women searching for wealthy husbands" yielded *Three Blind Mice* (William A. Seiter, 1938), *Moon over Miami* (Walter Lang, 1941), and *Three Little Girls in Blue* (H. Bruce Humberstone, 1946) before director Jean Negulesco revived this comic formula at Fox with *How to Marry a Millionaire* (1953).[17] Negulesco then proceeded with a second generation of films about "three attractive young women" to show off a new cavalcade of female-star trios on the backdrops of real locations (New York City, Rome), shot in color and widescreen processes: *Three Coins in the Fountain* (1954), *Woman's World*, and *The Best of Everything* (1959). Dropping the "searching for wealthy husbands" angle, these films instead focused on the women's romantic adventures in urban-professional settings and played the formula for melodrama. Around the same time that MGM rolled out its own youth-oriented variation with *Where the Boys Are* (Henry Levin, 1960), *Come Fly with Me* (Henry Levin, 1963), and *Follow the Boys* (Richard Thorpe, 1963), Negulesco remade *Three Coins in the Fountain* with Fox's musical *The Pleasure Seekers* (1964), "guest starring" Tierney in her last big-screen role.[18]

Woman's World took a similar approach to *On the Riviera* in its reproduction of the *Laura* portrait as a studio hallmark. Clifton Webb plays Ernest Gifford, the president of a major car company, who has invited three candidates to New York City to interview for the position of general manager. What is more, Gifford asks each of the men to bring his wife, believing that the spouse of the new hire will perform an equal role in representing the public face of the company. This sardonic, queer-coded character is not unlike Webb's Waldo Lydecker from *Laura*, the New York City columnist who transforms Laura into an ornamental object, a projection of his own desire for decorative self-presentation. To make the *Laura* connection explicit, Negulesco's CinemaScope frame shows us a small black-and-white reproduction of the *Laura* portrait in Gifford's study, hanging among portraits of his other female idols (fig. 38). Contrasted against the color and widescreen cinematography that Hollywood embraced in the 1950s, the portrait not only puts Fox's current

Fig. 38. The *Laura* portrait (*upper-left corner*) in *Woman's World* (Jean Negulesco, 1954).

output in a historical relationship with the beloved films of the studio's past (e.g., *Laura*) but also links Webb with his most famous character (Waldo) and the studio's "woman's film" canon to secure the perception of *Woman's World* as a film from the Fox tradition of quality.[19]

After the collapse of the studio system, the *Laura* portrait circulated less as a way of reinscribing Fox's brand identity and more in the service of invoking film noir, a retroactive category for studio-era filmmaking that had entered the parlance of U.S. film culture by the 1970s. Films then labeled "film noir" were, in the 1940s and 1950s, stylish vehicles for coolly glamorous stars who reflected the fashion trends of the time and therefore became privileged sources of midcentury nostalgia. Fox's *The Man with Bogart's Face* (Robert Day, 1980), part Hollywood-nostalgia film, part noir parody, may be one the strangest places to find the portrait. Robert Sacchi plays a movie buff who, à la the film noir *Dark Passage* (Delmer Daves, 1947), undergoes plastic surgery to look like Bogart (Sacchi made a career of doing Bogart impressions in films, television shows, and commercials). Named after Bogart's private-eye characters Sam Spade from *The Maltese Falcon* (John Huston, 1941) and Philip Marlowe from *The Big Sleep* (Howard Hawks, 1946), Sacchi's Sam Marlow opens a Los Angeles detective agency where, decked out in a trench coat and fedora, he can follow in the footsteps of his favorite star. He also hangs the *Laura* portrait on the wall of his office to complete the transformation. "Dana Andrews was swell in *Laura*," he remarks gazing at the portrait, "but what if Bogart had played Lieutenant McPherson? Yeah, Bogart. Smoking a cigarette and looking up at that portrait. Thinking Laura was dead, but still in love with her. What a love scene—and neither of them naked."

Much like McPherson, Marlow comes face-to-face with the girl in the picture, or at least a Gene Tierney lookalike, the film's nominal femme fatale. Michelle Phillips, one of the founding members of the 1960s folk group The Mamas & the Papas, plays the Tierney-esque Gena Anastas. "She didn't look exactly like Gene Tierney," Marlow concedes, "but close, close enough: eyes a little Chinese; red, red lips with teeth a little too large, and long, lovely legs." Marlow's description presumes knowledge of her roles in *The Shanghai Gesture* (Josef von Sternberg, 1941) and *China Girl* (Henry Hathaway, 1942), her lip-sticked overbite highlighted by the Technicolor of *Leave Her to Heaven* (John M. Stahl, 1945), and her modeling for wartime pinup photos. At other moments, Marlow compares Gena's clothes to the "sort of silky costume" Tierney wore walking across the desert in *Sundown* (Henry Hathaway, 1941) and describes her face as having "the same Isabel look that tempted Tyrone Power" in *The Razor's Edge* (Edmund Goulding, 1946). *Bogart's Face* deploys the *Laura* portrait as a logo for Hollywood film noir, and the frequent references to the real Tierney conflate the star with the characters she played.

Tierney and Bogart never starred together in a film noir, but their fantasy pairing acknowledges the place they share in the cultural memory of film noir as stars in the same canon. Naremore has argued that "even when parody ridicules a style, it feeds on what it imitates."[20] Further still, "parody helps to define and even create certain styles, giving them visibility and status."[21] The film's campy sendups of Tierney and Bogart demonstrate the pedagogical function of parody, reflecting and shaping how audiences recognized and understood film noir, for example, through certain acting styles, star personae, costumes, makeup, accessories, and props. Parody does not lay its subject to rest but instead allows "certain motifs to survive and enter new combinations."[22] Noir parodies such as *Bogart's Face*, *Dead Men Don't Wear Plaid* (Carl Reiner, 1982), and *Fatal Instinct* (Carl Reiner, 1993)—along with a host of cartoons, commercials, and episodes of television sitcoms—exploit and exaggerate noir character types such as the detective and the femme fatale to seize on a popular tradition, subjecting it to comic ridicule and paying sincere homage in equal measure.[23] Appearing in urban environments and low-key lighting, speaking in hard-boiled dialogue and narration, they imitate midcentury

Hollywood stars down to the cigarettes, alcohol, and period fashions. *Dead Men Don't Wear Plaid* was shot in black and white and intercuts footage of Steve Martin with scenes from classic films starring Bogart, Barbara Stanwyck, and Lana Turner, among others, while *Fatal Instinct* features a dark-haired heroine played by Sherilyn Fenn and named (what else?) Laura.

Laura's legacy persists in media and popular culture both through visual citation and more general examples of intertextuality. A satire on Hollywood, *The Player* (Robert Altman, 1992) substitutes the portrait for the film poster hanging in the office of studio executive Griffin Mill (Tim Robbins), but *Laura* is only one of many citations in the film. Under the guise of a neo-noir, *The Player* satirizes Hollywood as an industry run by people who have seen a lot of movies but fail to understand cinema as an art form (for Griffin, a mass-produced poster is as good as a painting). Mark Frost and David Lynch paid homage to *Laura* in their canceled ABC series *Twin Peaks* (1990–1991), a murder mystery set in small-town Washington that expanded on *Laura*'s themes of male fantasy projection and challenged audiences with the question "Who killed Laura Palmer?" Most often in the show, the teenage murder victim Laura (Sheryl Lee) was seen through the photographic representation of her ubiquitous homecoming-queen portrait, but the feature-film prequel *Twin Peaks: Fire Walk with Me* (David Lynch, 1992) gave her the role of protagonist and recounted the events that led up to her death. With Frost and Lynch's limited event series on Showtime, *Twin Peaks: The Return* (2017), Laura Palmer has since proven her own lasting presence.[24] The original *Laura* portrait turned up most recently in 2017, on cinephile social media, thanks to a tweet from Jan-Christopher Horak, the director of the UCLA Film & Television Archive. Horak discovered it in the collection of the late *Hollywood Reporter* columnist and television host Robert Osborne, a longtime Tierney fan who kept her films in the spotlight on Turner Classic Movies. As these examples illustrate, the *Laura* portrait ensures an ongoing visibility and reproducibility of Tierney's image as an instantly recognizable source of Hollywood nostalgia—distinguished by a studio pedigree and vintage film style—that vanishes, like Laura herself, only to return.

Acknowledgments

One of the most gratifying experiences of my career has been to see this book develop at Wayne State University Press. Acquisitions editor Marie Sweetman was one of my earliest and strongest advocates, and I owe her my deepest thanks for her commitment to the project. My two peers who reviewed the manuscript—Philippa Gates and Amanda Konkle—offered important suggestions for improvement and appreciated the project's goals with generosity, devoting their time and attention in a year when the COVID-19 pandemic had already demanded so much of it. Barry Keith Grant enthusiastically recommended publication, and I am honored to have a place in his excellent Contemporary Approaches to Film and Media Series. Stephanie Williams, Emily Nowak, Kristin Harpster, Carrie Teefey, Kelsey Giffin, Vi-An Nguyen, Jude Grant, and Rachel Lyon diligently shepherded the project through its final stages. The strengths of their labor cannot be overstated.

I gratefully acknowledge the College of Arts and Sciences at Syracuse University for its generous support of my research and the book's production. Research for the book required looking at historical material related to Tierney's promotion, publicity, and reception. The following librarians, archivists, and research facilities made accessing these primary sources possible: Sophia Lorent and the Moving Image Department at the George Eastman Museum; the Billy Rose Theatre Division at the New York Public Library for the Performing Arts; Ashley Swinnerton and the Film Study Center at the Museum of Modern Art; the Margaret Herrick Library of the Academy of Motion Picture Arts and Sciences; Kristine Krueger and the National Film Information Service of the Margaret Herrick Library; and Patrick Williams and the Syracuse University Libraries. Eric Hoyt deserves a special mention as the director of the Media History Digital Library, which allowed me to conduct a substantial amount of research right from my office. For selecting me as one of the spring 2021 Faculty Fellows, I am also indebted to Vivian May and the Syracuse University Humanities Center. The fellowship came with funding that I could apply toward the book's production expenses and released me from a semester of teaching so that I could finish writing in a timely manner.

I had the great fortune of working with colleagues in the Department of English at Syracuse University who helped create an environment in which writing a new book seemed actually manageable. Roger Hallas and my retired predecessor Steve Cohan were patient and encouraging mentors. Without their advice, especially in the early stages of writing, it is hard to imagine this book as it currently exists. Chris Hanson was always available to answer my questions about teaching and technology, and he remains a font of much-needed humor. If working in the department's Film and Screen Studies track feels like more than a job, it is because Roger and Chris prove that being friends and colleagues are not mutually exclusive relationships. Writing this book spanned the terms of two department chairs—Erin Mackie and Coran Klaver—and I thank them both for their ample support.

Colleagues outside of Syracuse University contributed to my progress on the book in various ways. Adrienne McLean and Katherine Fusco read and commented on drafts of chapters. Steve Rybin joined me for part of my visit to the Margaret Herrick Library and also brought *Screen Romances* magazine to my attention. I rehearsed excerpts from chapters at the Society for Cinema and Media Studies conferences held in Atlanta (2016), Chicago (2017), Seattle (2019), and online (2020), as well as the Modernist Studies Association conferences held in Pasadena (2016) and Amsterdam (2017). Philippa Gates and Katherine Spring organized the conference Classical Hollywood Studies in the 21st Century at Wilfrid Laurier University in 2018, and Sheri Chinen Biesen organized the "Stars and Screen" Film and Media History Conference at Rowan University later the same year, providing additional opportunities for me to present on Tierney. Closer to home, I engaged in regular conversations with my film studies neighbors, Matt Fee, Phil Novak, and Julie Grossman at Le Moyne College. Julie read and gave feedback on the entire manuscript, sending a vote of confidence before it went to press (her influence on this project has been profound since its beginning). An early version of chapter 1 was published in *Camera Obscura* 22, no. 2 (98) (2018), and an early version of chapter 4 was published in *Resetting the Scene: Classical Hollywood Revisited* (2021), edited by Philippa Gates and Katherine Spring. That material has been republished here by permission of Duke University Press and Wayne State University Press, respectively.

My acknowledgments would not be complete without recognizing the larger community I am lucky to have in Syracuse, including Crystal Bartolovich, Mike Goode, Eric Grode, Kate Hanson, Jolynn Parker, Kendall Phillips, Eevie Smith, Matt Spitzmueller, Farha Ternikar, Cath Thomas, Travis Vande Berg, and Bob and Dawn Wilson.

Finally, Andrea Scheibel was there when I first had the idea to do this project, and she carefully read every iteration of the manuscript that followed. I dedicate the book to her, as it was her admiration for and insights on Gene Tierney that really showed me how to write it.

Notes

Abbreviations

AMPAS = Margaret Herrick Library of the Academy of Motion Picture Arts and Sciences, Beverly Hills, CA.

GEM = George Eastman Museum, Rochester, NY.

MoMA = Museum of Modern Art, New York, NY.

NYPL = New York Public Library for the Performing Arts, New York, NY.

Introduction

1 When referring to a film for the first time in a chapter, I have cited the director's name and year of release in parentheses unless this information is given in the text. A chronological list of Gene Tierney's film and television credits can be found on page 249.

2 Johnny Mercer, *Laura: Theme Melody from the 20th Century-Fox Picture* Laura (New York: Robbins Music Corporation, 1945), personal collection.

3 Kristin Thompson, *Breaking the Glass Armor: Neoformalist Film Analysis* (Princeton, NJ: Princeton University Press, 1988), 162.

4 Foster Hirsch, *The Dark Side of the Screen: Film Noir* (Cambridge, MA: Da Capo Press, 2008), 121.

5 Thompson, *Breaking the Glass Armor*, 164. Kathryn Kalinak explains how the unexpected popularity of Raksin's theme "gave rise to the phenomenon known as the theme score, a stylistic approach to film scoring which privileged a single musical theme. The studio had a marketable commodity that could be lifted from the score and function as an integral piece of music." Kalinak, *Settling the Score: Music and the Classical Hollywood Film* (Madison: University of Wisconsin Press, 1992), 170.

6 At the time of Raksin's death in 2004, more than four hundred artists had recorded *Laura*'s theme, making it one of the most rerecorded songs in popular-music history and securing Raksin's reputation as the "grandfather of film music." Tamara Conniff, "*Laura*'s Composer Raksin Dies," *Hollywood Reporter*, August 10, 2004.

7 Gene Tierney with Mickey Herskowitz, *Self-Portrait* (New York: Berkley, 1980), 120.

8 James Naremore, *More than Night: Film Noir in Its Contexts*, 2nd ed. (Berkeley: University of California Press, 2008), 13.

9 "Complete National Film Registry Listing," Library of Congress, www .loc.gov/programs/national-film-preservation-board/film-registry/ complete-national-film-registry-listing/.

10 "The AFI List," American Film Institute, www.afi.com/afi-lists/.

11 In 1950, Tierney willed her famous eyes to the Eye-Bank for Sight Restoration in New York City. "Gene Tierney Wills Eyes to Sightless," *Hollywood Citizen-News*, May 23, 1950. Gene Tierney Clipping File, AMPAS.

12 Richard Harland Smith, "Gene Tierney Biography," TCM: Turner Classic Movies, https://www.tcm.com/tcmdb/person/191988%7C57782/ Gene-Tierney/#biography.

13 Leonard Maltin, *Leonard Maltin's Movie Encyclopedia* (New York: Penguin, 1995), 879.

14 David Thomson, *The New Biographical Dictionary of Film*, 2nd ed. (New York: Knopf, 2010), 969; Otto Friedrich, *City of Nets: A Portrait of Hollywood in the 1940's* (Harper, 2014), 155.

15 Bosley Crowther, "The Screen in Review: *The Ghost and Mrs. Muir*, with Rex Harrison, Gene Tierney, and George Sanders Opens at Radio City Music Hall," *New York Times*, June 27, 1947.

16 Bosley Crowther, "The Screen," *New York Times*, April 11, 1946.

17 Bosley Crowther, "The Screen in Review: Six New Films Arrive on the Holiday in Midtown Houses—Gene Tierney Appears in *Leave Her to Heaven* at Roxy," *New York Times*, December 26, 1945.

18 Amanda Konkle, *Some Kind of Mirror: Creating Marilyn Monroe* (New Brunswick, NJ: Rutgers University Press, 2019), 2.

19 Ibid., 7.

20 Biography of Gene Tierney, 1940, Core Collection Files, AMPAS.

21 Tierney with Herskowitz, *Self-Portrait*, 121–122.

22 Scott Eyman, *Ernst Lubitsch: Laughter in Paradise* (Baltimore: Johns Hopkins University Press, 2000), 354–359.

23 Megan Minarich, "Abortion's Coded Visibility: The Failed Censorship and Box-Office Success of *Leave Her to Heaven*," *Feminist Media Histories* 6, no. 4 (2020): 144.

24 Fredda Dudley, "Leave Heaven to Her," *Modern Screen*, August 1946, 59.

25 Thomas Schatz, *Boom and Bust: American Cinema in the 1940s* (Berkeley: University of California Press, 1999), 356, 363.

26 Tierney with Herskowitz, *Self-Portrait*, 157–158; and David Coleman, *The Bipolar Express: Manic Depression and the Movies* (Lanham, MD: Rowman & Littlefield, 2014), 98.

27 Sean Griffin, "Introduction: Stardom in the 1940s," in *What Dreams Were Made Of: Movie Stars of the 1940s*, ed. Sean Griffin (New Brunswick, NJ: Rutgers University Press, 2011), 2.

28 See Martin Shingler, *Star Studies: A Critical Guide* (London: BFI, 2012). The single-star volumes in British Film Institute's "Film Stars" series, ed. Shingler and Susan Smith, demonstrate the field's continued investment in Hollywood stars and its recent expansion to analyze stars from around the world.

29 See, for example, the following: Adrienne L. McLean, *Being Rita Hayworth: Labor, Identity, and Hollywood Stardom* (New Brunswick, NJ: Rutgers University Press, 2004); Karen McNally, *When Frankie Went to Hollywood: Frank Sinatra and American Male Identity* (Urbana: University of Illinois Press, 2008); Amy Lawrence, *The Passion of Montgomery Clift* (Berkeley: University of California Press, 2010); Tamar Jeffers McDonald, *Doris Day Confidential: Hollywood, Sex and Stardom* (London: I. B. Tauris, 2013); Elisabetta Girelli, *Montgomery Clift, Queer Star* (Detroit: Wayne State University Press, 2014); Kristen Hatch, *Shirley Temple and the Performance of Girlhood* (New Brunswick, NJ: Rutgers University Press, 2015); Victoria Sturtevant, *A Great Big Girl Like Me: The Films of Marie Dressler* (Urbana: University of Illinois Press, 2016); Gillian Kelly, *Robert Taylor: Male Beauty, Masculinity, and Stardom in Hollywood* (Jackson: University Press of Mississippi, 2019); Konkle, *Some Kind of Mirror*; Olympia Kiriakou, *Becoming Carole Lombard: Stardom, Comedy, and Legacy* (London: Bloomsbury, 2020); and Lisa Stead, *Reframing Vivien Leigh: Stardom, Gender, and the Archive* (New York: Oxford University Press, 2021).

30 McLean, *Being Rita Hayworth*, 3.

31 Richard Dyer, *Stars*, 2nd ed. (London: BFI, 1998), 60.

32 *The Ghost and Mrs. Muir* Pressbook, 1947, Department of Film Special Collections, MoMA.

33 Dyer, *Stars*, 61.

34 Tierney with Herskowitz, *Self-Portrait*, 48.

35 Dyer, *Stars*, 62–63.

36 Ibid., 61.

37 Ibid., 61–62.

38 Richard Dyer, *Only Entertainment*, 2nd ed. (London: Routledge, 2002), 79.

39 Ibid., 80.

40 McLean, *Being Rita Hayworth*, 16.

41 Ibid., 25.

42 Adrienne McLean, "Introduction," in *Headline Hollywood: A Century of Film Scandal*, ed. Adrienne L. McLean and David A. Cook (New Brunswick, NJ: Rutgers University Press, 2001), 9.

43 Cynthia Baron and Sharon Marie Carnicke, *Reframing Screen Performance* (Ann Arbor: University of Michigan Press, 2008), 17.

44 Ibid., 18. Popular discourse on acting began to shift in the early 1950s. Even a magazine such as *Photoplay* emphasized the labor of acting lessons as an ingredient in turning Hollywood newcomers into stars, a topic that Fredda Dudley covered in her "How a Star Is Born" series. See Konkle, *Some Kind of Mirror*, 14.

45 Virginia Wright Wexman, *Creating the Couple: Love, Marriage, and Hollywood Performance* (Princeton, NJ: Princeton University Press, 1993), 143.

46 Ibid., 144–145.

47 See McLean, *Being Rita Hayworth*; Konkle, *Some Kind of Mirror*; and Therese Grisham and Julie Grossman, *Ida Lupino, Director: Her Art and Resilience in Times of Transition* (New Brunswick, NJ: Rutgers University Press, 2017).

48 See Emily Carman, *Independent Stardom: Freelance Women in the Hollywood Studio System* (Austin: University of Texas Press, 2016); and Dyer, *Stars*, 54–59.

49 Schatz, *Boom and Bust*, 363.

50 For more on female performance related to song and dance, see McLean, *Being Rita Hayworth*; Priscilla Peña Ovalle, *Dance and*

the Hollywood Latina: Race, Sex, and Stardom (New Brunswick, NJ: Rutgers University Press, 2011); and Kirsten Pullen, *Like a Natural Woman: Spectacular Female Performance in Classical Hollywood* (New Brunswick, NJ: Rutgers University Press, 2014). See Konkle, *Some Kind of Mirror*, 147–187, for more on Monroe's training in the Method.

51 Konkle, *Some Kind of Mirror*, 13.

52 Written and directed by Clara and Julia Kuperberg, *Gene Tierney: A Forgotten Star* was produced by Wichita Films and aired in 2017 on the French network OCS.

53 See David M. Lugowski, "Claudette Colbert, Ginger Rogers, and Barbara Stanwyck: American Homefront Women," and Adrienne L. McLean, "Betty Grable and Rita Hayworth: Pinned Up," in *What Dreams Were Made Of: Movie Stars of the 1940s*, ed. Sean Griffin (New Brunswick, NJ: Rutgers University Press, 2011), 96–119, 166–191. See also Jeanine Basinger, "The Wartime American Woman on Film: Home-Front Soldier," in *A Companion to the War Film*, ed. Douglas A. Cunningham and John C. Nelson (Malden, MA: Wiley-Blackwell, 2016), 89–105.

54 Biography of Gene Tierney, 1946, Core Collection Files, AMPAS.

55 McLean, *Being Rita Hayworth*, 16.

56 Miriam Hansen, *Babel and Babylon: Spectatorship in American Silent Film* (Cambridge, MA: Harvard University Press, 1991), 91.

57 Ibid., 245–268.

58 Ibid., 116.

59 Ibid., 117.

60 Clayton R. Koppes and Gregory D. Black, *Hollywood Goes to War: How Politics, Profits and Propaganda Shaped World War II Movies* (Berkeley: University of California Press, 1990), 142–184.

61 Jeanine Basinger, *A Woman's View: How Hollywood Spoke to Women, 1930–1960* (New York: Knopf, 1993), 93. The concept of the "woman's picture" or "woman's film" has been queried and discussed at length by the following feminist film scholars: Pam Cook, "Melodrama and the Woman's Picture," in *Imitations of Life: A Reader on Film & Television Melodrama*, ed. Marcia Landy (Detroit: Wayne State University Press, 1991), 248–262; Pam Cook, "No Fixed Address: The Women's Picture from *Outrage* to *Blue Steel*," in *Contemporary Hollywood Cinema*, ed. Steve Neale and Murray Smith (London: Routledge, 1998),

229–246; Mary Ann Doane, *The Desire to Desire: The Woman's Film of the 1940s* (Bloomington: Indiana University Press, 1987); Molly Haskell, *From Reverence to Rape: The Treatment of Women in the Movies*, 3rd ed. (Chicago: University of Chicago Press, 2016), 153–188; Andrea S. Walsh, *Women's Film and Female Experience, 1940–1950* (New York: Praeger, 1984); and many of the contributors to *Home Is Where the Heart Is: Studies in Melodrama and the Woman's Film*, ed. Christine Gledhill (London: BFI, 1987).

62 Philippa Gates, "Home Sweet Home Front Women: Adapting Women for Hollywood's World War II Home-Front Films," *Americana: The Journal of American Popular Culture* 15, no. 2 (2016): www.americanpopularculture.com/journal/articles/fall_2016/gates.htm.

63 Thomas Doherty, *Projections of War: Hollywood, American Culture, and World War II*, 2nd ed. (New York: Columbia University Press, 1999), 153–154, 164–174.

64 Helen Hanson, *Hollywood Heroines: Women in Film Noir and the Female Gothic Film* (London: I. B. Tauris, 2007), 12.

65 Ibid., 15.

66 Ibid., 14. For more on U.S. women working during World War II, see Andrea S. Walsh, *Women's Film and Female Experience, 1940–1950* (New York: Praeger, 1984), 49–88; and Michael Renov, *Hollywood's Wartime Woman: Representation and Ideology* (Ann Arbor, MI: UMI Research Press, 1988), 33–47.

67 See Dana Polan, *Power and Paranoia: History, Narrative, and the American Cinema, 1940–1950* (New York: Columbia University Press, 1986).

68 Doherty, *Projections of War*, 155–158.

69 Tim Snelson, *Phantom Ladies: Hollywood Horror and the Home Front* (New Brunswick, NJ: Rutgers University Press, 2015), 7.

70 Ibid., 5, 6.

71 Ibid., 5.

72 Ibid., 7.

73 Biography of Gene Tierney, 1940, Core Collection Files, AMPAS. Fox's biography cited November 20 as her birthday and the press repeated this error, but Tierney later corrected the record (in addition to disputing rumors about her life and career) in a *Hollywood Reporter* piece. See Gene Tierney, "Fact and Fiction," *Hollywood Reporter*, December 31, 1945.

74 Biography of Gene Tierney, 1943, Core Collection Files, AMPAS.

75 Paul Benedict, "Gene with a Capital G!," *Silver Screen*, February 1941, 39.

76 Sidney Skolsky, "Hollywood Is My Beat: Go-Getter," *New York Post*, March 21, 1954.

77 Tierney with Herskowitz, *Self-Portrait*, 8–18.

78 Ibid., 19–28.

79 Ibid., 36–42.

80 Ibid., 44–46.

81 Biography of Gene Tierney, 1943, Core Collection Files, AMPAS.

82 Tierney with Herskowitz, *Self-Portrait*, 84.

83 See "March Mode-Makers," *Photoplay*, March 1942, 57–61.

84 Steven Dillon, *Wolf-Women and Phantom Ladies: Female Desire in 1940s US Culture* (Albany: State University of New York Press, 2015), 141, 144.

85 Tierney with Herskowitz, *Self-Portrait*, 48.

86 From 1956 to 1962, Zanuck worked as a semi-independent producer who distributed his films through Fox, and in 1962 he replaced Spyros Skouras as president. Peter Lev, *Twentieth Century–Fox: The Zanuck-Skouras Years, 1935–1965* (Austin: University of Texas Press, 2013), 4, 23–24.

87 Ibid., 48.

88 Tierney with Herskowitz, *Self-Portrait*, 124.

89 *Rings on Her Fingers* Pressbook, 1942, Department of Film Special Collections, MoMA.

90 Tierney with Herskowitz, *Self-Portrait*, 91.

91 Publicity release for *Rings on Her Fingers*, 1942, Core Collection Files, AMPAS.

92 *Rings on Her Fingers* Pressbook, 1942, Department of Film Special Collections, MoMA.

93 Ibid.

94 Basinger, "The Wartime American Woman on Film," 89.

95 Ibid., 93.

96 Maria Elena Buszek, *Pin-Up Grrrls: Feminisms, Sexuality, Popular Culture* (Durham, NC: Duke University Press, 2006), 224.

97 See Rebecca Bell-Metereau and Colleen Glenn, "Introduction," in *Star Bodies and the Erotics of Suffering*, ed. Rebecca Bell-Metereau and Colleen Glenn (Detroit: Wayne State University Press, 2015), 1–25.

Chapter 1

1 "We Point with Pride to Gene Tierney," *Silver Screen*, November 1942, 58.
2 Gene Tierney, "Fact and Fiction," *Hollywood Reporter*, December 31, 1945.
3 "We Point with Pride to Gene Tierney," 58.
4 "Dress Up—Not Down!" *Silver Screen*, July 1942, 45.
5 "*Modern Screen* Goes Easter Shopping," *Modern Screen*, May 1943, 48–51.
6 *China Girl* Pressbook, 1942, Department of Film Special Collections, MoMA.
7 Gene Tierney with Mickey Herskowitz, *Self-Portrait* (New York: Berkley, 1980), 92.
8 Ibid., 92–93.
9 "Countess from Brooklyn," *Photoplay*, March 1946, 55.
10 At a time when the studios were afraid of offending southern moviegoers, Trotti (a white southerner transplanted in Hollywood) served as a consultant on films set in the South. He was a former journalist who began his career in movies doing public relations for the Motion Picture Producers and Distributors of America, the industry trade association. In 1932, he followed his boss Col. Jason Joy to the Fox Film Corporation story department, and he worked at Twentieth Century–Fox as a screenwriter and producer until 1952, when he died prematurely from a heart attack. See Matthew H. Bernstein, "A 'Professional Southerner' in the Hollywood Studio System: Lamar Trotti at Work, 1925–1952," in *American Cinema and the Southern Imaginary*, ed. Deborah E. Barker and Kathryn McKee (Athens: University of Georgia Press, 2011), 122–147.
11 Peter Lev, *Twentieth Century–Fox: The Zanuck-Skouras Years, 1935–1965* (Austin: University of Texas Press, 2013), 72–74.
12 Along with John Lund and Richard Widmark, Tierney's costars in later films, Wellman was one of the three men she most admired in Hollywood because they made her the most comfortable. Tierney with Herskowitz, *Self-Portrait*, 151.
13 Dorothy Townsend, "William Wellman, Director, Dies," *Los Angeles Times*, December 10, 1975.
14 Lev, *Twentieth Century–Fox*, 74.
15 David M. Lugowski, "Claudette Colbert, Ginger Rogers, and Barbara Stanwyck: American Homefront Women," in *What Dreams Were*

Made Of: Movie Stars of the 1940s, ed. Sean Griffin (New Brunswick, NJ: Rutgers University Press, 2011), 119; Adrienne L. McLean, "Betty Grable and Rita Hayworth: Pinned Up," in *What Dreams Were Made Of: Movie Stars of the 1940s*, ed. Sean Griffin (New Brunswick, NJ: Rutgers University Press, 2011), 169.

16   Jeanine Basinger, "The Wartime American Woman on Film: Home-Front Soldier," in *A Companion to the War Film*, ed. Douglas A. Cunningham and John C. Nelson (Malden, MA: Wiley-Blackwell, 2016), 94.

17   Ibid., 94, 97.

18   John Truesdell, "Gene Tierney Insists on Working Hard," *Boston Post*, Aug. 24, 1941.

19   *Thunder Birds* Pressbook, 1942, Department of Film Special Collections, MoMA.

20   Ibid.

21   Ibid.

22   Ibid.

23   Ibid.

24   The term *metteur-en-scène* was used by the *Cahiers du Cinéma* critics in the 1950s to refer to technically proficient directors who lack the distinctive personal visions of auteurs.

25   This wartime "conversion narrative" was a common rhetorical strategy in 1940s Hollywood cinema. See Dana Polan, *Power and Paranoia: History, Narrative, and the American Cinema, 1940–1950* (New York: Columbia University Press, 1986), 75–76.

26   *China Girl* Pressbook, 1942, Department of Film Special Collections, MoMA.

27   Ibid.

28   Steven Dillon, *Wolf-Women and Phantom Ladies: Female Desire in 1940s US Culture* (Albany: State University of New York Press, 2015), 152.

29   Ibid.

30   I have not been able to determine the origin of this poem and have transcribed it directly from the film.

31   Lev, *Twentieth Century–Fox*, 79.

32   *China Girl* Pressbook, 1942, Department of Film Special Collections, MoMA.

33   Ibid.

34 Sarah Berry, *Screen Style: Fashion and Femininity in 1930s Hollywood* (Minneapolis: University of Minnesota Press, 2000), 94.

35 Ibid., 95.

36 Ibid., 117.

37 Ibid., 111.

38 Ibid., 112.

39 *China Girl* Pressbook 1942, Department of Film Special Collections, MoMA.

40 Karla Rae Fuller, *Hollywood Goes Oriental: CaucAsian Performance in American Film* (Detroit: Wayne State University Press, 2010), 1–2.

41 Ibid., 31.

42 Ibid., 31–32.

43 Paul Benedict, "Gene with a Capital G!," *Silver Screen*, February 1941, 39, 87.

44 Sean Griffin, "The Wearing of the Green: Performing Irishness in the Fox Wartime Musical," in *The Irish in Us: Irishness, Performativity, and Popular Culture*, ed. Diane Negra (Durham, NC: Duke University Press, 2006), 64, 65.

45 Aubrey Malone, *Maureen O'Hara: The Biography* (Lexington: University of Kentucky Press, 2013), 31.

46 Ibid., 33.

47 Rudy Behlmer, *America's Favorite Movies: Behind the Scenes* (New York: Frederick Ungar, 1982), 197.

48 Sheri Chinen Biesen, *Blackout: World War II and the Origins of Film Noir* (Baltimore: Johns Hopkins University Press, 2005), 160.

49 Vera Caspary, "My *Laura* and Otto's," *Saturday Review*, June 1971, 36.

50 Behlmer, *America's Favorite Movies*, 180–181.

51 For feminist insights into the adaptation of Caspary's novel, see Julie Grossman, "Women and Film Noir: Pulp Fiction and the Woman's Picture," in *Kiss the Blood Off My Hands: On Classic Film Noir*, ed. Robert Miklitsch (Urbana: University of Illinois Press, 2014), 37–61; and Margaret A. Toth and Teresa Ramoni, "'Their Voices Ring in My Ears: *Laura*, the Fugue, and Adaptation," *Adaptation* 14, no. 1 (2020): 136–156.

52 Behlmer, *America's Favorite Movies*, 182–184.

53 Peter Bogdanovich, "The Making of *Laura* by Otto Preminger as Told by Peter Bogdanovich," *On Film* 1, no. 0 (1970): 49.

54 Behlmer, *America's Favorite Movies*, 184.

55 Darryl F. Zanuck to Otto Preminger, November 1, 1943, in *Memo from Darryl F. Zanuck: The Golden Years at Twentieth Century–Fox*, ed. Rudy Behlmer (New York: Grove Press, 1993), 68.

56 Ibid., 69.

57 Darryl F. Zanuck to Otto Preminger, Rouben Mamoulian, and Samuel Hoffenstein, March 20, 1944, in *Memo from Darryl F. Zanuck: The Golden Years at Twentieth Century–Fox*, ed. Rudy Behlmer (New York: Grove Press, 1993), 70.

58 Beginning with Petrarch in the fourteenth century, *Laura* was a recurring name in lyric poetry for an idealized and unattainable love object (from Robert Tofte to Lord Byron and Friedrich Schiller). Caspary has denied any significance to the name in her novel beyond simply liking it. Behlmer, *America's Favorite Movies*, 177.

59 Stephen Michael Shearer, *Beautiful: The Hedy Lamarr Story* (New York: St. Martin's Griffin, 2013), 177; Paul Green, *Jennifer Jones: The Life and Films* (Jefferson, NC: McFarland, 2011), 61, 220–221.

60 Tierney with Herskowitz, *Self-Portrait*, 121.

61 For more on postwar "semidocumentaries," see Thomas Schatz, *Boom and Bust: American Cinema in the 1940s* (Berkeley: University of California Press, 1999), 378–386.

62 Caspary, "My *Laura* and Otto's," 37.

63 Kathryn Kalinak, *Settling the Score: Music and the Classical Hollywood Film* (Madison: University of Wisconsin Press, 1992), 166, 171.

64 Qtd. in ibid., 167. For more on the music in *Laura*, see Richard Ness, "A Lotta Night Music: The Sound of Film Noir," *Cinema Journal* 47, no. 2 (2008): 52–73.

65 Caspary, "My *Laura* and Otto's," 37.

66 Chris Fujiwara, *The World and Its Double: The Life and Work of Otto Preminger* (New York: Faber & Faber, 2008), 37.

67 Ibid., 40–44; Otto Preminger, *Preminger: An Autobiography* (Garden City, NY: Doubleday, 1977), 75–76.

68 Caspary, "My *Laura* and Otto's," 37.

69 Behlmer, *America's Favorite Movies*, 193–197.

70 Bogdanovich, "The Making of *Laura*," 52.

71 Tierney with Herskowitz, *Self-Portrait*, 124.

72 Shari Roberts, "'The Lady in the Tutti-Frutti Hat: Carmen Miranda, a Spectacle of Ethnicity," *Cinema Journal* 93, no. 32 (1993): 4.

73　Ibid.

74　Ronald L. Davis, *Hollywood Beauty: Linda Darnell and the American Dream* (Norman: University of Oklahoma Press, 1991), 96–97. Tierney described the story as "trash" and chose not to pursue it. Tierney with Herskowitz, *Self-Portrait*, 143–144.

75　Davis, *Hollywood Beauty*, 68–69, 81.

76　Ibid., 96–104.

77　Lev, *Twentieth Century–Fox*, 165.

78　Philip K. Scheuer, "La Tierney Hints Bolt to Comedy," *Los Angeles Times*, February 10, 1946. Gene Tierney Clipping File, AMPAS.

79　Ula Lukszo, "Noir Fashion and Noir as Fashion," in *Fashion in Film*, ed. Adrienne Munich (Bloomington: Indiana University Press, 2011), 62.

80　Robert Osborne, "Rambling Reporter," *Hollywood Reporter*, June 19, 1990.

81　Biesen, *Blackout*, 160.

82　Donna Peberdy, "Acting and Performance in Film Noir," in *A Companion to Film Noir*, ed. Andrew Spicer and Helen Hanson (Malden, MA: Wiley-Blackwell, 2013), 327–328.

83　Ibid., 328.

84　Kristin Thompson, *Breaking the Glass Armor: Neoformalist Film Analysis* (Princeton, NJ: Princeton University Press, 1988), 183.

85　Gene Tierney, "Farewell to the Orient," *Hollywood Reporter*, November 5, 1945.

86　Gene Tierney, "Fact and Fiction," *Hollywood Reporter*, December 31, 1945.

87　Rosalind Galt, *Pretty: Film and the Decorative Image* (New York: Columbia University Press, 2011), 124.

88　Ibid., 122.

89　Ibid., 145, 147.

90　Darryl F. Zanuck to Otto Preminger, Rouben Mamoulian, and Samuel Hoffenstein, March 20, 1944, in *Memo from Darryl F. Zanuck: The Golden Years at Twentieth Century–Fox*, ed. Rudy Behlmer (New York: Grove Press, 1993), 70.

91　For more on the "working-girl investigator" in Hollywood's wartime film noir productions, see Hanson, *Hollywood Heroines: Women in Film Noir and the Female Gothic Film* (London: I. B. Tauris, 2007), 18–32. Fox later remade *I Wake Up Screaming* as *Vicki* (Harry Horner,

1953) and switched blondes for brunettes by casting Jeanne Crain as the "working-girl investigator" and Jean Peters as the murdered woman. *Vicki* also pays homage to *Laura* when Vicki's press agent (Elliott Reid), a suspect in her murder case, hides from the police in a movie theater and we hear dialogue spoken by Gene Tierney and Dana Andrews from the film playing off-screen.

92 Newman first composed this melody for Samuel Goldwyn's *Street Scene* (King Vidor, 1931), and Fox recycled it in film noir throughout the 1940s: *The Dark Corner* (Henry Hathaway, 1946), *Kiss of Death* (Henry Hathaway, 1947), *Cry of the City* (Robert Siodmak, 1948), and *Where the Sidewalk Ends*. It was also used as the overture in Fox's New York City comedy *How to Marry a Millionaire* (Jean Negulesco, 1953) to demonstrate the stereo sound of its first film shot in CinemaScope. When Fox remade *I Wake Up Screaming*, Ken Darby and Max Showalter composed a brand-new theme, à la Raksin's "Laura," titled "Vicki," that accompanies the opening credits playing over Vicki's painted portrait.

93 Preminger, *Preminger*, 73–74.

94 Behlmer, *America's Favorite Movies*, 178–179.

95 Benedict, "Gene with a Capital G!," 82.

96 Truesdell, "Gene Tierney Insists on Working Hard."

97 Kirtley Baskette, "Fugitive from the Four Hundred," *Modern Screen*, March 1941, 39.

98 *The Ghost and Mrs. Muir* Pressbook, 1947, Department of Film Special Collections, MoMA.

99 Thorstein Veblen, *The Theory of the Leisure Class* (New York: Penguin, 1994), 68–101.

100 "Countess from Brooklyn," 55.

101 Ethel King, "Bonnie Cashin," *Guardian*, Feb. 8, 2000, www .theguardian.com/news/2000/feb/09/guardianobituaries4.

102 Stephanie Lake, *Bonnie Cashin: Chic Is Where You Find It* (New York: Rizzoli, 2016), 42.

103 Maureen Turim, "Designing Women: The Emergence of the New Sweetheart Line," in *Fabrications: Costume and the Female Body*, ed. Jane Gaines and Charlotte Herzog (London: Routledge, 1990), 212–213.

104 King, "Bonnie Cashin."

105 Lake, *Bonnie Cashin*, 42.
106 Bonnie Cashin, "Notes from a Designer's Diary," *Screenland*, June 1945, 37.
107 Ibid., 35.
108 Ibid., 66.
109 Jane Gaines, "Costume and Narrative: How Dress Tells the Woman's Story," in *Fabrications: Costume and the Female Body*, ed. Jane Gaines and Charlotte Herzog (London: Routledge, 1990), 181.
110 Ibid., 191–192.
111 Ibid., 200.
112 Mary Desjardins, "Classical Hollywood, 1928–1946," in *Costume, Makeup, and Hair*, ed. Adrienne L. McLean (New Brunswick, NJ: Rutgers University Press, 2016), 70.
113 Tamar Jeffers McDonald, *Hollywood Catwalk: Exploring Costume and Transformation in American Film* (London: I. B. Tauris, 2010), 66.
114 Ibid., 61.
115 Ibid., 66.
116 A major Fox star, yet often unavailable due to pregnancies, Crain was another one of the few brunettes under contract at the studio in the 1940s (she played the younger sister of Tierney's character in *Leave Her to Heaven*). *In the Meantime, Darling* was the first film that gave her top billing and, unlike Tierney, she starred primarily in musicals and comedies. Crain was not recognized as a dramatic actress until she played a light-skinned African American woman who passes for white in *Pinky* (Elia Kazan, 1949), a role that led to her an Oscar nomination for Best Actress; she also costarred with Linda Darnell and Ann Sothern in *A Letter to Three Wives*. After losing her box-office draw by 1953, she moved to Universal.
117 Barry Gifford, *Out of the Past: Adventures in Film Noir* (Jackson: University Press of Mississippi, 2001), 108.
118 "*Laura*'s Set Score," *Variety*, May 3, 1944.
119 Lila Stuart, "Gene Tierney—Hollywood's Best Dressed Star," *Screen Stars*, May 1945.
120 Elizabeth Wilson, "Gene Tierney Has Her Troubles Too!," *Screenland*, August 1945, 20.
121 "Temporary Blonde," *Silver Screen*, August 1945, 26.
122 Wilson, "Gene Tierney Has Her Troubles Too!," 20.

123 Tierney with Herskowitz, *Self-Portrait*, 124–125.

124 For more on this postwar film cycle, see R. Barton Palmer, *Shot on Location: Postwar American Cinema and the Exploration of Real Place* (New Brunswick, NJ: Rutgers University Press, 2016), 17–23.

125 "$250,000 Libel Suit Started by Army Officer against Author of *A Bell for Adano*, Others," *New York Times*, March 14, 1946.

126 "Toscani Who Claimed He Was 'Joppolo' on *Adano* Loses in Important Decision for Scripters on Civil Rights Issue," *Variety*, December 4, 1946.

127 Douglas Martin, "F. E. Toscani, 89, Dies; Model for Hero of *Bell for Adano*," *New York Times*, January 28, 2001.

128 "$250,000 Libel Suit," *New York Times*, March 14, 1946.

Chapter 2

1 Andrea S. Walsh, *Women's Film and Female Experience, 1940–1950* (New York: Praeger, 1984), 76.

2 Ibid., 75.

3 Ibid., 76.

4 Ibid., 78.

5 Michael Renov, *Hollywood's Wartime Woman: Representation and Ideology* (Ann Arbor, MI: UMI Research Press), 33.

6 Ibid., 46.

7 See Julie Grossman, *Rethinking the Femme Fatale in Film Noir: Ready for Her Close-Up* (London: Palgrave Macmillan, 2013).

8 Renov, *Hollywood's Wartime Woman*, 46. For more on the psychological concept of double binding, see Michael Renov, "*Leave Her to Heaven*: The Double Bind of the Post-War Woman," in *Imitations of Life: A Reader on Film & Television Melodrama*, ed. Marcia Landy (Detroit: Wayne State University Press, 1991), 227–236.

9 Hedda Hopper, "Gene Tierney and Cassini Start Test Separation," *Los Angeles Times*, November 12, 1946; "Gene Tierney Files Suit for Divorce," *Los Angeles Daily News*, January 15, 1947; "Gene Tierney Asks for Divorce," *Los Angeles Examiner*, January 15, 1947; "Gene Tierney Divorce Suit Charges Cruelty," *Los Angeles Times*, January 15, 1947; "Gene Tierney Wins Divorce, Complains of Cassini's Temper," *Hollywood Citizen-News*, March 10, 1947; "Gene Tierney Wins Divorce," *Los*

Angeles Examiner, March 11, 1947; "Actress Sites Mate's Hot Temper, Night Life Urge," *Los Angeles Herald Express*, March 11, 1947; "Gene Tierney Says Husband Used Her as Tossing Target," *Los Angeles Daily News*, March 11, 1947; Louella O. Parsons, "Gene Tierney, Cassini Make Up," *Los Angeles Examiner*, April 9, 1948; Hedda Hopper, "Gene Tierney and Mate Reconciled," *Los Angeles Times*, April 9, 1948; "Gene Tierney Asks for Divorce," *Hollywood Citizen-News*, January 16, 1952; "Gene Tierney Sues for Divorce," *Los Angeles Daily News*, January 16, 1952; "Gene Tierney Seeks Divorce From Cassini," *Los Angeles Times*, January 16, 1952; "Gene Tierney Suit Answered," *Los Angeles Examiner*, February 15, 1952; "Gene Tierney Nearer Divorce," *Los Angeles Times*, February 15, 1952; "Cassini Files Suit Reply," *Los Angeles Examiner*, February 16, 1952; "Gene Tierney Suit on Divorce Delayed," *Los Angeles Times*, February 20, 1952; "Gene Tierney Gets Divorce," *Hollywood Citizen-News*, February 28, 1952; "Gene Tierney Given 2nd Cassini Decree," *Los Angeles Examiner*, February 29, 1952; "Gene Tierney Given Divorce Decree," *Los Angeles Times*, February 29, 1952. Gene Tierney Clipping File, AMPAS.

10   "Gene Tierney Given Divorce Decree," *Los Angeles Times*, February 29, 1952. Gene Tierney Clipping File, AMPAS.

11   Renov, *Hollywood's Wartime Woman*, 47.

12   Gates, "Home Sweet Home Front Women: Adapting Women for Hollywood's World War II Home-Front Films," *Americana: The Journal of American Popular Culture* 15, no. 2 (2016), www.americanpopularculture.com/journal/articles/fall_2016/gates.htm.

13   Elisabeth Bronfen, *Specters of War: Hollywood's Engagement with Military Conflict* (New Brunswick, NJ: Rutgers University Press, 2012), 44, 45.

14   Ibid., 48.

15   Mary Jane Manners, "Love in a Cottage," *Silver Screen*, March 1942, 64.

16   "Gene Tierney's Honeymoon Home," *Screenland*, March 1942, 64.

17   James Reid, "Mister Cassini's War Bride," *Silver Screen*, September 1942, 42.

18   Ibid., 43, 72.

19   Ibid.

20   Elizabeth Wilson, "My Problems as a War Wife," *Screenland*, August 1943, 60.

21   Elizabeth Wilson, "Gene Tierney Has Her Troubles Too!," *Screenland*, August 1945, 77.

22 Ibid., 78–79.

23 Ibid., 79.

24 Reid, "Mister Cassini's War Bride," 42, 43.

25 Ibid., 73.

26 To help Leonardo DiCaprio prepare for his role in *Shutter Island*
    (2010), a neo-noir set in the 1950s, director Martin Scorsese report-
    edly screened *Laura* and advised DiCaprio to study Dana Andrews's
    performance. DiCaprio's character is introduced as a U.S. marshal
    and World War II veteran investigating the disappearance of a patient
    in a psychiatric hospital, but we eventually learn that he is, in fact,
    a patient himself, who killed his wife (Michelle Williams) after she
    drowned their children in the lake next to their house. It is revealed
    that his wife suffered from a bipolar disorder. David Coleman con-
    siders the film an homage not to Andrews in *Laura* but to Tierney in
    Leave Her to Heaven, one of Scorsese's favorite films. See David Cole-
    man, *The Bipolar Express: Manic Depression and the Movies* (Lanham,
    MD: Rowman & Littlefield, 2014), 108–109.

27 The Hays Code implicitly forbade the on-screen representation of and
    explicit reference to abortion, which is condemned in the Catholic
    Church. Note that the code was created by Catholics Martin J. Quig-
    ley and Daniel A. Lord (the latter a Jesuit priest) and overseen by the
    Production Code Administration (then led by the Catholic Joseph
    Breen). To prevent boycotts from the church and receive the code seal
    of approval to ensure distribution, filmmakers had to disguise abortion
    and, accordingly, Ellen's feticide in *Leave Her to Heaven* is presented as
    a "miscarriage." Megan Minarich argues that despite the conservative
    regulations of the time, audiences and reviewers still recognized the
    abortion as such, acknowledging Ellen's agency in choosing to termi-
    nate her pregnancy, and they responded positively to the film. Contin-
    ued resistance to abortion censorship on the part of filmmakers in the
    Hollywood studio system led to a code amendment in 1951 that explic-
    itly made abortion forbidden. See Megan Minarich, "Abortion's Coded
    Visibility: The Failed Censorship and Box-Office Success of *Leave Her to
    Heaven*," *Feminist Media Histories* 6, no. 4 (2020): 121–150.

28 Darryl F. Zanuck to William Bacher, December 4, 1944, in *Memo from
    Darryl F. Zanuck: The Golden Years at Twentieth Century–Fox*, ed. Rudy
    Behlmer (New York: Grove Press, 1993), 80.

29　Production Notes on *Leave Her to Heaven*, 1945, Core Collection Files, AMPAS.

30　Jason Altman, "10 Things I Learned: *Leave Her to Heaven*," *Criterion Collection*, April 15, 2020, www.criterion.com/current/posts/6910-10 -things-i-learned-leave-her-to-heaven.

31　A former playwright and lyricist, Swerling returned to Broadway to cowrite the book for the musical *Guys and Dolls* (1950) with Abe Burrows and won a Tony Award.

32　Darryl F. Zanuck to William Bacher, December 4, 1944, in Behlmer, *Memo from Darryl F. Zanuck*, 81.

33　Michael Walker contends that *Leave Her to Heaven* is different from Stahl's other films and that he worked less as an auteur than "as a coordinator and enabler, serving, with his cast and crew, to bring out the force of the melodrama implicit in the script." See Walker, "*Leave Her to Heaven*," in *The Call of the Heart: John M. Stahl and Hollywood Melodrama*, ed. Bruce Babington and Charles Barr (East Barnet, Herts: John Libbey, 2018), 229–241.

34　Altman, "10 Things I Learned."

35　Production Notes on *Leave Her to Heaven*, 1945, Core Collection Files, AMPAS.

36　Ibid.

37　Minarich, "Abortion's Coded Visibility," 144; Peter Lev, *Twentieth Century–Fox: The Zanuck-Skouras Years, 1935–1965* (Austin: University of Texas Press, 2013), 102.

38　See Martin Scorsese's discussion of the Technicolor cinematography in his essay film *A Personal Journey with Martin Scorsese through American Movies* (1995), produced by the British Film Institute. When introducing *Leave Her to Heaven* at the 45th New York Film Festival in 2007, he said that he referred to the film's color palette and design while shooting *New York, New York* (1977) and cited the costumes as an influence on Kate Beckinsale's wardrobe in *The Aviator* (2004). See Adam Schartoff, "Scorsese Introducing *Leave Her to Heaven*," YouTube video, 6:10, October 20, 2007, www.youtube.com/watch?v=ATfhKmkM-rE.

39　Production Notes on *Leave Her to Heaven*, 1945, Core Collection Files, AMPAS.

40　Ibid.

41　Ibid.

42 Jennifer Peterson, "The Front Lawn of Heaven: Landscape in Holly-wood Melodrama circa 1945," *Camera Obscura* 74/25, no. 2 (2010): 129–133.

43 Ibid., 121.

44 Ibid., 142.

45 Ibid., 122.

46 Ibid., 144.

47 Ibid., 142.

48 Ibid., 144.

49 Ibid., 142.

50 Ibid., 143.

51 Production Notes on *Leave Her to Heaven*, 1945, Core Collection Files, AMPAS.

52 Marshall Deutelbaum, "Costuming and the Color System of *Leave Her to Heaven*," *Film Criticism* 11, no. 3 (1987): 17.

53 Mark Jancovich, "Female Monsters: Horror, the 'Femme Fatale' and World War II," *European Journal of American Culture* 27, no. 2 (2008): 133–139.

54 Peterson, "The Front Lawn of Heaven," 124.

55 Ibid., 125.

56 On the dust jacket, Richard's author biography informs her that he was the editor of the *Harvard Lampoon*, which in real life had named Tierney the "Worst Female Discovery of 1940." Perhaps Ellen's revenge on Richard was forecasted from the beginning.

57 Production Notes on *Leave Her to Heaven*, 1945, Core Collection Files, AMPAS.

58 Darryl F. Zanuck to Jules Furthman, April 2, 1947, in *Memo from Darryl F. Zanuck: The Golden Years at Twentieth Century-Fox*, ed. Rudy Behlmer (New York: Grove Press, 1993), 127.

59 James Agee, "The New Pictures," *Time*, January 7, 1946.

60 Qtd. in Jancovich, "Female Monsters," 141.

61 Production Notes on *Leave Her to Heaven*, 1945, Core Collection Files, AMPAS.

62 Jancovich's research shows how critics recognized Fox's effort to cast Tierney "against type in an attempt to extend her range" but "presented her beauty as incompatible with her ambitions to be taken seriously as an actress." Jancovich, "Female Monsters," 141, 142.

63 Philip K. Scheuer, "La Tierney Hints Bolt to Comedy," *Los Angeles Times*, February 10, 1946. Gene Tierney Clipping File, AMPAS.

64 Production Notes on *Leave Her to Heaven*, 1945, Core Collection Files, AMPAS.

65 Grossman, *Rethinking the Femme Fatale in Film Noir*, 23.

66 Gene Tierney with Mickey Herskowitz, *Self-Portrait* (New York: Berkley, 1980), 127.

67 Ibid., 126–127.

68 Grossman, *Rethinking the Femme Fatale in Film Noir*, 79.

69 Renov, "*Leave Her to Heaven*," 28–29.

70 Ibid., 28.

71 Production Notes on *Leave Her to Heaven*, 1945, Core Collection Files, AMPAS.

72 Walker, "*Leave Her to Heaven*," 239.

73 At Bar Harbor, Ellen will call out to Richard when she notices him by the seashore in a state of depression, but the only sound we hear when she opens her mouth is nondiegetic: a lone woodwind note. The underscoring of the scene has replaced the sound of her voice.

74 Tierney with Herskowitz, *Self-Portrait*, 29–35, 153–154.

75 Margaret Blair, "Eye View: Laura—Later," *Women's Wear Daily*, May 10, 1976; Bill Burt, "Actress Gene Tierney: JFK and I Were Deeply in Love," *National Enquirer*, March 16, 1976. Gene Tierney Clipping File, MoMA. See also Tierney with Herskowitz, *Self-Portrait*, 128–142.

76 Jeanine Basinger, *The Star Machine* (New York: Knopf, 2007), 167.

77 *The Razor's Edge* Pressbook, 1946, Core Collection Files, AMPAS.

78 Production Notes on *The Razor's Edge*, 1946, Core Collection Files, AMPAS.

79 Basinger, *The Star Machine*, 151.

80 Ibid., 166–167.

81 Production Notes on *The Razor's Edge*, 1946, Core Collection Files, AMPAS.

82 Darryl F. Zanuck to unnamed recipient, June 16, 1944, in *Memo from Darryl F. Zanuck: The Golden Years at Twentieth Century–Fox*, ed. Rudy Behlmer (New York: Grove Press, 1993), 93.

83 Darryl F. Zanuck to George Cukor, November 14, 1945, in *Memo from Darryl F. Zanuck: The Golden Years at Twentieth Century–Fox*, ed. Rudy Behlmer (New York: Grove Press, 1993), 97.

84 Ibid., 96.

85 Ibid., 95.

86 Ibid., 96.

87 Production Notes on *The Razor's Edge*, 1946, Core Collection Files, AMPAS.

88 Thomas Schatz, *Boom and Bust: American Cinema in the 1940s* (Berkeley: University of California Press, 1999), 467.

89 Tierney with Herskowitz, *Self-Portrait*, 136–137.

90 "Unanimous Reviewer Raves Greet *Razor's* in New York," *Hollywood Reporter*, November 22, 1946. Core Collection Files, AMPAS.

91 "*Razor's* Smashing Triumph of Expert Craftsmanship," *Hollywood Reporter*, November 20, 1946. Core Collection Files, AMPAS.

92 Maugham's novel was adapted a second time for a 1984 Columbia Pictures film directed by John Byrum. Bill Murray and Catherine Hicks starred in the roles previously played by Power and Tierney, respectively. This version disappointed critics and underperformed at the box office.

93 Zanuck first offered the role of Isabel to Maureen O'Hara in strict confidence, but when she spilled the news to Linda Darnell and word got back to Zanuck, he withdrew the offer and extended it to Tierney. O'Hara and Power had already costarred in the Fox swashbuckler *The Black Swan* (Henry King, 1942). See Aubrey Malone, *Maureen O'Hara: The Biography* (Lexington: University of Kentucky Press, 2013), 60.

94 Production Notes on *The Razor's Edge*, 1946, Core Collection Files, AMPAS.

95 Herb Howe, "Design for Delight," *Photoplay*, December 1946, 129.

96 Ibid., 45.

97 Ibid., 129.

98 Fredda Dudley, "Glamour Is Her Business," *Movies*, January 1947, 26.

99 Ibid., 74.

100 "Gene Tierney's Wedding Gown Finally Gets to Real Wedding," *Hollywood Citizen-News*, October 3, 1946. Gene Tierney Clipping File, AMPAS.

101 See Oleg Cassini, *The Wedding Dress* (New York: Rizzoli, 2018).

102 Tierney with Herskowitz, *Self-Portrait*, 135.

103 "Film Love Real Thing Now to Gene and Ty," October 26, 1946. Gene Tierney Clipping File, AMPAS.

104 Tierney with Herskowitz, *Self-Portrait*, 135.

105 Schatz, *Boom and Bust*, 369.

106 The unnamed Indian holy man is played by the white British actor Cecil Humphreys.

107 For more on modernism's Othering of "female" mass culture, see Andreas Huyssen, *After the Great Divide: Modernism, Mass Culture, Postmodernism* (Bloomington: Indiana University Press, 1986), 44–64.

108 Jack D. Grant, "*Razor's* Smashing Triumph of Expert Craftsmanship," *Hollywood Reporter*, November 20, 1946. Core Collection Files, AMPAS.

109 *The Razor's Edge* Pressbook, 1946, Core Collection Files, AMPAS.

110 Production Notes on *The Razor's Edge*, 1946, Core Collection Files, AMPAS.

111 For a full discussion of this concept, see *Masked Men: Masculinity and the Movies in the Fifties* (Bloomington: Indiana University Press, 1997), 34–78.

112 Ibid., 87.

113 Ibid., 88.

114 Ibid., 50.

115 Ibid., 54.

116 Ibid., 56.

117 Ibid., 58.

118 David Bordwell, "Lighting Up with Hildy Johnson," in *His Girl Friday*, directed by Howard Hawks (1940; New York: The Criterion Collection, 2017), Blu-ray.

119 Matthew C. Ehrlich, *Journalism in the Movies* (Urbana: University of Illinois Press, 2004), 20.

120 Tamar Jeffers McDonald, *Romantic Comedy: Boy Meets Girl Meets Genre* (London: Wallflower Press, 2007), 19.

121 Ibid., 20.

122 Ehrlich, *Journalism in the Movies*, 48.

123 Ibid., 49.

124 Mel Gussow, *Don't Say Yes until I Finish Talking: A Biography of Darryl F. Zanuck* (New York: Doubleday, 1971), 99.

125 Ibid., 99–100.

126 *Sweet Rosie O'Grady* was actually the second time Grable succeeded Young. In the Fox musical *Springtime in the Rockies* (Irving Cummings, 1942), a remake of *Second Honeymoon*, Grable and John Payne starred in roles previously played by Young and Power, respectively.

127 Basinger, *The Star Machine*, 323–324.

128 Fredda Dudley, "Laugh or Go Mad," *Silver Screen*, November 1948, 63.

129 Gene Schrott, "Gene's Greatest Triumph," *Screenland*, May 1949, 55.

130 For more on the *Paramount* decree, see Schatz, *Boom and Bust*, 323–328.

131 Ibid., 329–333.

132 Basinger, *The Star Machine*, 178.

133 McDonald, *Romantic Comedy*, 38.

134 Ibid., 43–44.

135 Ibid., 44.

136 Ibid., 39.

137 For more on Kinsey's findings in both books, see Cohan, *Masked Men*, 57–61.

138 McDonald, *Romantic Comedy*, 40–44.

139 Ibid., 38–39. For more on "the sexual display" in 1950s U.S. film and culture, see Barbara Klinger, *Melodrama and Meaning: History, Culture, and the Films of Douglas Sirk* (Bloomington: Indiana University Press, 1994), 51–57.

140 The *Police Gazette* was a precursor to heterosexual men's lifestyle magazines such as *Playboy*.

141 Thanks to Sean Griffin for bringing this "switcheroo" to my attention.

142 "The Screen in Review," *New York Times*, December 22, 1948.

Chapter 3

1 For more on Hollywood genres and production trends of the 1940s, see Thomas Schatz, *Boom and Bust: American Cinema in the 1940s* (Berkeley: University of California Press, 1999), 79–127, 203–261, 353–394.

2 See, for example, the following: Pam Cook, "Duplicity in *Mildred Pierce*," in *Women in Film Noir*, 2nd ed., ed. E. Ann Kaplan (London: BFI, 1998), 68–82; Mary Ann Doane, *The Desire to Desire: The Woman's Film of the 1940s* (Bloomington: Indiana University Press, 1987), 70–95; Lucy Fischer, "Three-Way Mirror: *Imitation of Life*," in *Imitation of Life: Douglas Sirk, Director*, ed. Lucy Fischer (New Brunswick, NJ: Rutgers University Press, 1991), 3–28; Sandy Flitterman-Lewis,

"*Imitation*(s) of Life: The Black Woman's Double Determination as Troubling 'Other,'" in *Imitation of Life: Douglas Sirk, Director*, ed. Lucy Fischer (New Brunswick, NJ: Rutgers University Press, 1991), 325–335; Marina Heung, "'What's the Matter with Sarah Jane?' Daughters and Mothers in Sirk's *Imitation of Life*," in *Imitation of Life: Douglas Sirk, Director*, ed. Lucy Fischer (New Brunswick, NJ: Rutgers University Press, 1991), 302–324; E. Ann. Kaplan, "The Case of the Missing Mother: Maternal Issues in Vidor's *Stella Dallas*," in *Issues in Feminist Film Criticism*, ed. Patricia Erens (Bloomington: Indiana University Press, 1991), 126–136; Joyce Nelson, "*Mildred Pierce* Reconsidered," in *Movies and Methods, Volume II*, ed. Bill Nicholas (Berkeley: University of California Press), 450–458; and Linda Williams, "'Something Else besides a Mother': *Stella Dallas* and the Maternal Melodrama," in *Imitations of Life: A Reader on Film & Television Melodrama*, ed. Marcia Landy (Detroit: Wayne State University Press, 1991), 307–330.

3　Lucy Fischer, *Cinematernity: Film, Motherhood, Genre* (Princeton: Princeton University Press, 1996), 6.

4　Ibid., 8.

5　Andrea S. Walsh, *Women's Film and Female Experience, 1940–1950* (New York: Praeger, 1984), 67.

6　Ibid., 68.

7　Ibid.

8　Ibid., 69.

9　Ibid., 70–72.

10　Dana Polan, *Power and Paranoia: History, Narrative, and the American Cinema, 1940–1950* (New York: Columbia University Press, 1986), 80.

11　Ibid., 81.

12　Ibid., 82.

13　Ibid., 83.

14　Ibid., 85.

15　Ernest R. Haydon, "The High Cost of Star Babies," *Movies*, December 1943, 21.

16　Ibid.

17　Ibid., 22–23.

18　Gene Tierney with Mickey Herskowitz, *Self-Portrait* (New York: Berkley, 1980), 147.

19　Ibid., 102–108.

20 Andrea Sarvady, "Gene Tierney," in *Leading Ladies: The 50 Most Unfor-gettable Actresses of the Studio Era*, ed. Frank Miller (San Francisco: Chronicle Books, 2006), 195.

21 Tierney with Herskowitz, *Self-Portrait*, 108.

22 "Daria Makes Debut," *Hollywood Citizen-News*, May 9, 1944. Gene Tierney Clipping File, AMPAS.

23 Fredda Dudley, "Leave Heaven to Her," *Modern Screen*, August 1946, 102.

24 Ibid., 100.

25 Ibid., 101.

26 Ibid., 102.

27 Elizabeth Wilson, "Gene Tierney Has Her Troubles Too!," *Screenland*, August 1945, 77.

28 Ibid., 78.

29 Twentieth Century–Fox Press Release, 1947, Core Collection Files, AMPAS.

30 Twentieth Century–Fox Press Release, 1947, Core Collection Files, AMPAS.

31 "Big Sister," *Modern Screen*, December 1942, 46–47, 99, 100–102.

32 Lyle Wheeler, "Treasure House," *Photoplay*, October 1950, 54.

33 Ibid., 96.

34 Ibid.

35 Sean Griffin, "The Wearing of the Green: Performing Irishness in the Fox Wartime Musical," in *The Irish in Us: Irishness, Performativity, and Popular Culture*, ed. Diane Negra (Durham, NC: Duke University Press, 2006), 64.

36 Qtd. in William Paul, "*Heaven Can Wait*: The Simple Act of Living," *Criterion Collection*, June 13, 2005, www.criterion.com/current/posts/371-heaven-can-wait-the-simple-act-of-living.

37 Ibid.

38 Raphaelson's previous scripts for Lubitsch included *Trouble in Paradise* (1932), *The Merry Widow* (1934), and *The Shop around the Corner* (1940). *The Merry Widow* was an adaptation of Franz Lehár's operetta of the same name that introduced the "Merry Widow Waltz," which can be heard in *Heaven Can Wait*.

39 Paul, "*Heaven Can Wait*."

40 Ibid.

41 Thomas Doherty, *Projections of War: Hollywood, American Culture, and World War II*, 2nd ed. (New York: Columbia University Press, 1999), 174.

42 Ibid.

43 On the popularity of occultism in the United States during World
    War II, see Tim Snelson, *Phantom Ladies: Hollywood Horror and the
    Home Front* (New Brunswick, NJ: Rutgers University Press, 2015),
    91–96.

44 Polan, *Power and Paranoia*, 189.

45 Ibid., 189–190.

46 Scott Eyman, *Ernst Lubitsch: Laughter in Paradise* (Baltimore: Johns
    Hopkins University Press, 2000), 348.

47 Although he played the titular monster in Universal's *The Invisible Man
    Returns* (Joe May, 1940), Price was known more as a character actor
    than an A-feature lead; prior to *Dragonwyck*, he acted with Tierney in
    supporting roles in *Hudson's Bay* (Irving Pichel, 1941), *Laura*, and *Leave
    Her to Heaven*. Thrilled by his experience playing a villain onstage in
    Patrick Hamilton's *Angel Street* (1938), a play that inspired film adapta-
    tions directed by Thorold Dickinson in 1940 and George Cukor in 1944
    under its original British title *Gaslight*, Price felt that a similar film role
    would make him a star. His daughter has quoted him on the challenge
    of landing the role of Nicholas Van Ryn: "I had to fight like the devil for
    this part. My bosses kept remembering me as the good-natured guy in
    Laura and I insisted I wasn't that type." Victoria Price, *Vincent Price: A
    Daughter's Biography* (Mineola, NY: Dover, 1999, 2018), 122.

48 Fischer, *Cinematernity*, 73–91. Contemporary horror films such as
    The Babadook (Jennifer Kent, 2014) and *Hereditary* (Ari Aster, 2018)
    demonstrate the genre's continued preoccupation with mother-
    hood that arguably exists on a continuum with the "woman's film"
    melodrama.

49 "Female Gothic" was coined by literary critic Ellen Moers to refer to
    work that arouses fear in the reader, featuring a young female protag-
    onist "who is simultaneously persecuted victim and courageous hero-
    ine." See Moers, *Literary Women* (London: The Women's Press, 1963),
    91. For more on women and the literary Gothic, see Tania Modleski,
    Loving with a Vengeance: Mass Produced Fantasies for Women, 2nd ed.
    (London: Routledge, 1990, 2008), 51–76.

50 Helen Hanson, *Hollywood Heroines: Women in Film Noir and the Female
    Gothic Film* (I. B. Tauris, 2007), 38–48.

51 Ibid., 74–75.

52 See Diane Waldman, "'At Last I Can Tell It to Someone!': Feminine
    Point of View and Subjectivity in the Gothic Romance Film of the
    1940s," *Cinema Journal* 23, no. 2 (1983): 29–40, and Doane, *Desire to
    Desire*, 123–154. For other theoretical considerations of this genre, see
    the following: Hanson, *Hollywood Heroines*, 48–62; Polan, *Power and
    Paranoia*, 273–284; and Walsh, *Women's Film and Female Experience*,
    167–193.

53 See Mark Jancovich, "Bluebeard's Wives: Horror, Quality and the
    Gothic (or Paranoid) Woman's Film in the 1940s," *Irish Journal
    of Gothic and Horror Studies* 12 (Summer 2013): 20–43.

54 Eyman, *Ernst Lubitsch*, 338.

55 Mankiewicz left MGM for the opportunity to direct at Fox and came
    aboard *Dragonwyck* as a replacement for his friend and mentor Ernst
    Lubitsch while Lubitsch recovered from a heart attack (horror would
    have been an equally unusual assignment for Lubitsch, a filmmaker
    who worked primarily in wry comedies such as *Heaven Can Wait*).
    Disagreements over the film led to a falling out between them, such
    that Lubitsch demanded his name be removed from the credits and
    promotion. Eyman, *Ernst Lubitsch*, 336, 338.

56 Ibid., 338.

57 Doane, *Desire to Desire*, 124.

58 Ibid., 123.

59 Waldman, "'At Last I Can Tell It to Someone!'" 29, 30.

60 Ibid., 30–31.

61 Ibid., 31.

62 Ibid., 33–36.

63 Ibid., 36.

64 Ibid., 38.

65 E. Ann Kaplan, *Motherhood and Representation: The Mother in Popular
    Culture and Melodrama* (London: Routledge, 1992), 12.

66 Adriana Trigiani, foreword to *The Ghost and Mrs. Muir* (New York: Vin-
    tage, 2014), xii.

67 Frieda Grafe, *The Ghost and Mrs. Muir* (London: BFI, 1995), 10.

68 Ibid.

69 Ibid., 19.

70 Ibid., 24–25, 36.

71 Ibid., 30.

72 Jack D. Grant, *"The Ghost and Mrs. Muir,"* *Hollywood Reporter*, May 16, 1947; "The Ghost and Mrs. Muir," *Variety*, May 16, 1947; "The Ghostly Lover," *Newsweek*, June 30, 1947; Harrison Carroll, *"Ghost* Yarn Is Different,"* *Los Angeles Herald Express*, July 4, 1947; Lowell E. Redelings, *"Ghost and Mrs. Muir* Delightful,"* *Hollywood Citizen-News*, July 4, 1947; Edwin Schallert, *"Ghost and Mrs. Muir* Scores as Novelty," *Los Angeles Times*, July 4, 1947; and *"The Ghost and Mrs. Muir,"* *Esquire*, September 1947.
73 Grafe, *The Ghost and Mrs. Muir*, 20, 46.
74 Alison L. McKee, *The Woman's Film of the 1940s: Gender, Narrative, and History* (London: Routledge, 2014), 104.
75 Ibid., 102.
76 Ibid., 110.
77 Ibid., 112.
78 Ibid., 113.

Chapter 4

1 Gene Tierney with Mickey Herskowitz, *Self-Portrait* (New York: Berkley, 1980), 34.
2 Ibid., 176.
3 Ibid., 155.
4 Ibid., 158.
5 "Gene Tierney Given Divorce Decree," *Los Angeles Times*, February 29, 1952. Gene Tierney Clipping File, AMPAS.
6 To master the basic techniques of ballet for *Never Let Me Go*, she trained for two hours per day during a six-week period, but a professional Russian ballet dancer doubled for her in long shots. Tierney with Herskowitz, *Self-Portrait*, 159.
7 Ibid., 210.
8 Ibid., 176.
9 "Gene Tierney Collapses with Virus Infection," *Los Angeles Times*, September 22, 1954. Gene Tierney Clipping File, AMPAS.
10 "On the Corner," *Sunday News*, November 6, 1955. Gene Tierney Clipping File, NYPL.
11 Cobina Wright, "Gene Took a Break," *Mirror Magazine*, June 24, 1956. Gene Tierney Clipping File, NYPL.

12 Tierney with Herskowitz, *Self-Portrait*, 179–186.

13 "Gene Tierney Again in Mental Hospital," *New York Journal-American*, January 21, 1958. Gene Tierney Clipping File, NYPL.

14 Tierney with Herskowitz, *Self-Portrait*, 193–194.

15 "Gene Tierney Back in Topeka Clinic," *Los Angeles Examiner*, January 22, 1959. Gene Tierney Clipping File, AMPAS.

16 Ed Misurell, "Gene Tierney Gets a Second Chance," *Pictorial Review*, December 21, 1958. Gene Tierney Clipping File, NYPL.

17 Ernest Tidyman, "Gene Tierney: Back in the Shadows," *New York Post*, January 22, 1959; "Actress Has Peace of Mind: Gene Tierney Now a Salesgirl," *New York Mirror*, October 15, 1959. Gene Tierney Clipping File, NYPL.

18 Warren Hall, "New Saleslady in Town," *The American Weekly*, December 13, 1959. Gene Tierney Clipping File, NYPL.

19 "Welcome for a Troubled Beauty: Long Ill, Gene Tierney Gets Back to Hollywood," *Life*, September 1958, 87.

20 Doug Brewer, "Gene Tierney Comes Home," *Modern Screen*, December 1958, 44.

21 Frank Ellis, "The Ordeal of Gene Tierney," *True Confessions*, June 1959, 4. Gene Tierney Clipping File, MoMA.

22 Cynthia Lowry, "Gene Tierney: 'I Had to Learn,'" *New York Daily Magazine*, November 12, 1958. Gene Tierney Clipping File, NYPL.

23 Frank Ellis, "The Ordeal of Gene Tierney," *True Confessions*, June 1959, 97. Gene Tierney Clipping File, MoMA.

24 A more recent example occurred in September of 2016 when the Democratic candidate for president of the United States, Hillary Clinton, received national attention from news media over her pneumonia diagnosis. See Mary Elizabeth Williams, "Hillary Powers through Pneumonia—Because That's What Women Do," *Salon*, September 12, 2016, http://www.salon.com/2016/09/12/hillary-powers-through -pneumonia-because-thats-what-women-do/.

25 Andrew Pulver, *Night and the City* (London: Palgrave Macmillan, 2010), 23.

26 Tierney with Herskowitz, *Self-Portrait*, 156.

27 Ibid., 160.

28 Ibid., 165, 171.

29 Ibid., 175.

30 Ibid., 176.

31 Fredda Dudley Balling, "No Tears for Tierney," *Movieland*, June 1954, 66.

32 Ibid., 51.

33 Ibid., 66.

34 Ibid., 68.

35 Fredda Dudley, "Laugh or Go Mad," *Silver Screen*, November 1948, 28.

36 Gene Tierney, "Fact and Fiction," *Hollywood Reporter*, December 31, 1945.

37 Cholly Knickerbocker, "Why Gene's Divorcing My Brother," *Modern Screen*, April 1947, 114.

38 Elizabeth Farrington, "Miss Tierney Regrets," *Modern Screen*, September 1947, 72.

39 "Gene Tierney, Mate in 'Spat,'" *Hollywood Citizen-News*, October 25, 1946; "Gene Tierney Hires Lawyer; Rift Rumored," *Los Angeles Times*, October 26, 1946. Gene Tierney Clipping File, AMPAS.

40 Louella O. Parsons, "Gene Tierney Rift Reported," *Los Angeles Examiner*, October 26, 1946. Gene Tierney Clipping File, AMPAS.

41 "Gene Tierney Divorce Suit Charges Cruelty," *Los Angeles Times*, January 15, 1947. Gene Tierney Clipping File, AMPAS.

42 "Gene Tierney Wins Divorce," *Los Angeles Examiner*, March 11, 1947. Gene Tierney Clipping File, AMPAS.

43 Ibid.

44 Hedda Hopper, "Looking at Hollywood with Hedda Hopper: Talented Tierney," *Chicago Sunday Tribune*, June 6, 1948. Gene Tierney Clipping File, AMPAS.

45 Edwin Schallert, "Fox Suspends Gene Tierney in Rift Over Role," *Los Angeles Times*, September 29, 1947. Gene Tierney Clipping File, AMPAS.

46 "20th Suspends Gene Tierney," *Variety*, Sep. 30, 1947. Gene Tierney Clipping File, AMPAS.

47 Tierney with Herskowitz, *Self-Portrait*, 160.

48 Ibid., 143.

49 Dudley, "Laugh or Go Mad," 29.

50 Tierney with Herskowitz, *Self-Portrait*, 144.

51 Ibid., 166.

52 Cynthia Lowry, "Gene Tierney: 'I Had to Learn,'" *New York Daily Magazine*, November 12, 1958. Gene Tierney Clipping File, NYPL.

53 Cynthia Lowry, "Gene Tierney: When Hope Was Lost . . . ," *New York Post*, November 13, 1958.

54 Cynthia Lowry, "Actress Grateful for Care," *Newark Evening News*, November 14, 1958.

55 "Welcome for a Troubled Beauty: Long Ill, Gene Tierney Gets Back to Hollywood," *Life* (September 1958), 87.

56 Ibid., 87, 88.

57 Ibid., 88, 92.

58 Ibid., 92.

59 Joe Hyams, "Gene Tierney Back at the Job," *New York Herald Tribune*, September 15, 1958; "Reborn Star," *Time*, September 29, 1958; Phyllis Battelle, "Gene Eager for Film Work," *New York Journal-American*, November 12, 1958; Ed Misurell, "Gene Tierney Gets a Second Chance," *Pictorial Review*, December 21, 1958. Gene Tierney Clipping File, NYPL.

60 Tierney with Herskowitz, *Self-Portrait*, 103–108.

61 Ibid., 223.

62 Doug Brewer, "Gene Tierney Comes Home," *Modern Screen*, vol. 52, no. 11 (December 1958): 44.

63 "Gene Tierney 'Thinking Over,' Says He's Dear," *Los Angeles Herald-Examiner*, December 8, 1953; "Aly Khan Mum on Marying," *Los Angeles Times*, May 6, 1953; "Should Gene Marry Aly? Tune in Next . . . ," *Los Angeles Daily News*, March 10, 1954; "Gene Tierney Admits She Loves Aly," *Los Angeles Times*, March 31, 1954; "Gene Tierney, Aly Here, Deny Stop for Wedding," *Los Angeles Times*, April 7, 1954. Gene Tierney Clipping File, AMPAS.

64 Phyllis Battelle, "The Long Road Back: How Gene Tierney Has Achieved Happiness after Years of Tragedy," *New York Journal-American*, November 9, 1958. Gene Tierney Clipping File, NYPL.

65 "Gene Tierney Psychiatric Patient in Kansas Clinic," *Los Angeles Examiner*, January 22, 1958. Gene Tierney Clipping File, AMPAS.

66 "Gene Tierney Patient at Psychiatric Clinic," *Los Angeles Times*, January 22, 1958. Gene Tierney Clipping File, AMPAS.

67 Jim Hoffman, "Something Terrible's Going to Happen to Me—Again," *Photoplay*, October 1960, 84, 86.

68 Ibid., 86.

69 Adrienne L. McLean, *Being Rita Hayworth: Labor, Identity, and Hollywood Stardom* (New Brunswick, NJ: Rutgers University Press, 2004), 17.

70 Ibid., 79.

71 Ibid., 102.

72 Tierney with Herskowitz, *Self-Portrait*, 201.

73 Janet Walker, *Couching Resistance: Women, Film, and Psychoanalytic Psychiatry* (Minneapolis: University of Minnesota Press, 1993), xvi, 8.

74 Ibid., 8, 10.

75 Ibid., 2, 12.

76 Ibid., 12–13.

77 Phyllis Battelle, "The Long Road Back: 'Cry,' Clinic Doctors Told Gene Tierney," *New York Journal-American*, November 10, 1958. Gene Tierney Clipping File, NYPL.

78 Fox's biography outlined these events and estimated the suit at $90,000, while the Battelle article referred to a $50,000 suit. The biography advised the press to "soft pedal" this story, "as Mr. Tierney is still boiling and would probably welcome a chance to sue somebody for something." Biography of Gene Tierney, 1943, Core Collection Files, AMPAS.

79 See Tierney with Herskowitz, *Self-Portrait*, 68–69, 72.

80 "Gene's Elopement Stirs Tierney War Council," *Los Angeles Examiner*, June 4, 1941. Gene Tierney Clipping File, AMPAS.

81 Biography of Gene Tierney, 1943, Core Collection Files, AMPAS.

82 Tierney with Herskowitz, *Self-Portrait*, 60, 65.

83 "Gene Tierney's Love Troubles May Make Her a Great Actress," *Los Angeles Examiner*, July 13, 1941. Gene Tierney Clipping File, AMPAS.

84 Louella O. Parsons, *Los Angeles Examiner*, November 25, 1941. Gene Tierney Clipping File, AMPAS.

85 Biography of Gene Tierney, 1943, Core Collection Files, AMPAS. The *Los Angeles Times* reported that Tierney sued her father for $15,000 damages, charging that he "converted $10,000 of her screen earnings to his own use while acting as her legal guardian." Fox's biography stated that Howard owed Tierney $40,000, but in *Self-Portrait*, she estimated that her father stole $30,000 from her over a two- to three-year period. "Gene Tierney Loses Her Suit against Her Father," *Los Angeles Times*, June 17, 1943; Tierney with Herskowitz, *Self-Portrait*, 71.

86 Tierney with Herskowitz, *Self-Portrait*, 68–71.

87 Phyllis Battelle, "The Long Road Back: Gene Felt Like Broken Woman in Clinic," *New York Journal-American*, November 11, 1958. Gene Tierney Clipping File, NYPL.

88 Battelle, "The Long Road Back: Gene Eager for Film Work."

89 Marie Torre, "Gene Tierney Tells How She Defeated 'G. E.' Jinx," *New York Herald Tribune*, September 30, 1960. Gene Tierney Clipping File, NYPL.

90 Atra Baer, "Slams Door on Painful Past: Gene Tierney Sees Rainbow," *New York Journal-American*, August 17, 1961. Gene Tierney Clipping File, NYPL.

91 *Advise & Consent* Pressbook, 1962, Moving Image Stills, Posters, and Paper Collection, GEM.

92 *Toys in the Attic* Pressbook, 1963, Moving Image Stills, Posters, and Paper Collection, GEM.

93 Tierney with Herskowitz, *Self-Portrait*, 224.

94 Peter Shelley, *Frances Farmer: The Life and Films of a Troubled Star* (Jefferson, NC: McFarland, 2011), 1–5.

95 Tierney with Herskowitz, *Self-Portrait*, 89.

96 Anne Helen Petersen, *Scandals of Classic Hollywood* (New York: Penguin, 2014), 169–171.

97 Ibid., 171, 175.

98 Ibid., 175.

99 Ibid., 177.

100 Thomas Schatz, "The New Hollywood," in *Film Theory Goes to the Movies*, ed. Jim Collins, Hilary Radner, and Ava Preacher Collins (London: Routledge, 1993), 8–36.

101 Tierney with Herskowitz, *Self-Portrait*, 166.

102 Ibid., 187.

103 Ibid., 183–186.

104 Ibid., 184.

105 Ibid., 186–187.

106 Ibid., 135.

107 Rebecca Bell-Metereau and Colleen Glenn, "Introduction," in *Star Bodies and the Erotics of Suffering*, ed. Rebecca Bell-Metereau and Colleen Glenn (Detroit: Wayne State University Press, 2015), 2.

108 Ibid., 5.

109 McLean, *Being Rita Hayworth*, 25. See also Danae Clark, *Negotiating Hollywood: The Cultural Politics of Actors' Labor* (Minneapolis: University of Minnesota Press, 1995).

110 Richard Dyer, *Only Entertainment*, 2nd ed. (London: Routledge, 2002), 80.

111   Ibid.

112   Bell-Metereau and Glenn, "Introduction," 20.

113   Ibid., 8.

114   Pressbook, *Whirlpool*, 1949, Department of Film Special Collections, MoMA.

115   The trailer for *Black Widow* used almost the same language, declaring, "Not since the unforgettable *Laura*, has there been such breath-taking suspense!" Tierney's role in *Black Widow* was quite small by comparison but still shows how Fox's repeated efforts to capitalize on the success of her earlier film noir relied to some degree on her screen presence.

116   "Commentary by Richard Schickel," in *Whirlpool*, directed by Otto Preminger (1949; Beverly Hills, CA: Twentieth Century Fox Home Entertainment, 2005), DVD.

117   Donald Spoto, *Possessed: The Life of Joan Crawford* (New York: Harper-Collins, 2010), 190.

118   Pressbook, *Whirlpool*, 1949, Department of Film Special Collections, MoMA.

119   Litvak was the same director who allegedly spotted Tierney during her trip to Hollywood as a youth (see Introduction).

120   Victoria Amador, *Olivia de Havilland: Lady Triumphant* (Lexington: University of Kentucky Press, 2019), 163.

121   See also Tim Snelson, *Phantom Ladies: Hollywood Horror and the Home Front* (New Brunswick, NJ: Rutgers University Press, 2015), 91-96.

122   Philippa Gates, "Home Sweet Home Front Women: Adapting Women for Hollywood's World War II Home-Front Films," *Americana: The Journal of American Popular Culture* 15, no. 2 (2016), www.americanpopularculture.com/journal/articles/fall_2016/gates.htm. See also Sheri Chinen Biesen, "Psychology in American Film Noir and Hitchcock's Gothic Thrillers," *Americana: The Journal of American Popular Culture* 13, no. 1 (2014), www.americanpopularculture.com/journal/articles/spring_2014/biesen.htm.

123   Philippa Gates, *Detecting Women: Gender and the Hollywood Detective Film* (Albany: State University of New York Press, 2011), 159–162, 185–188.

124   Mary Ann Doane, *The Desire to Desire: The Woman's Film of the 1940s* (Bloomington: Indiana University Press, 1987), 45.

125 Bosley Crowther, "The Screen in Review: Incredible Goings-On Feature *Whirlpool*, Mystery-Horror Picture Showing at Roxy," *New York Times*, January 14, 1950.

126 Richard L. Coe, "One on the Aisle: This Puzzler Has TWO Psychiatrists," *Washington Post*, February 3, 1950.

127 Mae Tinee, "Ferrer's First Starring Film Is Just Boring," *Chicago Daily Tribune*, January 19, 1950.

128 Philip K. Scheuer, "Jose Ferrer Fascinating Menace in *Whirlpool*," *Los Angeles Times*, January 14, 1950.

129 Chris Fujiwara, *The World and Its Double: The Life and Work of Otto Preminger* (New York: Faber & Faber, 2008), 117, 118.

130 Ibid., 117.

131 Ibid., 118.

132 Qtd. in ibid., 113.

133 Dave Kehr, "Critics Choice: New DVD's," *New York Times*, September 6, 2005. According to Raksin, Hecht thought the film was "terrible." Qtd. in Fujiwara, *The World and Its Double*, 114.

134 Ibid.

135 Walker, *Couching Resistance*, 66.

136 James Naremore, *Acting in the Cinema* (Berkeley: University of California Press, 1988), 86.

137 Ibid., 71, 72.

138 Fujiwara, *The World and Its Double*, 117.

139 Ibid., 116.

140 Ibid.

141 Walker, *Couching Resistance*, 64.

142 Tierney with Herskowitz, *Self-Portrait*, 225.

143 Biography of Gene Tierney, 1946, Core Collection Files, AMPAS.

144 "Gene Tierney Wins Divorce."

145 Battelle, "The Long Road Back: How Gene Tierney Has Achieved Happiness after Years of Tragedy."

146 Julie Grossman, *Rethinking the Femme Fatale in Film Noir: Ready for Her Close-Up* (London: Palgrave Macmillan, 2013), 82.

147 Ibid., 81, 87.

148 Ibid., 82.

149 Tierney with Herskowitz, *Self-Portrait*, 69.

150 Grossman, *Rethinking the Femme Fatale in Film Noir*, 87.

151 Mitchell S. Cohen, "Film Noir: The Actor: Villains and Victims," *Film Comment* (November/December 1974), 28.

Conclusion

1 Note that the traditional star system itself would soon be in decline. In the wake of the *Paramount* decree, studios responded to postwar economic pressures by letting go of their star contracts, while stars ran out their contracts and formed independent production companies. Talent agencies put stars in a "package" with a script and director that could be sold to a studio, which then leased the space of production to an independent company on a film-by-film basis and provided financing and distribution. See Denise Mann, *Hollywood Independents: The Postwar Talent Takeover* (Minneapolis: University of Minnesota Press, 2008).

2 Leonard Maltin, *Leonard Maltin's Movie Encyclopedia* (New York: Penguin, 1995), 879.

3 Walter Benjamin, "The Work of Art in the Age of Its Technological Reproducibility: Second Version," in *The Work of Art in the Age of Its Technological Reproducibility and Other Writings on Media*, ed. Michael W. Jennings, Brigid Doherty, and Thomas Y. Levin, trans. Edmund Jephcott, Rodney Livingstone, Howard Eiland, et al. (Cambridge, MA: Belknap Press of Harvard University Press, 2008), 22.

4 James Naremore, *Acting in the Cinema* (Berkeley: University of California Press, 1988), 25.

5 Ibid., 25–27. "Exhibition value" is Benjamin's term.

6 Steven Jacobs and Lisa Colpaert, *The Dark Galleries: A Museum Guide to Painted Portraits in Film Noir, Gothic Melodramas, and Ghost Stories of the 1940s and 1950s* (Ghent, Belgium: Aramer, 2014), 17.

7 Ibid., 23.

8 Ibid., 24–26.

9 Ibid., 23.

10 Ibid., 32.

11 The concept of remediation is defined in Jay Bolter and Richard Grusin, *Remediation: Understanding New Media* (Cambridge, MA: MIT Press, 1998, 2000).

12 Steven Rybin, *Gestures of Love: Romancing Performance in Classical Hollywood Cinema* (Albany: State University of New York Press, 2017), 132.

13 Ibid., 128.

14 Ibid., 130.

15 In the early 1950s, Hollywood had reduced production of its social-problem films and returned to a tradition of "pure entertainment" as a way of maintaining political neutrality during the House Un-American Activities Committee's investigation of the motion picture industry. See Brian Neve, "HUAC, the Blacklist, and the Decline of Social Cinema," in *The Fifties: Transforming the Screen, 1950–1959*, ed. Peter Lev (Berkeley: University of California Press, 2006), 73.

16 Aubrey Solomon, *Twentieth Century–Fox: A Corporate and Financial History* (Lanham, MD: Scarecrow Press, 1988, 2002), 46.

17 In addition, Solomon cites *Ladies in Love* (Edward H. Griffith, 1936) and the backstage musical *Sally, Irene and Mary* (William A. Seiter, 1938), although I would qualify their inclusion in this cycle. Only one of the women in the former is in pursuit of a wealthy husband, and all three women in the latter are more concerned with supporting themselves as singers than with getting married. *Three Blind Mice, Moon over Miami*, and *Three Little Girls in Blue* all share the same source material (a stage play by Stephen Powys), while *Ladies in Love* was based on a play by Leslie Bush-Fekete and *Sally, Irene and Mary* was an adaptation of a play by Edward Dowling and Cyrus Wood that MGM previously brought to the screen in 1925.

18 Fox's infamous *Valley of the Dolls* (Mark Robson, 1967), partly inspired by the life of the late Fox star Carole Landis, might be seen as the postscript to this eminently durable formula.

19 Webb also costarred in *The Dark Corner* (Henry Hathaway, 1946), a Fox film noir released two years after *Laura*, which combined elements of the Tierney film with *I Wake Up Screaming* (H. Bruce Humberstone, 1941). In *The Dark Corner*, Webb plays a sinister New York City art dealer, whose wife resembles the woman in one of his prized portraits.

20 James Naremore, *More than Night: Film Noir in Its Contexts*, 2nd ed. (Berkeley: University of California Press, 2008), 200.

21 Ibid., 201.

22 Ibid., 196.

23 *Who Framed Roger Rabbit* (Robert Zemeckis, 1988) is an example of an affectionately parodic film that combines live actors with cartoons,

including a private-eye in the Bogart mold, played by Bob Hoskins, and an animated femme fatale drawn like Rita Hayworth in *Gilda* (Charles Vidor, 1946). Kathleen Turner provided the voice of the latter not long after starring in the neo-noir *Body Heat* (Lawrence Kasdan, 1981).

24 For more on the relationship between *Twin Peaks* and *Laura*, see Julie Grossman and Will Scheibel, *Twin Peaks* (Detroit: Wayne State University Press, 2020), 36–37, 43.

Gene Tierney's Credits

Film

1940   *The Return of Frank James* (Fritz Lang, Twentieth Century–Fox)

1941   *Hudson's Bay* (Irving Pichel, Twentieth Century–Fox)

1941   *Tobacco Road* (John Ford, Twentieth Century–Fox)

1941   *Belle Starr* (Irving Cummings, Twentieth Century–Fox)

1941   *Sundown* (Henry Hathaway, Walter Wanger Productions/United Artists)

1941   *The Shanghai Gesture* (Josef von Sternberg, Arnold Productions, Inc./United Artists)

1942   *Son of Fury: The Story of Benjamin Blake* (John Cromwell, Twentieth Century–Fox)

1942   *Rings on Her Fingers* (Rouben Mamoulian, Twentieth Century–Fox)

1942   *Thunder Birds* (William A. Wellman, Twentieth Century–Fox)

1942   *China Girl* (Henry Hathaway, Twentieth Century–Fox)

1943   *Heaven Can Wait* (Ernst Lubitsch, Twentieth Century–Fox)

1944   *Laura* (Otto Preminger, Twentieth Century–Fox)

1945   *A Bell for Adano* (Henry King, Twentieth Century–Fox)

1945   *Leave Her to Heaven* (John M. Stahl, Twentieth Century–Fox)

1946   *Dragonwyck* (Joseph L. Mankiewicz, Twentieth Century–Fox)

1946   *The Razor's Edge* (Edmund Goulding, Twentieth Century–Fox)

1947   *The Ghost and Mrs. Muir* (Joseph L. Mankiewicz, Twentieth Century–Fox)

1948   *The Iron Curtain* (William A. Wellman, Twentieth Century–Fox)

1948   *That Wonderful Urge* (Robert B. Sinclair, Twentieth Century–Fox)

1950   *Whirlpool* (Otto Preminger, Twentieth Century–Fox)

1950   *Night and the City* (Jules Dassin, Twentieth Century–Fox)

1950   *Where the Sidewalk Ends* (Otto Preminger, Twentieth Century–Fox)

1951   *The Mating Season* (Mitchell Leisen, Paramount Pictures)

1951   *On the Riviera* (Walter Lang, Twentieth Century–Fox)

1951   *The Secret of Convict Lake* (Michael Gordon, Twentieth Century–Fox)

1951   *Close to My Heart* (William Keighley, Warner Bros.)

1952   *Way of a Gaucho* (Jacques Tourneur, Twentieth Century–Fox)

1952   *Plymouth Adventure* (Clarence Brown, Metro-Goldwyn-Mayer)

1953   *Never Let Me Go* (Delmer Daves, Metro-Goldwyn-Mayer)

1953   *Personal Affair* (Anthony Pelissier, Two Cities Films/United Artists)

1954   *Black Widow* (Nunnally Johnson, Twentieth Century–Fox)

1954   *The Egyptian* (Michael Curtiz, Twentieth Century–Fox)

1955   *The Left Hand of God* (Edward Dmytryk, Twentieth Century–Fox)

1962   *Advise & Consent* (Otto Preminger, Alpha Alpina S. A./Columbia Pictures)

1963   *Toys in the Attic* (George Roy Hill, Meadway-Claude Productions Company and The Mirisch Corporation/United Artists)

1964   *The Pleasure Seekers* (Jean Negulesco, Twentieth Century–Fox)

Television

Appearances on awards ceremony broadcasts and talk/variety shows are not included.

1957   *What's My Line?* (CBS series, 1950–1967), Season 8, Episode 52

1960   *General Electric Theater* (CBS series, 1953–1962), Season 9, Episode 10, "Journey to a Wedding"

1969   *The F.B.I.* (ABC series, 1965–1974), Season 4, Episode 23, "Conspiracy of Silence"

1969   *Daughter of the Mind* (ABC Movie of the Week)

1980   *Scruples* (CBS miniseries)

Selected Bibliography

See chapter notes for references to primary sources such as articles in newspapers, trade papers, general-circulation magazines, and fan magazines.

"The AFI List." *American Film Institute*, www.afi.com/afi-lists/.

Altman, Jason. "10 Things I Learned: *Leave Her to Heaven*." *Criterion Collection*, April 15, 2020, www.criterion.com/current/posts/6910-10-things-i-learned -leave-her-to-heaven.

Amador, Victoria. *Olivia de Havilland: Lady Triumphant*. Lexington: University of Kentucky Press, 2019.

Baron, Cynthia, and Sharon Marie Carnicke. *Reframing Screen Performance*. Ann Arbor: University of Michigan Press, 2008.

Basinger, Jeanine. *The Star Machine*. New York: Knopf, 2007.

———. "The Wartime American Woman on Film: Home-Front Soldier." In *A Companion to the War Film*, ed. Douglas A. Cunningham and John C. Nelson, 89–105. Malden, MA: Wiley-Blackwell, 2016.

———. *A Woman's View: How Hollywood Spoke to Women, 1930–1960*. New York: Knopf, 1993.

Behlmer, Rudy. *America's Favorite Movies: Behind the Scenes*. New York: Frederick Ungar, 1982.

———, ed. *Memo from Darryl F. Zanuck: The Golden Years at Twentieth Century–Fox*. New York: Grove Press, 1993.

Bell-Metereau, Rebecca, and Colleen Glenn. "Introduction." In *Star Bodies and the Erotics of Suffering*, ed. Rebecca Bell-Metereau and Colleen Glenn, 1–25. Detroit: Wayne State University Press, 2015.

Benjamin, Walter. "The Work of Art in the Age of Its Technological Reproducibility: Second Version." In *The Work of Art in the Age of Its Technological Reproducibility and Other Writings on Media*. Edited by Michael W. Jennings, Brigid Doherty, and Thomas Y. Levin, 19–55. Translated by

Edmund Jephcott, Rodney Livingstone, Howard Eiland, et al. Cambridge, MA: Belknap Press of Harvard University Press, 2008.

Bernstein, Matthew H. "A 'Professional Southerner' in the Hollywood Studio System: Lamar Trotti at Work, 1925–1952." In *American Cinema and the Southern Imaginary*, edited by Deborah E. Barker and Kathryn McKee, 122–147. Athens: University of Georgia Press, 2011.

Berry, Sarah. *Screen Style: Fashion and Femininity in 1930s Hollywood*. Minneapolis: University of Minnesota Press, 2000.

Biesen, Sheri Chinen. *Blackout: World War II and the Origins of Film Noir*. Baltimore: Johns Hopkins University Press, 2005.

———. "Psychology in American Film Noir and Hitchcock's Gothic Thrillers." *Americana: The Journal of American Popular Culture* 13, no. 1 (2014). www.americanpopularculture.com/journal/articles/spring_2014/biesen.htm.

Bogdanovich, Peter. "The Making of *Laura* by Otto Preminger as Told by Peter Bogdanovich." *On Film* 1, no. 0 (1970): 49–52.

Bolter Jay, and Richard Grusin. *Remediation: Understanding New Media*. Cambridge, MA: MIT Press, 1998, 2000.

Bordwell, David. "Lighting Up with Hildy Johnson." In *His Girl Friday*, directed Howard Hawks. 1940. New York: Criterion Collection, 2017. Blu-ray.

Bronfen, Elisabeth. *Specters of War: Hollywood's Engagement with Military Conflict*. New Brunswick, NJ: Rutgers University Press, 2012.

Buszek, Maria Elena. *Pin-Up Grrrls: Feminisms, Sexuality, Popular Culture*. Durham, NC: Duke University Press, 2006.

Carman, Emily. *Independent Stardom: Freelance Women in the Hollywood Studio System*. Austin: University of Texas Press, 2016.

Cassini, Oleg. *The Wedding Dress*. New York: Rizzoli, 2018.

Clark, Danae. *Negotiating Hollywood: The Cultural Politics of Actors' Labor*. Minneapolis: University of Minnesota Press, 1995.

Cohan, Steven. *Masked Men: Masculinity and the Movies in the Fifties*. Bloomington: Indiana University Press, 1997.

Coleman, David. *The Bipolar Express: Manic Depression and the Movies*. Lanham, MD: Rowman & Littlefield, 2014.

"Commentary by Richard Schickel." In *Whirlpool*, directed by Otto Preminger. 1949. Beverly Hills, CA: Twentieth Century Fox Home Entertainment, 2005. DVD.

"Complete National Film Registry Listing." Library of Congress. www.loc
    .gov/programs/national-film-preservation-board/film-registry/complete
    -national-film-registry-listing/.
Cook, Pam. "Duplicity in *Mildred Pierce*." In *Women in Film Noir*, 2nd ed.,
    edited by E. Ann Kaplan, 68–82. London: BFI, 1998.
———. "Melodrama and the Woman's Picture." In Landy, *Imitations of Life*,
    248–262.
———. "No Fixed Address: The Women's Picture from *Outrage* to *Blue Steel*."
    In *Contemporary Hollywood Cinema*, edited by Steve Neale and Murray
    Smith, 229–246. London: Routledge, 1998.
Davis, Ronald L. *Hollywood Beauty: Linda Darnell and the American Dream*.
    Norman: University of Oklahoma Press, 1991.
Desjardins, Mary. "Classical Hollywood, 1928–1946." In *Costume, Makeup, and
    Hair*, edited by Adrienne L. McLean, 47–74. New Brunswick, NJ: Rutgers
    University Press, 2016.
Deutelbaum, Marshall. "Costuming and the Color System of *Leave Her to
    Heaven*." *Film Criticism* 11, no. 3 (1987): 11–20.
Dillon, Steven. *Wolf-Women and Phantom Ladies: Female Desire in 1940s US
    Culture*. Albany: State University of New York Press, 2015.
Doane, Mary Ann. *The Desire to Desire: The Woman's Film of the 1940s*. Bloom-
    ington: Indiana University Press, 1987.
Doherty, Thomas. *Projections of War: Hollywood, American Culture, and World
    War II*. 2nd ed. New York: Columbia University Press, 1999.
Dyer, Richard. *Only Entertainment*. 2nd ed. London: Routledge, 2002.
———. *Stars*. 2nd ed. London: BFI, 1998.
Ehrlich, Matthew C. *Journalism in the Movies*. Urbana: University of Illinois
    Press, 2004.
Eyman, Scott. *Ernst Lubitsch: Laughter in Paradise*. Baltimore: Johns Hopkins
    University Press, 2000.
Fischer, Lucy. *Cinematernity: Film, Motherhood, Genre*. Princeton, NJ:
    Princeton University Press, 1996.
———. ed. Imitation of Life: *Douglas Sirk, Director*. New Brunswick, NJ: Rutgers
    University Press, 1991.
———. "Three-Way Mirror: *Imitation of Life*." In Fischer, Imitation of Life, 3–28.
Flitterman-Lewis, Sandy. "*Imitation*(s) of Life: The Black Woman's Double
    Determination as Troubling 'Other.'" In Fischer, Imitation of Life,
    325–335.

Friedrich, Otto. *City of Nets: A Portrait of Hollywood in the 1940's.* New York: HarperCollins, 1987, 2014.

Fujiwara, Chris. *The World and Its Double: The Life and Work of Otto Preminger.* New York: Faber and Faber, 2008.

Fuller, Karla Rae. *Hollywood Goes Oriental: CaucAsian Performance in American Film.* Detroit: Wayne State University Press, 2010.

Gaines, Jane. "Costume and Narrative: How Dress Tells the Woman's Story." In Gaines and Herzog, *Fabrications*, 180–211.

———, and Charlotte Herzog, eds. *Fabrications: Costume and the Female Body.* London: Routledge, 1990.

Galt, Rosalind. *Pretty: Film and the Decorative Image.* New York: Columbia University Press, 2011.

Gates, Philippa. *Detecting Women: Gender and the Hollywood Detective Film.* Albany: State University of New York Press, 2011.

———. "Home Sweet Home Front Women: Adapting Women for Hollywood's World War II Home-Front Films." *Americana: The Journal of American Popular Culture* 15, no. 2 (2016). http://www.americanpopularculture.com/journal/articles/fall_2016/gates.htm.

Gifford, Barry. *Out of the Past: Adventures in Film Noir.* Jackson: University Press of Mississippi, 2001.

Girelli, Elisabetta. *Montgomery Clift, Queer Star.* Detroit: Wayne State University Press, 2014.

Gledhill, Christine, ed. *Home Is Where the Heart Is: Studies in Melodrama and the Woman's Film.* London: BFI, 1987.

Grafe, Frieda. *The Ghost and Mrs. Muir.* London: BFI, 1995.

Green, Paul. *Jennifer Jones: The Life and Films.* Jefferson, NC: McFarland, 2011.

Griffin, Sean. "Introduction: Stardom in the 1940s." In *What Dreams Were Made Of: Movie Stars of the 1940s*, edited by Sean Griffin, 1–11. New Brunswick, NJ: Rutgers University Press, 2011.

———. "The Wearing of the Green: Performing Irishness in the Fox Wartime Musical." In *The Irish in Us: Irishness, Performativity, and Popular Culture*, edited by Diane Negra, 64–83. Durham, NC: Duke University Press, 2006.

———, ed. *What Dreams Were Made Of: Movie Stars of the 1940s.* New Brunswick, NJ: Rutgers University Press, 2011.

Grisham, Therese, and Julie Grossman. *Ida Lupino, Director: Her Art and Resilience in Times of Transition.* New Brunswick, NJ: Rutgers University Press, 2017.

Grossman, Julie. *Rethinking the Femme Fatale in Film Noir: Ready for Her Close-Up*. London: Palgrave Macmillan, 2013.

——, and Will Scheibel. *Twin Peaks*. Detroit: Wayne State University Press, 2020.

——. "Women and Film Noir: Pulp Fiction and the Woman's Picture." In *Kiss the Blood Off My Hands: On Classic Film Noir*, edited by Robert Miklitsch, 37–61. Urbana: University of Illinois Press, 2014.

Gussow, Mel. *Don't Say Yes until I Finish Talking: A Biography of Darryl F. Zanuck*. New York: Doubleday, 1971.

Hansen, Miriam. *Babel and Babylon: Spectatorship in American Silent Film*. Cambridge, MA: Harvard University Press, 1991.

Hanson, Helen. *Hollywood Heroines: Women in Film Noir and the Female Gothic Film*. London: I. B. Tauris, 2007.

Haskell, Molly. *From Reverence to Rape: The Treatment of Women in the Movies*. 3rd ed. Chicago: University of Chicago Press, 2016.

Hatch, Kristen. *Shirley Temple and the Performance of Girlhood*. New Brunswick, NJ: Rutgers University Press, 2015.

Heung, Marina. "'What's the Matter with Sarah Jane?' Daughters and Mothers in Sirk's *Imitation of Life*." In Fischer, Imitation of Life, 302–324.

Hirsch, Foster. *The Dark Side of the Screen: Film Noir*. Cambridge, MA: Da Capo Press, 2008.

Huyssen, Andreas. *After the Great Divide: Modernism, Mass Culture, Postmodernism*. Bloomington: Indiana University Press, 1986.

Jacobs, Steven, and Lisa Colpaert. *The Dark Galleries: A Museum Guide to Painted Portraits in Film Noir, Gothic Melodramas, and Ghost Stories of the 1940s and 1950s*. Ghent, Belgium: AraMer, 2014.

Jancovich, Mark. "Bluebeard's Wives: Horror, Quality and the Gothic (or Paranoid) Woman's Film in the 1940s." *The Irish Journal of Gothic and Horror Studies* 12 (Summer 2013): 20–43.

——. "Female Monsters: Horror, the 'Femme Fatale' and World War II." *European Journal of American Culture* 27, no. 2 (2008): 133–149.

Kalinak, Kathryn. *Settling the Score: Music and the Classical Hollywood Film*. Madison: University of Wisconsin Press, 1992.

Kaplan, E. Ann. "The Case of the Missing Mother: Maternal Issues in Vidor's *Stella Dallas*." In *Issues in Feminist Film Criticism*, edited by Patricia Erens, 126–136. Bloomington: Indiana University Press, 1991.

——. *Motherhood and Representation: The Mother in Popular Culture and Melodrama*. London: Routledge, 1992.

Kelly, Gillian. *Robert Taylor: Male Beauty, Masculinity, and Stardom in Holly-wood*. Jackson: University Press of Mississippi, 2019.

King, Ethel. "Bonnie Cashin." *Guardian*, February 8, 2000, www.theguardian .com/news/2000/feb/09/guardianobituaries4.

Klinger, Barbara. *Melodrama and Meaning: History, Culture, and the Films of Douglas Sirk*. Bloomington: Indiana University Press, 1994.

Konkle, Amanda. *Some Kind of Mirror: Creating Marilyn Monroe*. New Brunswick, NJ: Rutgers University Press, 2019.

Koppes, Clayton R., and Gregory D. Black. *Hollywood Goes to War: How Politics, Profits and Propaganda Shaped World War II Movies*. Berkeley: University of California Press, 1990.

Lake, Stephanie. *Bonnie Cashin: Chic Is Where You Find It*. New York: Rizzoli, 2016.

Landy, Marcia, ed. *Imitations of Life: A Reader on Film & Television Melodrama*. Detroit: Wayne State University Press, 1991.

Lawrence, Amy. *The Passion of Montgomery Clift*. Berkeley: University of California Press, 2010.

Lev, Peter. *Twentieth Century–Fox: The Zanuck-Skouras Years, 1935–1965*. Austin: University of Texas Press, 2013.

Lugowski, David M. "Claudette Colbert, Ginger Rogers, and Barbara Stanwyck: American Homefront Women." In Griffin, *What Dreams Were Made Of*, 96–119.

Lukszo, Ula. "Noir Fashion and Noir as Fashion." In *Fashion in Film*, edited by Adrienne Munich, 54–82. Bloomington: Indiana University Press, 2011.

Malone, Aubrey. *Maureen O'Hara: The Biography*. Lexington: University of Kentucky Press, 2013.

Maltin, Leonard. *Leonard Maltin's Movie Encyclopedia*. New York: Penguin, 1995.

Mann, Denise. *Hollywood Independents: The Postwar Talent Takeover*. Minneapolis: University of Minnesota Press, 2008.

McDonald, Tamar Jeffers. *Doris Day Confidential: Hollywood, Sex and Stardom*. London: I. B. Tauris, 2013.

———. *Hollywood Catwalk: Exploring Costume and Transformation in American Film*. London: I. B. Tauris, 2010.

———. *Romantic Comedy: Boy Meets Girl Meets Genre*. London: Wallflower Press, 2007.

McKee, Alison L. *The Woman's Film of the 1940s: Gender, Narrative, and History*. London: Routledge, 2014.

McLean, Adrienne L. *Being Rita Hayworth: Labor, Identity, and Hollywood Stardom*. New Brunswick, NJ: Rutgers University Press, 2004.

———. "Betty Grable and Rita Hayworth: Pinned Up." In Griffin, *What Dreams Were Made Of*, 166–191.

———. "Introduction." In *Headline Hollywood: A Century of Film Scandal*, edited by Adrienne L. McLean and David A. Cook, 1–26. New Brunswick, NJ: Rutgers University Press, 2001.

McNally, Karen. *When Frankie Went to Hollywood*: *Frank Sinatra and American Male Identity*. Urbana: University of Illinois Press, 2008.

Meeuf, Russell. *John Wayne's World: Transnational Masculinity in the Fifties*. Austin: University of Texas Press, 2013.

Minarich, Megan. "Abortion's Coded Visibility: The Failed Censorship and Box-Office Success of *Leave Her to Heaven*." *Feminist Media Histories* 6, no. 4 (2020): 121–150.

Modleski, Tania. *Loving with a Vengeance: Mass Produced Fantasies for Women*. 2nd ed. London: Routledge, 2008.

Moers, Ellen. *Literary Women*. London: Women's Press, 1963.

Naremore, James. *Acting in the Cinema*. Berkeley: University of California Press, 1988.

———. *More than Night: Film Noir in Its Contexts*. 2nd ed. Berkeley: University of California Press, 2008.

Nelson, Joyce. "*Mildred Pierce* Reconsidered." In *Movies and Methods, Volume II*, edited by Bill Nicholas, 450–458. Berkeley: University of California Press.

Ness, Richard. "A Lotta Night Music: The Sound of Film Noir." *Cinema Journal* 47, no. 2 (2008): 52–73.

Neve, Brian. "HUAC, the Blacklist, and the Decline of Social Cinema." In *The Fifties: Transforming the Screen, 1950–1959*, edited by Peter Lev, 65–86. Berkeley: University of California Press, 2006.

Kiriakou, Olympia. *Becoming Carole Lombard: Stardom, Comedy, and Legacy*. London: Bloomsbury, 2020.

Ovalle, Priscilla Peña. *Dance and the Hollywood Latina: Race, Sex, and Stardom*. New Brunswick, NJ: Rutgers University Press, 2011.

Palmer, R. Barton. *Shot on Location: Postwar American Cinema and the Exploration of Real Place*. New Brunswick, NJ: Rutgers University Press, 2016.

Paul, William. "*Heaven Can Wait*: The Simple Act of Living," *Criterion Collection*, June 13, 2005, www.criterion.com/current/posts/371-heaven-can-wait-the-simple-act-of-living.

Peberdy, Donna. "Acting and Performance in Film Noir." In *A Companion to Film Noir*, edited by Andrew Spicer and Helen Hanson, 318–334. Malden, MA: Wiley-Blackwell, 2013.

Petersen, Anne Helen. *Scandals of Classic Hollywood: Sex, Deviance, and Drama from the Golden Age of American Cinema*. New York: Penguin, 2014.

Peterson, Jennifer. "The Front Lawn of Heaven: Landscape in Hollywood Melodrama circa 1945." *Camera Obscura* 25, no. 2 (74) (2010): 118–159.

Polan, Dana. *Power and Paranoia: History, Narrative, and the American Cinema, 1940–1950*. New York: Columbia University Press, 1986.

Preminger, Otto. *Preminger: An Autobiography*. Garden City, NY: Doubleday, 1977.

Price, Victoria. *Vincent Price: A Daughter's Biography*. Mineola, NY: Dover, 1999, 2018.

Pullen, Kirsten. *Like a Natural Woman: Spectacular Female Performance in Classical Hollywood*. New Brunswick, NJ: Rutgers University Press, 2014.

Pulver, Andrew. *Night and the City*. London: Palgrave Macmillan, 2010.

Renov, Michael. *Hollywood's Wartime Woman: Representation and Ideology*. Ann Arbor, MI: UMI Research Press, 1988.

———. "*Leave Her to Heaven*: The Double-Bind of the Post-War Woman." In Landy, *Imitations of Life*, 227–236.

Roberts, Shari. "'The Lady in the Tutti-Frutti Hat: Carmen Miranda, a Spectacle of Ethnicity," *Cinema Journal* 93, no. 32 (1993): 3–23.

Rybin, Steven. *Gestures of Love: Romancing Performance in Classical Hollywood Cinema*. Albany: State University of New York Press, 2017.

Sarvady, Andrea. "Gene Tierney." In *Leading Ladies: The 50 Most Unforgettable Actresses of the Studio Era*, edited by Frank Miller, 192–195. San Francisco: Chronicle Books, 2006.

Schartoff, Adam. "Scorsese Introducing *Leave Her to Heaven*." YouTube video, 6:10. October 20, 2007. www.youtube.com/watch?v=ATfhKmkM-rE.

Schatz, Thomas. *Boom and Bust: American Cinema in the 1940s*. Berkeley: University of California Press, 1999.

———. "The New Hollywood." In *Film Theory Goes to the Movies*, edited by Jim Collins, Hilary Radner, and Ava Preacher Collins, 8–36. London: Routledge, 1993.

Shearer, Stephen Michael. *Beautiful: The Hedy Lamarr Story*. New York: St. Martin's Griffin, 2013.

Shelley, Peter. *Frances Farmer: The Life and Films of a Troubled Star*. Jefferson, NC: McFarland, 2011.

Shingler, Martin. *Star Studies: A Critical Guide*. London: BFI, 2012.

Smith, Richard Harland. "Gene Tierney Biography." TCM: Turner Classic Movies. https://www.tcm.com/tcmdb/person/191988%7C57782/Gene-Tierney/#biography.

Snelson, Tim. *Phantom Ladies: Hollywood Horror and the Home Front*. New Brunswick, NJ: Rutgers University Press, 2015.

Solomon, Aubrey. *Twentieth Century-Fox: A Corporate and Financial History*. Lanham, MD: Scarecrow Press, 1988, 2002.

Spoto, Donald. *Possessed: The Life of Joan Crawford*. New York: HarperCollins, 2010.

Stead, Lisa. *Reframing Vivien Leigh: Stardom, Gender, and the Archive*. New York: Oxford University Press, 2021.

Sturtevant, Victoria. *A Great Big Girl Like Me: The Films of Marie Dressler*. Urbana: University of Illinois Press, 2016.

Thompson, Kristin. *Breaking the Glass Armor: Neoformalist Film Analysis*. Princeton, NJ: Princeton University Press, 1988.

Thomson, David. *The New Biographical Dictionary of Film*. 2nd ed. New York: Knopf, 2010.

Tierney, Gene, with Mickey Herskowitz. *Self-Portrait*. New York: Berkley, 1980.

Toth, Margaret A., and Teresa Ramoni. "'Their Voices Ring in My Ears: *Laura*, the Fugue, and Adaptation." *Adaptation* 14, no. 1 (2020): 136-156.

Trigiani, Adriana. Foreword to *The Ghost and Mrs. Muir*, xi-xvi. New York: Vintage, 2014.

Turim, Maureen. "Designing Women: The Emergence of the New Sweetheart Line." In Gaines and Herzog, *Fabrications*, 212-13.

Veblen, Thorstein. *The Theory of the Leisure Class*. New York: Penguin, 1994.

Vogel, Michelle. *Gene Tierney: A Biography*. Jefferson, NC: McFarland, 2009.

Waldman, Diane. "'At Last I Can Tell It to Someone!': Feminine Point of View and Subjectivity in the Gothic Romance Film of the 1940s." *Cinema Journal* 23, no. 2 (1983): 29-40.

Walker, Janet. *Couching Resistance: Women, Film, and Psychoanalytic Psychiatry*. Minneapolis: University of Minnesota Press, 1993.

Walker, Michael. "*Leave Her to Heaven*." In *The Call of the Heart: John M. Stahl and Hollywood Melodrama*, edited by Bruce Babington and Charles Barr, 229-241. East Barnet, Herts: John Libbey, 2018.

Walsh, Andrea S. *Women's Film and Female Experience, 1940-1950*. New York: Praeger, 1984.

Wexman, Virginia Wright. *Creating the Couple: Love, Marriage, and Hollywood Performance*. Princeton, NJ: Princeton University Press, 1993.

Williams, Mary Elizabeth. "Hillary Powers Through Pneumonia—Because That's What Women Do." *Salon*. September 12, 2016. http://www.salon .com/2016/09/12/hillary-powers-through-pneumonia-because-thats-what -women-do/.

Williams, Linda. "'Something Else Besides a Mother': *Stella Dallas* and the Maternal Melodrama." In Landy, *Imitations of Life*, 307–330.

Index

CPSIA information can be obtained
at www.ICGtesting.com
Printed in the USA
JSHW042009260622
27361JS00005B/20